THE WAR ON DADS AND CHILDREN

How to fight it, and win

by

Vincent McGovern

Grosvenor House
Publishing Limited

This book is published by
Grosvenor House Publishing Ltd
Link House
140 The Broadway, Tolworth, Surrey, KT6 7HT.
www.grosvenorhousepublishing.co.uk

A CIP record for this book
is available from the British Library

ISBN 978-1-83975-450-0

Acknowledgements

There are a great many people whom I am indebted to for their invaluable and priceless support to myself and the children.

First of all, I wish to thank my parents Joe and Ann McGovern for their unlimited help and support always towards our children and myself. Steadfast does not begin to describe them. My two sisters, Irene and Carmel, my two brothers Pat and Des and their spouses/partners, John, Nick, Katrina and Cathy, for their huge practical support and assistance at all times.

I also wish to thank my personal friends from school days, the three remarkable and very generous Cornyn brothers from Ballinagleragh County Leitrim, Anthony, Michael and Pauric plus their wives Maureen, Maureen and Geraldine. Yes, two Maureens!

My old and generous racing friends Jimmy Burke and his wife Paula from Baltinglass Co Wicklow, Tony Hudziak and his wife Jackie now in Newbridge Co Kildare. With such wonderful people I felt greatly enabled to fight for the protection of the children and myself, and without them... well, let's not go there!

In Wembley I wish to thank all who wrote witness statements and, in particular, those who were prepared to go to court as witnesses on my behalf. Truly outstanding were John and Judy

Woods, also Kathryn Bartlett and Steve Kempson, the late Jim O Sullivan and his wife Mary. Pivotal here was and is my IT guru, Peter Adebowale. The amount of times he has saved my skin on the computer!! And from Ealing since 2018, I thank my wonderful fiancée Sunita for her support and insight. Knowledge and beauty! Thanks darling.

Special thanks to my main McKenzie Friend Noel Robinson, whom I met through the shared parenting charity Families Need Fathers. He is also quite good at editing!

It cannot be sufficiently described by me what a legend Erin Pizzey is. Her knowledge and insight are truly illuminating. I'm deeply appreciative of her advice and support, and what an incredible foreword!

Further thanks to the remarkable writer Louis De Berneires, and deepest appreciation for his support and foreword. A true master of words! Martin Daubney (ex MEP) and I restored his 1981 Yamaha LC350 while discussing the book and preparation. Thanks for the advice and the foreword Martin, and I hope we can bring this issue to much wider attention. Those giants in this business, William Collins and Nick Langford, were kind enough to lend me some of their best work, to use as I deemed best! Their work should be compulsory reading for all who are concerned about children and society.

Other notables who gave support towards the book were the remarkable writers John Waters of Ireland and Neil Lyndon, now in Scotland. If you want brains just look at the work done by all those people I've mentioned above.

I wish to thank the children's mother for having given me the wonderful gift of fatherhood and allowing me to look after our three beautiful children for nine years. I have no hatred against her, my hatred is against the highly bigoted agencies and personnel who ideologically and financially profit so much from children's misery and fathers' despair. I hope to drive your institutional malpractice into the dustbin of history!

But I do acknowledge that without them this book and its reason would never exist.

And lastly but certainly not least, thanks to Grosvenor House Publishing. Information means nothing without being distributed. Knowledge is power!

Foreword by Erin Pizzey

"But what I hope to demonstrate is the deep systemic malpractice which runs from top to bottom of the UK family court system and myriad associated services."

When I was sent this manuscript and looked at the title, I confess that my initial reaction was one of dread. In the ensuing almost fifty years since I opened the first refuge in the world in 1971, I was well aware of the inadequacies of the Family Courts, and all the allied agencies, to such an extent that I listed all their failings in the back of my book *'Scream Quietly or the Neighbours will Hear'*. My attempt to rectify the abuse and damage they inflicted upon troubled families was met with unbridled rage and a long list of the guilty agencies lining up to sue me in a court of law.

My book was the first to blow wide open the years of secrecy (but well known to all the agencies) concerning the plight of all victims of domestic violence which had so far been met with a solid wall of silence. Since that time, I have been fighting at the coal face of the appalling injustice experienced by those who have been scorched and burnt and often driven to suicide by a war that is waged against them if they dare raise their heads above the parapet and say, just as the author of this book is saying, the UK courts and the myriad associated services are not fit for purpose. My feeling of dread evaporated because I found to my delight and astonishment that Vincent McGovern has written a totally absorbing testament, not only to his own years of harrowing abuse and persecution at the hands of those that are entrusted with protecting the rights of the individual but also to, in so many cases, the vindictive deliberate stone-walling of his search for justice.

If you read this book because you too are one of the many thousands of people in this country who have had the forces of injustice unleashed against you, then not only will you be able to walk in the author's footsteps but you will be able to recognise the signposts that you believed were there to map the road to salvation, and then turned the whole journey into a cruel joke.

Thanks to this utterly honest, courageous account of one man's efforts to be reunited with the children that he loved and who loved him, he will take you by the hand and walk beside you step by step along the paths he took and help you find your way through the sticky morass of lies and distortions that he lists so vividly in this book. If you are reading this book because you are a seeker of truth, believe me that this book is written without rage or vindictiveness. This is a sober well-balanced account of the state of affairs in the family courts in this country at the present time.

I sincerely hope that this book is the precursor of an international dialogue seeking to adduce the cause of destructive activism that has worm-holed its way into supposedly the least susceptible of all institutions, the Family Court. We need to examine the steps that were taken all those years ago to dismantle the role of the family in our lives and the exiling of fathers not only from their homes, but also from their children. I leave you with a remark made to me by a prison governor: 'Every child born into a dysfunctional family is a point on my pension.' Fifty years of the planned destruction of the family allows her to think of this remark as perfectly normal and, until Vincent McGovern wrote this book, her ignorance and unconcern is echoed by most people working in the most delicate of all relationships, that which exists between children and their parents.

Introduction for Vincent

Louis de Berneires

In 1989 everything changed for Britain's fathers. Up until that time they had automatically been their children's guardian, but then, suddenly and casually, the Children's Act came into force, and neither parent was. Children, it seemed, had become the property of the state, to dispose of as its institutions saw fit. Families were now at the mercy of the courts and the social workers who advised them. As is always the case, terms got changed, pointlessly, and 'custody' became 'residence'.

As far as I know there had been no intention to sideline fathers, but this is what happened overnight. It was already customary for fathers to go out to work whilst women stayed at home to care for the children, and something called 'attachment theory' had become popular with 'experts' in the 1950s. From then on everybody in the know' knew' that children could only form a deep bond with one person.

Even though 'attachment theory' has long been discredited, it became axiomatic that children belonged with their mothers, who realised that the more they could keep their children away from their fathers, the more maintenance they could claim from them.

Most, I would think, must have been egged on by their solicitors, who adore their adversarial system in which they coin money whilst being the only ones who do not get hurt. An entire industry has sprung up around the notion that all women are sweet and gentle victims, and all fathers are depraved and brutal abusers, against whom children have to be protected. We live in a society that used to disparage women, but now despises men. Even the male social workers have Stockholm syndrome.

There are plenty of 'deadbeat dads' of course, and the assumption is that all of us are. It is forgotten that for the majority, our children love and need us as much as we love and need them. Without us they grow up with no intimate male role model. Boys succumb to the idiocies of peer pressure, and girls have no idea what sort of man to fall in love with. The Right to a Family Life that is enshrined in our law only applies in print, too often; it doesn't apply to so many children who are forced to grow up virtually fatherless, or to fathers whose terrible despair can lead them to fall into an abyss of rage, madness and suicide. When your children have been heisted with the collusion of an entire legal and bureaucratic machine, it is all but impossible to retain any hope or will to live. I speak from experience. I also know that if I had not had enough money to pay lawyers, I might well have had to give up. Justice has always been for sale, but never more so than in the British Family Justice system. In our courts it is simply a competition to see whose money runs out first. The most recent attempts at reform were blocked in the House of Lords by the very people who caused all the problems in the first place, before they were promoted to the Westminster snoozorium.

Judges never get to meet the children over whose fate they preside, and there really are some who think that reasonable contact can consist of talking on Skype once in a blue moon. These ones were presumably brought up by nannies and private schools, and see no point in parents or parenting anyway.

The ideologues who poison our family lives forget that when a father is got rid of, so are all the children's female relatives on his side. The children lose their grandmothers, cousins, and aunts, and this is why campaigns for a child's right to have a proper relationship with their father have so many female supporters. Fatherhood is a feminist issue.

Nobody knows more than Vincent McGovern about the scandalous mismanagement and institutional sexism of our system. The fact that the situation is slowly but continuously improving is thanks to the dogged dedication of campaigners like him.

You will find in this volume an impressive marshalling of facts, and busting of myths. Readers almost certainly would have had no idea that 40% of domestic abuse is committed by women, or that murdered children are most frequently killed by their mothers, or that single pregnant women who are given council accommodation are given it on condition that the father cannot move in. This book should be read by policymakers, judges, and social workers, and by anyone who wants to know what is really going on, and wants to see what can be done about it.

Martin Daubney's Foreword!

The War On Dads & Children – How To Fight it, and Win is part personal polemic and part how-to-beat a legal system that has turned British fathers into outcasts at the fundamental expense of children's rights.

It is the story of how Vincent McGovern, an ordinary stay-at-home, father-of-three, found himself the unwitting target of the entire rigged British family court, legal, social care and domestic violence industries – but fought back and triumphed.

In 2007, Vincent's then-wife accused him of killing a family dog that never existed (well, it did only *to the local council's female-only domestic violence agency)*. With his typical black Irish humour, Vincent dubbed this fictional hound 'Shadow' when he learned of it, and soon he found himself living in a garage, childless and the target of the full arsenal of the state.

His response? *"I swore that so long as I lived, I would kick the malpractice out of these bastards"*.

Against all the odds, Vincent fought back. Despite not even owning a computer, and sleeping on a blow up mattress on his garage floor, Vincent became a self-taught expert in the dark arts of British family law.

Vincent became much more than a thorn in the system's side: first, he succeeded in winning a staggering and unprecedented five Ombudsman investigations: one Local Govt and one

Parliamentary Ombudsman against Brent Council, two Parliamentary against Cafcass (Children and family court advisory support service), and also one against the Solicitors Regulatory Authority via the Legal Services Ombudsman.

Next, in 2014, after personally addressing the European Union's Petitions Commission, Vincent was pivotal in forcing an EU first-ever investigation into a nation state's family court system – particularly into the grotesque practice of "enforced adoption" of children – when children are removed from unsuitable mothers and placed into foster care without fathers having a say in the matter – leading to a 53% reduction in one year.

(Ref: Cen Lon Branch webpage video on Families Need Fathers website)

Vincent went on to become Chair of Central & North London branches of the shared parenting charity Families Need Fathers in 2011 and has assisted over 1000 attendees per year since 2008 – meaning he's helped over 12,000 attendees.

This means Vincent has helped more separated fathers than anybody else in the UK since 2007, as well as grandmothers, aunts and children.

With the unparalleled knowledge Vincent has accrued, the final section of the book will become a unique "how to beat the system" guide.

Currently, data shows that child separation due to relationship breakdown is the single biggest driver of male suicide - which is the biggest killer of men aged under 45.

With figures from The Samaritans released during the coronavirus pandemic proving it is middle-aged, poorer men most at-risk, there has never been a more timely release of a book.

As well as not only saving the UK's army of separated fathers countless £1000s, this book could literally save their lives.

THE AUTHOR

A mountain man from the Cuilcagh mountains on the Irish border, Vincent McGovern is one of the most respected men's voices on the UK child protection scene – and a perpetual thorn in the side to the establishment.

Few people can talk with such passion on behalf of, or connect with, downtrodden, forgotten dads – having literally walked in their shoes to the edges of despair and back.

Formerly a motorcycle racer, then a motorbike courier who gladly gave up his career for "the best job on the planet" – to rear his three children while his professional wife, a doctor, worked – Vincent became the victim of a rigged system, yet refused to play the role of the victim.

Instead, he turned his despair to hope by learning how to win.

Few individuals know as much about the UK Family Court system. Vincent does not call himself a men's rights activist. He has no interest in bashing feminism. Instead, he is all about child protection.

"The needs of the child come first, second and always," he says. "But the British child protection system only wishes to protect itself. Fathers are mere grist to the mill. This must change".

Introduction

The War on Dads and Children.

My name is Vincent McGovern and I was a house-husband/ primary carer of three children from May 1st 1998 until 20th June 2007, when it rather abruptly came to an end. We can blame a phantom dog for being pivotal. Prior to looking after children, I was a motorbike courier for 13 years, a barman, scaffolder, labourer for MacAlpine engineering and a mechanic. As you can see an excellent background grounded in academia!

This book was written between 2013 and 2020, mostly in the 2016/2017 winter while recovering after I received a much-needed 2nd hip from the NHS. Much of the book is quite serious with an overall tone laced with satire: some chapters are quite comic. The shortest Chapter has 1 word, sufficiently descriptive. Three of the longer chapters are copied from highest quality published work done by others, with their blessing.

Since June 2007 I have obtained in my favour five Ombudsman Investigations, three of which were Parliamentary and Health Service Ombudsman (PHSO), two of these were into the Children and Family Court Advisory Service (Cafcass). I have also addressed the European Parliament Petitions Commission twice in March and November 2014 on its motion 'Systemic Failings in The UK Family Court System'. This led to the first ever investigation of a sovereign nation children's services by the EU Commission. I have also had eighteen or so official enquiries into systemic failings including kickstarting an O.F.S.T.E.D investigation into Brent Council's Children's Services and a GMC enquiry.

I have been Chair both of Central and North London Branches of the shared parenting charity Families Need Fathers (FNF) since 2011, in a voluntary capacity. Central London is the original, busiest, and largest branch within FNF. I have also had 43 hearings in my own case, 38 as a Litigant In Person. I obtained a Shared Residence Order in April 2009 for my children: enforcement however was woeful. I also worked part time as a McKenzie Friend, a lay adviser in the Family Courts, and have attended over 350 hearings. I have McKenzied for both mothers and fathers, though usually fathers. I have neither a caution, charge nor conviction to my name. I have been a school governor since 2006 and as such I hold an enhanced Disclosure and Barring Service Certificate. I was also an invited attendee to the All-Party Parliamentary Group on Children in the House of Lords.

The book has approximately 78,000 words introductory paragraphs are in bold for most chapters, and is divided into four sections:

1. **My Story, Chapters 1 – 6.** This includes the 2 Ombudsman and 3 PHSO enquiries plus an overview and comments regarding failings. Chapter 1 is quite long and has a philosophical overview on the systemic failings within the family court process and laughable regulation.

2. **Systemic Failings in the UK Family Court System, Chapters 7 – 14.** This section contains some wonderful part chapters by others who are in the lead on this subject. Some chapters are heavy duty and professional of viewpoint.

3. **Campaigning: mine and others, Chapters 15 – 22.** This includes the preparation and experience from twice addressing the European Parliament in 2014. The outcome is that others and I, for the first time ever in the EU, helped them to decide a situation within a country was sufficiently serious to warrant an investigation by the EU into Children's services. The text varies from the deadly serious to the totally flippant!

4. **Solutions, Chapters 23 – 28.** This contains a chapter on how to make a complaint, a chapter on being a Litigant in Person within Family Courts, and a chapter on being a McKenzie Friend. So few parents, especially fathers, can afford proper representation, and virtually never receive Legal Aid. I deeply believe that apart from abuse of the system by vested interests there is absolutely no reason why the UK cannot replicate best practice regarding children's outcomes as is common post-divorce or separation in so much of the EU and especially Scandinavian countries.

I am NOT a men's rights activist, neither am I an eternal whiner. I seek the proper implementation of the Children Act 1989 and the removal of institutional malpractice. This Act clearly states that the right to a proper relationship with both parents and wider family post-divorce or separation is the child's right: otherwise one has parental alienation.

My target within this book is to bring to as wide an audience as is possible how the noble intentions of Parliament and the Children Act 1989 has been so severely subverted by vested interests and inadequate regulation to the detriment of children. More importantly, I want others to take this knowledge on board by removing institutional malpractice and create better outcomes for children and dads.

If someone like me, who has spent 22 years of their adult life either working as a motorbike courier or a house-husband can do what I have done to investigate, expose, and effectively challenge what I call 'child endangering gender discrimination', then there is no excuse for many others to not do better. I have long believed that it is women and mothers who are in the lead of bringing about the much-needed change and improvement so necessary in this arid landscape. Men, fathers, brothers, sisters, mothers, grandparents, now is the time to stand up and be counted in the protection of children. This book has the how and why. You need to supply the will and ability after reading it. Knowledge is power. Now use the power!

Regards
Vincent McGovern.

Chapter 1

Unregulators

.it needs to be accepted, with honesty and candour, that there have been in recent years in the family courts shocking examples of professional malpractice......" Sir James Munby President of the Family Division, in B (A Child) [2016] EWCA Civ 1088

Chapter 1 was written in October 2013, along with two and three. The purpose of Chapter 1 being titled Unregulators, is to demonstrate the vast difference between the average person's perceptions of morals, right and wrong, the concept of right to a fair trial, innocent until proved guilty, and where this is so obviously breached, the incredible efforts the system will use to protect institutional malpractice. My thanks to Stuart Hontree for the above quotation from Sir James Munby which is taken from a draft version of Stuarts book; 101 Dirty Tricks of the secret family courts.

In a sense chapter 1 is the philosophical foundation for this book. It is the longest and serves also to demonstrate the 'how and why.' I was initially asked to write it as part of someone else's book meant to be called 'Unregulators.' Ten people were supposed to contribute a chapter each. I was the only one who wrote a chapter, this one, and so I then decided to write my own book at a later date. To me, the system i.e. the tax funded public services are supposed to help and protect its citizens, especially children. They are not meant to be a semi-secret cabal of virtually unregulated self-administering bastion of self-protection which macerates citizens who point out it is far too often as in this case institutionally endangering vulnerable children because of their warped ideology and innumerable vested interest fellow travellers.

All people are equal is an absolute principal of mine. Here you will discover that equality is dependent on gender. And as a father I was ticking the wrong box. And I don't accept children suffering because of a warped ideology. This is the 21st century, not the 11th.

You may well ask, what has the term Unregulators got to do with Parental Alienation and Institutional Malpractice in the UK. The simple answer is everything. Local Authority institutional malpractice is pivotal in the outcome of family law proceedings. My journey through this minefield is why these next chapters, deep and personal though they are, are crucial to understanding this malpractice. I am not looking for sympathy, many have been subject to much worse than I have been. But what I hope to demonstrate is the deep systemic malpractice which runs from top to bottom of the UK family court system and myriad associated services. If anyone knows more than I do about this, please make contact and let us meet so I can learn more.

By unregulators, I mean regulators who do not regulate. Which means effectively, they are fraudsters. This may seem too strong a word, so let us use another term - unfit for purpose. Much depends on what purpose they are meant to serve. I have always believed that regulatory authorities were meant to regulate whatever they were meant to regulate for the good of society, using such standards as common decency, average understanding of values, morals, needs, equality in law, equality of opportunity for access to such service, and if wronged, equality of opportunity to seek redress via the established regulatory bodies.

Such was my belief before I needed them in 2007. My belief in 2017 as I write this is that regulators are not meant to regulate, they are meant to protect those involved in malpractice from regulation. Why should I have such a cynical view? Well, fifteen official inquiries, five Ombudsman investigations three of which were Parliamentary and Health Services Ombudsman with findings in my favour, some of which makes absolutely wonderful reading. However, the difference any of this has made to the malpracticing, pseudo professional government bodies involved? Disappointingly little so far, but I'm working on it!

Perhaps you've made a judgement that I'm one of those always unhappy professional complainers, highly educated in local and national government policies or even used to earn a living in one - an educated whistleblower if you like. An individual with insider information or who has access to such. Sorry to disappoint you, but until 2007 I was in one of the most under-appreciated jobs known to man or woman for over nine years, and before that I was an under-valued motorbike courier for thirteen years.

From 1998 until 2007 I was a house-husband, a stay at home, look after children, bring them to and from school, do the cooking, cleaning, shopping, change nappies, mow the lawn, prepare an evening meal most evenings, do some house decorating, motorbike and car maintenance and home renovation subject to the kindly assistance of the children, you get the picture, I was a lowly house father. Which means that in the social order I had a status lower than slave, as I later found out to mine and the children's cost.

The dull moronic brain-dead job before that for thirteen years? I was a motorbike courier. Twenty-two years of adult life totally under the radar, no job application forms, no human resources meetings and definitely no career path.

I believe I was what's known as a John Smith, a nobody from nowhere going anywhere. Another average, boring married man who instead of being the primary earner, was the primary carer. I had never even managed to get arrested, cautioned, or charged by the police, in fact at the time of writing this is still the situation. Just another simple law-abiding citizen, creating no waves, causing no problems. I had never made a formal or informal complaint in my life until my late forties about anyone or anything. I was a school governor and on the committee of the local resident's association, unlikely to be top of any government watch list for terrorist activities due to my membership.

My education, well if you wish to exercise humour, primary school was in a standard small two-room rural school in remote north-west Ireland, with an outside toilet that was like the unregulators mentioned, totally unfit for purpose intended. That's because the only plank with the hole in the only boys toilet was always full of….what is that substance called when people lower their trousers, sit down, make a smell and leave a substance behind? And there was neither top or bottom to the door, but there was a middle section. I almost forgot, there was a wall, three feet from the door which matched the door frame in height, ideal for ruffians and uncouth boys to gaze and comment in an ungracious manner. The teacher, now there's a story in poor regulation.

The reason for this lengthy description? My experiences in that semi open plan toilet were identical to the experiences I endured many, many years later due to the misbehaviour of the regulatory authorities in the UK.

My secondary education is very high, Summerhill College in Co. Sligo is on top of a hill. I left school in Ireland aged seventeen in 1976 with what is called a Leaving Certificate. Scraped a pass in five subjects, the minimum necessary.

I believed that possession of a Leaving Cert entitled me to leave the country, after all that is what it says, you can leave.

My higher-level education was fascinating. I attended Sir Alfred MacAlpines Construction school of higher education in Birmingham, UK. You see I was often up, but more often down a ladder in my duty as a 'general site operative'. That is a posh name for 'labourer.' Some labourers, usually when drunk which meant they could speak more clearly, would describe themselves as 'labourologists'. I decided that my trusty shovel had insufficient gravitas for such grandiose titles, the bloody thing was heavy enough to dig with without making it any worse.

Now we come to the government bodies, local and national unregulators in the UK charged with and quite often highly paid and educated, at tax-payers expense of course, who are supposed to regulate government services for the good of society. I used to believe that. Please don't laugh, I seriously believed it.

I now realise that such innocence ranks with believing in Santa, the earth is flat, if you do good you will go to heaven, bad people will go to hell, and so on. The problem on earth where you have protectionist local and national government is that protectionist people have nice comfortable unsackable positions within these authorities, and the more protectionist they are, the more likely they are to become members of a statutory regulatory body. That's right, a 'statutory regulatory body'. Government set up, government funded, government controlled, government aims and objectives, subject to government regulation for the benefit of all. All of the last sentence is correct apart from the last big three letter word, all.

All is not you and me, the man or woman in the street, the coal mine, the building site, the office, the factory or indeed the kitchen. 'All', in this case means all who are within the system. And all others, those who work and pay taxes to fund all this, the all which is society, are not just not getting the protection we should be getting. We are being abused, used, misused and misled because we are necessary to fund the necessary pretend regulators who have wonderful publicity departments, perfect mission statements, and above all, a totally fireproof system of self -preservation. And self -preservation is the total opposite of general good. We have the pigs from Animal Farm and we, the general public, are the horse who keeps telling himself or herself we must work harder, must make more sacrifices, must eat less, must drink less, must, must, must, until someone comes along and exposes the whole sorry unregulated mess for the self-serving farrago that it is.

The services I have yet to mention, you may be curious what they are. Something about bee keeping, or drain flow in waterless areas, surely only such irrelevancies would have such useless regulators in charge. Sadly not. The services in question are among the most important in society, the regulators charged with the most sacred of all duties, the duty to protect children.

Am I the first to have exposed such, or to believe I am the only one who knows just how rotten these regulators are? Oh no, this has been known for decades in the UK, Royal Commissions, official Government investigations including Lord Laming's of 2001, numerous special case reviews, serious case reviews, autopsies, coroner's reports, newspaper headlines and articles stretching everywhere and going nowhere, politicians earnestly promising change and all of society saying, never again! And what do the regulators say each time? 'Lessons have been learnt".

Since 1948 there have been almost eighty public inquiries into major cases of child abuse in the UK where institutional and regulatory failures were dominant. Learning is good, the problem is, when does it stop? When are the lessons learnt after such appalling failures going to be put into practice? Well actually they are being learnt and being put into practice all the time, but not the lessons any reasonable person would consider. The lessons being learnt and put into practice are the lessons of how to avoid getting caught, how to avoid responsibility, how to pass the buck and the best lesson of all, the lesson to always say whenever an investigation is taking place by the police or some occasional public response to a horrific lack of accountability or regulation which resulted in yet another poor innocent vulnerable child's death, the best lesson of all is when these government bodies and their regulators keep saying, 'the proper procedures were followed'. Who created the procedures? What procedures? why, the procedures of self- preservation of course. We are so important we will take on board in our own time what lessons we need to learn to prevent the same thing from ever happening again - this is what the public are told. What this really means is, we will improve our firewall of protection, and you and yours will be a temporary little problem that we have always overcome.

Of course, this means the regulators need more money to conduct an internal review, engage private and public consultants from the same culture, do strategic management reviews, and guess what, nobody anywhere did anything wrong is quite remarkably the outcome.

It was the system you see that was wrong. Not us, the people within the regulatory system, because we did not know what we now know. And now that they know what they do know, the one guarantee is they will not know enough to protect the vulnerable from the next situation. Because every situation is different is their response, and we need more funding and less interference from the very well meaning, but uninformed public so that we can continue as we were before. It amounts to the perfect scam, give us more for your good, you never give enough, so we cannot protect or do our statutory duty to your satisfaction. But we can certainly do it to our satisfaction. It is the mushroom system of management, keep the public in the dark and keep throwing muck at them. And what happens if a member of the public pokes his nose into our business? Well then, all the forces of hell with government backing are let loose on the miscreant, the maverick, because he dared, dared to try and make the government regulatory bodies do their job according to their own statutory obligations. And this is where I arrive in the tale, and I hope it is a wake-up call for all those who read it.

Proof? I have far too much of it. But getting it, well hopefully others can learn from my experience. And the systemic abuse and denigration suffered while looking for what is meant to be always available to the public, as these bodies are all public funded, demonstrate very clearly that only the most diligent of people taking unbelievable risks have any slim chance of getting a result. The unbelievable risk I hear you say, what was it, a fine, arrest, imprisonment? No, much, much worse than those. For daring to try and hold these public bodies and regulators to account I was threatened by letter and verbally twice with the prospect of my children being taken into care. And if you want to know what feeling sick feels like, I assure you being told that is a shortcut to putrefying sickness. It psychologically kills you.

So how did we arrive at this barbaric situation, what terrible action or horrible crime had I committed? I challenged the institutional and unregulated maladministration of local and national authority. And when a private citizen challenges the state with some effect, then the beast of unlimited government power will be released and set on you. Straightforward naked crude abuse of position because I asked government services and regulators to do what they are supposed to do.

On the first Sunday of February 2007 my then wife said to me, totally out of the blue, 'I want a divorce'. First and only time in my life those words had ever been said to me. Many have heard them before, and no doubt many more will. What's the big deal you may ask? Lots of couples' divorce and separate - take it like a man and stop whining you may say.

Well the big deal is, a week later I was told to abandon the children, get out of the house, or I would be destroyed with the help of local services. Despite the shock, I actually thought it would be good to have them involved for the children's sake, and also mine. Matters became steadily worse and in April 2007 I decided I needed help. I knew there were lurid allegations being made against me to the local services as my then wife regularly threatened me with having done so. I telephoned the local domestic violence agency and also the national domestic violence helpline. And guess what, they refused to help me. I was advised to speak to my solicitor.

I contacted a recently retired solicitor in Uxbridge and he informed me the local DV agencies would help my wife to get me booted from the family home using any pretext and the best I could hope for was weekend contact with my children, possibly also an evening after school visit. I stuttered some comments about due process and innocent until proved guilty. He just laughed at my innocence. While waiting at Uxbridge tube station a horrible blackness overcame me. I decided to wait for a passing express train. After 20 minutes or so I realised Uxbridge was an end of line station. I phoned my parents upon returning home. My mother's assurances of support lifted me enormously, family are best!

Afterwards I found out this is their standard signposting technique when a father contacts a domestic violence agency. You see, in constitution and practice they discriminate on grounds of gender when providing a service. Their names are

Brent Domestic Violence Agency Project – Advance (BDVAP-Advance) London Borough of Brent Domestic Violence Corporate Strategy 2005 - and the UK National Domestic Violence Helpline.

I knew that the children's services in the Borough of Brent were renowned for their hostile, anti-father attitude and extraordinary incompetence. Lord Laming in 2001/03 had been commissioned by the UK government to hold a major inquiry into maladministration by among others, London Boroughs of Brent and Haringey, the Police, National Society for The Protection of Children and the NSPCC. This was known as the Victoria Climbie inquiry. It cost the UK taxpayer £3.8 million, delivered a four-hundred-page report, was empowered by three Acts of Parliament and made 108 recommendations, many of which were supposed to be implemented within six months as a matter of urgency. In 2009 following the brutal death of Baby P (Peter Connolly) who like Victoria Climbie was well known to all of the children's services in Haringey, Lord Laming was asked to do a review. His report was that his recommendations were not implemented.

My fears regarding children's services in Brent were well founded. They decided at a few days notice to call a Case Conference after my then wife had contacted them. Some difference in service based on gender right there. The constitution of the panel was, shall we say, a cause for concern. The panel comprised of, among others, my then wife's business partner who was the children's GP, a junior member of staff from their jointly owned GP premises, and three work colleagues. Ref: London Borough of Brent Case Conference 15th June 2007, Rosie Atwal was the Chair.

I was informed by a social worker on the 7th June that my wife had been in contact with the BDVAP, yes indeed the very same local and national government funded agency that had suggested I contact a solicitor. The BDVAP in constitution and practice will only work with females. Ref: Letter addressed to me after repeated intervention on my behalf from the local Member of Parliament, Barry Gardiner, date; 22nd September 2009 from the Brent Head of Community Safety. The Council repeatedly refused to comply with their statutory duty under Freedom of Information Act. Fortunately, very fortunately, I had a good member of parliament Barry Gardiner, Member of Parliament Brent North who insisted on Brent Council fulfilling their statutory duty here. It still took many months for all this to happen with many letters, reminders and follow ups.

I complained strongly to the local council, Brent, about this totally improper panel and process in June 2007. I also complained about Brent social services handing me another vulnerable child's file on one occasion, and also posting yet another child's file to me. By this time I had found out via the family court what the principal allegations against me were. The most dangerous one, was that I had repeatedly kicked and then killed the family dog in front of our three children and my wife, terrifying everyone. The B.D.V.A.P. had much to say about this grotesque act of cruelty. Their verdict on this and other evidence was that after their Multi Agency Risk Assessment Conference (M.A.R.A.C), held in secret and of which I knew absolutely nothing about, the verdict *only* on this evidence should be presented to the case conference.

The case conference was set up and chaired by Brent social services at very short notice after my then wife approached them via her member of staff. The verdict reached was, that on the evidence received I was a risk to the children. With social services assistance my then wife approached a Court ex–parte (without notice to me) and I was booted from the family home. I was also going to be immediately arrested if

I attempted to contact the children or their mother or caused anyone else to do so. And pending the local services risk assessment, and complying with what domestic violence perpetrator courses they insisted upon, I would be unlikely to see the children until they were satisfied I was not a danger.

You might believe all was done properly, everything being accurate and above board, with no lies told and the laws of the land being strictly followed, with justice being served on a brutal terrifying man. Well, not quite, you see, we never had a family dog. Which also meant I had never kicked or killed the phantom family dog.

My family, possessing excess dark humour, when hearing this absurd allegation, promptly christened the phantom dog, Shadow. I have nineteen witness statements confirming this. And I was despite being the children's father and primary carer for over nine years, (twenty-nine witness statements), barred because of my gender from access to domestic violence and hence the gateway to children's services in Brent. Under London Borough of Brent Domestic Violence Corporate Strategy 2005-2008, all agencies in Brent have to refer and defer to the BDVAP. It is the only official agency for domestic violence in Brent. And it is funded from local and national government which greatly helps it to attract funding from various charities and foundations. And these agencies are pivotal in determining outcome in UK family courts.

Nevertheless, the response from the Local Government Chief Executive of Brent, one Gareth Daniel, when I complained about this unbelievable child endangering gender discrimination, was very reassuring in the manner of all bad jokes. It was crystal clear from his letters to me one of which threatened to put our children into care and later another one describing me as 'unhelpfully tendentious.'. For those who wish to believe I am exaggerating consider the following.

Nevres Kamal was a front line social worker within the Borough of Haringey's laughable social services department. The same Borough, along with Brent, that Lord Laming some years earlier had been the head of such an in-depth inquiry into. Fat lot of good that did. For months before Baby P became public knowledge she had been trying to get the council to stop having social services staff going on foreign junket trips while serious cases were building up and other malpractices.

Share

Baby P council falsely accused me of abusing a child, reveals whistleblower who feared she'd lose her daughter

By EILEEN FAIRWEATHER
UPDATED: 13:51, 16 November 2008

Read more: http://www.dailymail.co.uk/news/article-1086196/Baby-P-council-falsely-accused-abusing-child-reveals-whistleblower-feared-shed-lose-daughter.html#ixzz4Vq0CylPt
Follow us: @MailOnline on Twitter I DailyMail on Facebook

An employment tribunal heard that she had been singled out by her bosses because she was a whistleblower. Haringey eventually dropped the case and paid her undisclosed compensation.

Read more: http://www.dailymail.co.uk/news/article-1086196/Baby-P-council-falsely-accused-abusing-child-reveals-whistleblower-feared-shed-lose-daughter.html#ixzz4Vpy zaYBG

Follow us: @MailOnline on Twitter | DailyMail on Facebook

In May 2020 Haringey children's services were once again making headlines, and as usual for the wrong reasons. This is the service that was so hopeless at protecting children it led to, along with Brent council the setting up of the Lord Laming Inquiry, empowered by Parliament changes in law, huge cost to the public etc. That was in 2001. Later on in 2007 we had the Baby P (Peter Connolly) situation in Haringey of unimaginable horror with politicians and other jobsworths assuring us all that nothing like this would ever happen again. And now we arrive at 2020 to discover that Haringey children's services have allowed this to happen,

Social workers from the local authority with the worst reputation for child protection failures in the country allowed a mother of two boys to develop a relationship with a paedophile.

Staff from Haringey Council put their sympathy for the woman before the needs of the children, whose lives have been seriously damaged, High Court judge Mr Justice Hayden said.

The case – said by the judge to be the worst failure by social workers he had ever come across – carries echoes of the scandal over the death of Baby P in 2007.

Ref: Daily Mail, May 20th 2020. Steve Doughty.

The younger boy now lives with his father, the older boy who has severe needs has been place in a care home by the court. Haringey children's services had refused to listen to the (separated since 2018) fathers concerns about a paedophile recently released from prison having a relationship with the mother.

Obviously no lessons were learnt from any of the official inquiries conducted into the disastrous children's services of Haringey.

But we return to Brent.

Incidentally, this was the same Gareth Daniel who had been in charge of Brent at the time of Victoria Climbie. He told the Lord Laming inquiry that he was in charge of council strategy, we now know what that strategy consisted of.

The response from the then Head of Children's services in Brent, John Christie, when I complained about their general malpractice through my local Councillor was quite incredible. I had also complained about the handing over of other vulnerable children's files to a member of the public, me. What followed was an email from the Deputy Director of Brent Social Services, one Janet Palmer, to local councillors stating that I had entered their offices (the public are never allowed) and stolen these files which I now sought to gain advantage from. Ref: Janet Palmer/SOCSERVICES/BRENT/ GB 10/07/2007 08:49.

When one complains to local government the initial responses are risible. Pretend cloying concern, deep sympathy expressed, told that matters will be fully investigated or have already been, no stone will be left unturned and finally you will be informed about their lengthy complaints procedure. This nebulous say everything and nothing document, some of them huge, then enables the local authority to state they have fully complied with procedure. How good of them. One could be forgiven for blushing in appreciation. Until you read through this epistle of nothingness and realise it is just a time-wasting bluff on their part. Specifically, because it omits all of what has happened to you. A bit like going to a scrapyard, you see everything you don't want, but not the part you do want.

My six complaints against Brent Social Services.

1. They operated a system that automatically discriminates against fathers. Ref: London Borough of Brent Domestic Violence Corporate Strategy 2005-
2. Brent processed my case in their secret M.A.R.A.C (Multiple Agency Risk Assessment Conference) process without me ever knowing what the evidence was.
3. Despite me being the children's primary carer for over nine years I was still blocked because of my gender from access to Brent Services. Incidentally I was also blocked by the National Domestic Violence Hotline when I approached them for help in 2007.
4. Brent processed me in secret based on laughably false allegations e.g kicking and killing non-existent family dog.
5. This M.A.R.A.C process and Brent's institutional discrimination against fathers (and all men) makes a complete mockery of the phrase "Welfare of The Child Is Paramount" Section 1 Children Act 1989. Brent had facilitated in the removal of a loving parent and primary carer for over nine years to three children without one iota of evidence against him during those nine years. Suddenly, the primary earner who is female and seeking a more favourable divorce, decides to make allegations against him and Brent accepts them as truthful without any attempt at verification.
6. Brent demonstrated complete contempt for any concept of justice or child welfare with their above process.

At this stage, your complaints will usually be dealt with by the, shall we say, lower staff of the council. And they will probably respond close enough to their own time scales. It is standard practice for them to do the concerned undertaker bit where you may feel how can you continue attacking these nice people. But matters change when you persist. Suddenly the level you are dealing with becomes very high. High in standard you may ask. Oh no, high in self protectionism for the council and authority.

I suddenly found myself dealing with a consultant, no less. Very flattering for the person looking to have their complaint dealt with professionally, until you realise that this is standard on their part when someone persists with a complaint. The intellectual level you are dealing with is suddenly very high, and incredibly difficult for a private person of average education to absorb. In other words, you are outgunned, blown out of the water, sunk without trace, dealt with as far as the council are concerned. You rattled their cage, now the big beast that costs a lot more to feed has been released and you will of course be finished off. Just another unhappy complainer who had nothing really to go with, easily dismissed at this stage.

It is then that you have the horrible empty pit feeling in your stomach. Family and friends have up to the point been supportive and very helpful, but they can no longer keep up with it. They have lives to lead, this has gone on for months so far, a massive wrong has been done to you and your children, but now emotion is a handicap because it is not nearly sufficient for where you now are. Everything and every value you hold dear is irrelevant, you are now in their make-believe world and it makes Alice In Wonderland appear logical.

These are the authorities responsible for maintaining and setting standards for the good of society. Huge taxes are required to educate, house, train, maintain, and all for what? The public good we are told. It reminds me of the scene in The

Wizard of Oz, when, near the end, the Great Oz is blustering and bluffing when they are in his magnificent castle, his voice and indignation is thunderous and very frightening, and then the little dog Toto pulled apart the curtain and the entire bluff was revealed. The problem is the Wizard of Oz and Alice In Wonderland are fairy tales where good triumphs over evil. In life when dealing with corrupt local government and their compliant regulators there is no happy ending, no triumph of good over evil. There is just horrible trench warfare, where they have all the advantage because you and I, and all the other mugs in society have paid and are paying for them. While that continues, coupled with aggressive protectionism of malpractice by the regulators who feed from the same trough, the average citizen is going to keep being dumped on.

We now arrive at what I consider my personal crossroads. From June 2007 until August I was only trying to get Brent council and its agencies to look at where they had gone wrong and correct it where possible in my case. I genuinely believed I was just in the wrong place at the wrong time and matters would be looked at from a child centred logical viewpoint. After all, this is their job and they are professionals. I was trying to protect myself and get back into the children's lives as I knew they missed me terribly. In fact, during the weeks I was not allowed to see them I started to panic that I would not remember what they looked like and I posted pictures of them in several places in the semi converted garage I was living in. The social worker was kind, she described it as a flat. They were probably describing the floor where I slept on a blow-up airbed, that was the flat part I presume.

The Family Courts were very angry about this back-door justice as they saw it and the Judge promptly ordered supervised contact to begin immediately. At last I thought, a human with a brain and common sense, who can see through this nonsense and are focused on the children. The children had repeatedly requested to all who would listen, that they wanted to go on holiday with me to see my parents in Ireland, something they had done every summer. To my astonishment and utter delight at a hearing in August 2007, the Judge ordered that I have the children for a week and could take them out of the jurisdiction to Ireland for eight days. Joy of joys, all the pain was worth it so far, the children could enjoy something normal after the horrible year and matters would only get better for them and I, and indeed both parents.

I had foolishly underestimated the sheer savagery and determination of Brent officers and social services to do what they want, irrespective of court orders and whatever damage that would and did cause to our children. At my ex-wife's request, a social worker from Brent was despatched to the nursery where our then three-year-old child was having a nap. The social worker woke him up, and repeatedly asked him how he felt about going to Ireland on holidays with his dad. She also kept asking him if he preferred to stay with his mother. At the third question, the little boy said his mother before his father. After interviewing our oldest boy then aged nine, who was under horrendous pressure, the Brent social worker, wrote that she did not recommend the two boys travel with me. I implored the social worker and the council to put the children first and assist in carrying out the court order, which after all was made in the children's interest. I was repeatedly ignored and fobbed off. During that holiday whilst not with me, the oldest boy started self-harming and talked about killing himself. There was a social services case conference scheduled for one week after the holiday. This horrifying information had come to my attention regarding the eldest boy. What do you think was the action of social services at the case conference? Case closed, the children were taken off the At Risk Register. The father was no longer in the family home and now the children were deemed safe.

My protestations about what was happening to our eldest were totally ignored. I had become present, but invisible.

I had never known real anger in my life until then. I had often felt irritated, annoyed, disgruntled about various matters, but never real anger. After the events described, I felt an anger that I realised would consume me if I did not control it. My way of dealing with it was to smash the unregulated wilful child endangering policies and actions of the local council. I was determined to make them do their job properly according to the guidelines and laws of the land. I decided to approach the proper regulatory authorities...

Looking back, it was actually quite stupid of me to approach the regulators. It is obvious with hindsight that these agencies were doing what they were doing with the effective collusion of the regulatory bodies. Collusion either in turning a blind eye to institutional malpractice or wilful incompetence on their part, which amounts to the same thing.

I found myself becoming invisible. That is to say the local authority decided to make me invisible. Letters were not acknowledged, phone calls were not answered, sometimes junior members of staff would take my calls and assure me the matter would be dealt with. I persisted and therefore discovered the contempt professionals hold when a member of the public tries to hold them accountable. By this stage I had acquired a computer and printer from a very good friend, and had started to use a mobile phone earlier in the year. I was very slowly and purely through lack of choice moving into the twenty-first century. This meant I could type letters as opposed to handwriting them. It also meant I could access information and guidelines relevant to the many government agencies and regulatory authorities involved. Much of this information was nebulous and wishy washy, say everything and said nothing of value. Nevertheless, there were still many clear breaches and examples of malpractice among the pseudo professionals employed by the local council or affiliated to them.

I persisted in my complaints against the local council and started to make some headway. Another very good friend spent many hours with me explaining how malpractice is standard practice where the local social services and council are concerned. His most telling comment when he became involved will always live with me. He said, 'social services and local council are like a bad dog, they will do anything to anyone to get what they want because they have no fear of regulation'.

He explained at length the procedures I would have to go through before my complaints would get anywhere of significance. This procedural knowledge was invaluable, it is not available to members of the public and effectively it armed me. I owe a huge debt to his assistance, and indeed many other friends and family members who enabled me to be far more effective at exposing malpractice and proceeding through the various and many regulatory procedures. I was deeply touched and still am by the unswerving assistance I have always been able to call upon from family members, friends and neighbours. I even had support from some people who did not like me. They were sickened by the obvious child endangering malpractice among the self-styled professionals employed by the local council and their assistance was and is deeply appreciated. The average person in society is a high-quality individual, deeply child focused. Unfortunately, the local government children's services and the level of regulation about them is the complete opposite. It is self-serving, in the main.

I could provide several ring binders of information and correspondence with regulators and authorities. Personally, I find them stomach turning when I have to read them, even now. Suffice to say that there is copious documented evidence of my complaints history which corroborates everything I write here. But I do not want to sicken readers by providing infinite detail, many of you may believe you have had quite enough already. I sympathise where this is felt and thank you for reading this far.

Some of you may feel I have anger or unresolved issues of anger against my children's mother. I have no anger whatsoever against her, she has given birth to three beautiful children which I fathered. Because of her I had nine wonderful years being our children's primary carer, without question the best years of my life and indeed the children thrived during these years. Being angry with her is like being angry with bad weather, what's the point? Her later diagnosis of bipolar personality disorder explains much of what I suspected, but such is life.

However, my contempt for the unprofessional work of court appointed agencies who wilfully ignored this official diagnosis and focused purely on presenting me as being a man of violence, despite court findings exonerating me is the focus of my anger. My anger is also against the local authorities and their regulators who absolutely refuse to perform their duty to our children, and which numerous investigations and official inquiries have repeatedly exposed but to no avail. I am not trying to change the world, change law or anything else. Besides I would not have a clue how to do so. I simply focus on holding these authorities accountable to their statutory guidelines, and if regulators are complicit with malpractice, them also. I am a simple person and I like to keep things simple. Circles are for the bewildered.

I mentioned earlier about Alice In Wonderland and now we have Vincent in Brent.

During my complaints against the local government and its many agencies now involved in my case, I discovered the real meaning of dishonesty. I always believed that the local authority would only tell a lie if they could not be caught out - a huge overestimation on my part. The real problem is, local government and its myriad regulators have virtually no standard of honesty. Which perversely means, they have no standard of dishonesty. The truth is whatever they wish it to be. It is totally pliable, infinitely variable, but always, and I mean always, beneficial to them.

For one example of distortion, the local head of children's psychotherapy told me, "the truth, whatever it is, is infinitely variable". In short, they bring lying into disrepute. Years later I was told that in social services training there is no such thing as the 'truth,' only 'power.'

I spent several months trying to contact this man, always rebuffed. He had presented a statement to the case conference on 15th June 2007 stating I had blocked treatment for the children. He had never met me, never contacted me by letter or phone, and I never knew of his or his department's existence until then. I knew absolutely nothing about his alleged willingness to treat our children. He certainly had my address and home telephone number, in fact he told the case conference that he was asked to help remove me from the family home by my ex-wife, who just so happened to be a work colleague of his. When I finally met him several months later after the family courts had insisted and overruled the local professional's reports, his included, he started taking deep breaths and saying he did not know why he had said what he had in his report to the 15th June case conference. At a later Local Government Ombudsman investigation he was forced to apologise and I also received an apology from the North-West London head of Children and Adolescent Mental Health Services, letter of 18.12.08. And, of course we had the sincere commitment that the service would be improved as lessons had been learnt and procedural change would follow. Now, where have I heard that one before?

Ironically, he was set up by the local council. When I continued my complaints against this institutional local malpractice in Brent, the council had a very bright idea. At this stage, I was getting near to the Local Government Ombudsman which happens after Stage 3 of a complaint. Oh yes, you have to learn their bureaucratic language. A complaint goes nowhere unless it has the magic words, 'I wish to make a formal Stage 1, 2, or 3 complaint'. Then it will be quite often be lost! You see, these agencies have many very large desks. And these desks have several trays. Also, they have temporary staff, interns, work experience personnel, and guess what? Some of these staff do not know which tray is the proper tray for placing your formal complaint in. And, quite incredibly, at night time when nobody is present, leprechauns or poltergeists remove your complaint from the proper filing cabinet and place them at the back of different filing cabinets, or the cleaners accidentally put them in the bin!

As a rule of thumb, if a complaint goes missing, that means it is too hot to handle. Many of mine have been lost, but I used to work as a motorbike courier and at the time I still had the clipboard and some delivery sheets left over. Quite remarkably I rediscovered my love for couriering once again. A busy, scruffy and impatient courier would enter the reception of these local authorities and get a signature from security or reception. And as I am a slightly disbelieving individual where local government is concerned, I used to politely ask the individual who had provided their signature what their name is and carefully note it beside the spider's web they had casually provided me with. After a while they cottoned onto this, and suddenly there was an administrative problem. I would be asked to wait for someone to come down. I would still be waiting if they had their way. On a couple of occasions, a local helpful councillor delivered them to reception for me. And then we had the beautiful email from the Deputy Director of Brent Social Services to local Councillors describing me in terms of blushing flattery.

I was faced with the problem of how could I deliver, and prove I had delivered letters of complaint to the local Council. I put my issue to the local sub Postmaster and the solution was beautiful. Registered letters were expensive and would be brought before the council's legal department. Which meant they were virtually guaranteed to be, very sadly, lost somewhere in their wonderfully busy system. Every time I posted a letter I obtained proof of postage, which in UK law is also proof of delivery. And the best part is, they had no way of knowing this. I would send the complaint letter keeping proof of postage, ask them in a week or so if they had received it, and get a standard response of, 'very sorry, we cannot help you as we cannot find it'. Then I sent a copy of the letter with proof of postage to the local Council Chief Executive, local Councillors etc, and unbelievably, my original letter was quite often found. Subject to all the administrative difficulties encountered above, you understand. Which is when I learned of these administrative difficulties.

By now I was having temporary delusions of competence. I could type with two fingers, I could persuade a printer to print, I had discovered proof of postage, and best of all I could hold the council accountable. A one-man campaign you may think. Well the council had a surprise for me. At stage 3 of my first complaint Brent decided to really treat me to the best they could manage. They hired a consultant, who obviously spent many hours poring over my complaint. This ex local Government Ombudsman investigator wrote an incredibly detailed and very closely typed twenty-seven -page response to me. Three days before a major three-day hearing in the Family

Court where due to no money I was a Litigant In Person, I miraculously also have this to deal with.

The small brain was overwhelmed. This would have to wait until after the court hearing. By now my excuse for a brain was becoming really frazzled. And when I recovered from the shock of reading such an avalanche of print from the local council, I discovered Eureka. Detailed and massive though it was, when I unpicked it line by line, well hidden in the middle of a huge paragraph relating to separate matter, was the line I was looking for. They had lied and compounded the lie. Talk about hard work, tunnelling with a spoon came to mind. I continued with my complaint to the Local Government Ombudsman.

It was then I discovered the cosy relationship between Local Government and Government regulators. You see, the Local Government Ombudsman (LGO) decided that Brent had done nothing wrong in the kangaroo case conference of 15th June 2007. In fact, the LGO rebuked me for not fully participating with it. At that time, my very experienced family law solicitor and an ex judge had advised me against participating with such an improperly constituted panel and to request an independent panel. I made this request in writing and verbally. And with regard to the libellous emails from the Deputy Director of Brent Social Services to local Councillors about me, that was a 'regrettable error'. The only apparent cause of concern was Social Services in Brent handing me other vulnerable children's files. That was described as deplorable. I'm sure Brent Social Services were terrified at such strong condemnation.

However, the local head of children's psychotherapy was now in the firing line. I was advised by the LGO that under Special Amendments 2006 of the Children Act 1989 I could pursue my complaint, if I so wished. And I did. By now I had really improved my complaints. No longer long heart-rending letters complaining about brutal malpractice. At this stage, I had discovered the really effective mechanism of complaining. My complaint under Special Amendments 2006 of the Children Act was much better written. Very short, to the point, no loose language or so I believed. But my new best friend, Gareth Daniel, Chief Executive of Brent Council had a special surprise for me.

Remember this is the same Gareth Daniel who was chief executive of Brent at the time of the very expensive and thorough Lord Laming inquiry. And Mr Daniel undertook to implement all necessary recommendations from the Lord Laming inquiry. Lessons were learnt, there would be no repeat, beacon of good practice and so on. And, oh yes, children's services were underfunded and they would need more money. Mr Daniel had the idea that my complaints were getting somewhere, and he came up with a brilliant plan to stop them. He simply decided that most of my complaints had already been dealt with by the council. So therefore, there was only a small part of my complaint outstanding. All the big ones were just thrown in the bin. Executive decision, made no doubt for sound procedural reasons. You see, he had learned how to deal with complaints, and was putting it to good use. Ref: letter Gareth Daniel to me; 17th December 2008. His excuse of convenience was that the Local Government Ombudsman had decided the council were correct.

Let us look at the bigger picture here. A local council has received the most serious of complaints regarding vulnerable children's safety, and this council aggressively pursuing a gender discriminatory policy where half of all children's parents are blocked from access to the gateway services. Two complaints managers hired by the council to deal with the complaint formerly worked in the Local Government Ombudsman office. And surprise surprise, the Local

Government Ombudsman finds that the council did nothing wrong of importance, just a few minor misdemeanour's. I would hate to appear cynical about regulatory.

If Lord Laming's Victoria Climbie enquiry, several government investigations and huge financial input has led to such a hopelessly inadequate system, why are the powers that be in society letting this happen and why is there no pressure being put on them by the public?

I then proceeded with the tiny part of my complaint still allowed by the local council, Brent. This meant that an outside independent investigator with an assistant would be involved. Credit is due here because despite the tiny remit allowed, they did a very good job under the circumstances. On the virtually irrelevant portion of the complaint outstanding they found fault with the local Head of Children and Adolescent Mental Health Service, CAMHS and Brent Social Services. I received a letter of partial apology from the North-West London head of CAMHS, and also a partial apology from the Director of Children's Services in Brent. The council were very smart here, a tiny procedural matter was found against them, which is exactly as they had intended. The equivalent of a bank robber being issued with a parking ticket for parking his car illegally while inside robbing the bank.

I persisted with the complaint, always trying to get the principal complaints heard. And Brent then treated me to a 'Independent Panel report: Stage Three Complaints Review Panel under the Children Act 1989 Complaints Procedure. What really annoyed me here was that my concern for the children was being administratively hijacked by bureaucratic jargon.

This panel had three senior consultants in management, who were now 'panel members'. One of them was the Chair. The review was fixed for 24th February 2009. I was allowed to bring a friend, so I borrowed one with a good brain. And guess who was representing Brent, my former admirer, Janet Palmer, she who had sent the very flattering email mentioned earlier about me to Local Councillors, and who had investigated herself when I formally complained about her to Brent where she found she had done nothing wrong. Such a surprise that the investigated was the investigator and cleared herself of any wrongdoing. And the second person representing Brent was, Christine Bridgett, Head of Service. And therein lies a story which describes so much of what is wrong with local government self-regulation.

After the Brent kangaroo, and I apologise to all kangaroos, case conference of 15th June 2007, I started writing complaints about this reckless child endangering malpractice by Brent. And one head of service, in fact the only one to this day, who decided to meet me was Christine Bridgett, I believe then Head of Children In Need. We met in her office on 24th July 2007. And Alice in Wonderland was also present, and dominated the meeting. You see, one of my biggest complaints was about Brent processing me in secret for repeatedly kicking and then killing the non-existent family dog. When I mentioned about this phantom dog and produced the witness statements corroborating that as a family we never had a dog, what was the response from Ms Bridgett? My wife should have reported the matter to the RSPCA, Royal Society for The Protection of Cruelty to Animals.

Two years later I attended an open event at Willesden Magistrates Court. By now I was representing a shared parenting charity and various stands were also in attendance. One of them was the Local Children Safeguarding Board, represented by, Christine Bridgett. The LCSB have a duty to regulate local children's services as provided by the council. Let us hope she does not get bitten by a phantom dog in the course of her duties. And that was when I began to understand just how cosy the relationship is between malpracticing local government authorities and their 'statutory regulatory authorities'.

Also present at the review panel meeting was the independent investigator and his assistant. Here was a man who had been a former senior social worker, poacher turned gamekeeper if you like. I protested about the presence of, Janet Palmer, and also attempted to have my principal complaints dealt with. You can guess the result, zero on both counts. I sat back and witnessed the independent investigator process my case on the relatively tiny outstanding matter left. And boy oh boy, did I learn. This man was brilliant at understanding nuances of language, written and spoken. The review panel hit him from several angles, but he had the wit and ability to always deflect their attempts and re-enter mine. In the context of where I was and my ability to survive and develop my case, was the equivalent of an ignorant man playing air guitar and pretending to be Jimi Hendrix. The difference was that stark.

My friend in attendance helping me then made one simple and rather obvious statement. He stated that Brent were facilitating and promoting false allegations based on grounds of gender. The result was totally unexpected. Janet Palmer went immediately into extreme outrage that such a possibility could ever be considered. Christine Bridgett supported her, at a much lower decibel. I realised then that so much of a council's rage and effort is being used to protect themselves. These people had as far as I could see unlimited access to public funds to protect themselves from my complaint. And the fear was all in front of me. Problem was, I did not know how to pursue this any further.

The wonderful man assisting me on the day was involved in similar action with London Borough of Haringey, the twin of

Brent that had due to brutal malpractice regarding Victoria Climbie caused the Lord Laming investigation in 2001-2003 after a public outcry. This man had an intellect so far ahead of mine it would be the equivalent of comparing a wooden post to a senior university lecturer. Unlike me, he decided to take court action against the malpractising local authority. We estimate the local authority used huge amount of public funds to equip themselves with the best legal protection possible. How much would invite ridicule if I print it, so I won't. Sadly, the poor man ended up having a major mental breakdown trying to deal with this and his children's matters were also in court. I learnt a vital lesson. A private person has no hope seeking protection from the courts in this business. That just plays into the hands of the local authority who will out manoeuvre you and then hit you for costs. After all, they can hire the best legal mercenaries, we fund them.

Incidentally, I lost at the aforementioned review panel on an interpretation of action. I had complained about the local head of children's psychotherapy telling a court that I was blocking treatment for my children. If you cast your mind back this was related to the kangaroo case conference on 15th June 2007 and his statement was then lodged in the bundle for court as evidence against me. The disadvantage of average education and an element of over emotion is that when writing my complaint, I used the word 'telling'. The council and social services had great joy informing the review panel that this man was not present in court, so therefore he could not have told the court anything. On a technicality of language interpretation, I lost on that point. And I learnt from losing. Because at that point I realised the council were persecuting me. And persecution is the deliberate systemic planned act of oppression to neutralise via intimidation. One of the few advantages I had in life was many, many years riding a motorbike for a living. And as I teenager I had read the remarkable book by Robert M Pirsig, 'Zen and the Art of

Motorcycle Maintenance'. I actually bought it to learn more about maintaining bikes. I was so disgusted I threw it aside for several years until I read a review about it by a motorcycling journalist I really admired. I then read it again to understand it better. And now out of absolute necessity I re-entered that deep thinking process.

That was my first Ombudsman investigation on my behalf. And a pretty sorry excuse for regulation if I say so. So how did I end up with four more Ombudsman investigations, three of which were Parliamentary and Health Services Ombudsman, the Ombudsman in charge of everything? The best quote I can think of is by Thomas Edison. He once replied when asked about genius, 'it is ninety-nine per cent perspiration and one per cent inspiration'. Well, I could do the sweating all right.

Then I realised my inspiration is not just the children's needs, I would use the repeat malpractice of these unregulated services as inspiration. I figured that as a Litigant In Person in family proceedings the pain is a given, I had time as I was living in a semi-converted garage and awaiting a large diameter hip resurfacing. The rent was affordable as I owned the garage. I was seeing the children quite regularly, albeit with problems and had confidence that the Judges in Family Courts were far more professional in their work than the children's services I had encountered. And once again my delusions of confidence were misplaced. Not so much by the Judges themselves, but particularly by the family court support agency.

Chapter 2

Cafcass Part One

Unquestionably one of the most shocking experiences in my life was meeting Cafcass, the Children and family court advisory support service. Despite growing up in the bottom of Ulster during the 60's and 70's which was when the 'troubles' started, and also having a keen knowledge of history, nothing prepared me for the visceral naked child endangering gender discrimination that I experienced with Cafcass. Without question they are the biggest obstacle to reform and improvement within the family courts. But then, what can one expect when the domestic violence agency they so eagerly and often commission, insists that only men can be guilty of domestic abuse. Cafcass and Brent children's services, are definitely the gruesome twosome where children and fathers are concerned.

Cafcass stands for Children and Family Court Advisory and Support Services. They are the eyes and ears of the family court. Cafcass investigate families and report their findings to the court. And Judges cannot stray from their recommendations without giving reason. From April 2016 to March 2017 Cafcass in England and Wales received 40,534 private family law applications.

'Hell is not hot enough, nor eternity long enough for those miscreants,' thundered an Irish bishop once when preaching from the pulpit giving out about Irish nationalists, who later became the government of Ireland after independence. I am absolutely confident this bishop had never met Cafcass. If he had, his language might not have been so moderate. At some time in history when intelligent people review all the many faults within children's services and the family court system in the UK, Cafcass' institutional malpractice will loom large. If you believe that my experiences in Brent were bad, you were correct. But Cafcass in my case demonstrated why Brent did what they did. And the reason they did it is quite simple. It is the system - *their* system. Safe from prying eyes or public interference, hiding behind secrecy, protected by the ultimate mission statement, 'Welfare of the child is paramount'. And they have a phenomenal protection system, the Courts themselves. Cafcass were set up on April Fool's Day 2001. A worse joke was never more perpetrated upon children in the UK than this lot.

To help you better understand what an absurd joke Cafcass are at vulnerable children's expense consider this: 82% of Cafcass officers are female and their Domestic Violence Perpetrator Programme/Domestic Violence Intervention Project is for *male* perpetrators only. A lovely introduction to their institutional thinking.

A special Children's Guardian, called a Guardian Ad Litem, had been appointed by a family court as they deemed the allegations so severe neither party could be depended on to adequately represent the children. The children would have their own solicitor and the Guardian would have the service of a Barrister in court. All well and good one might say and also publicly funded. I was delighted with what I considered proper professionals becoming involved after my experiences with the clowns in Brent: Until I met the guardian outside court for the first time. She introduced herself in a friendly manner, and commented I had a very good relationship with the children. I responded that as I had been their primary carer I should have. 'Oh no, you were not', was her reply. Dumbstruck by that comment I said nothing more. It had the effect of almost making me wish for Brent. Just for a little while, you understand.

Everything in the family courts is protected vigorously by those courts. Their eagerness to bring contempt proceedings against those who publish or speak publicly is well known. I will have to keep my comments only to what happened outside of the family courts. After all, no need to tease them, is there. That said, more importantly, my children and I owe a great deal to the Judges who eventually, nineteen hearings later, effectively disregarded all of the recommendations from the myriad agencies in Brent, and especially Cafcass, in granting me shared residence of our three children. Although I am not too impressed at their refusal to enforce that order when later necessary regarding our eldest boy and also when aged nine, his younger brother.

The guardian requested a meeting with me a few weeks later at her office in central London. Upon entering the building security asked me where I was going. I replied Cafcass. The man then said the best of luck and offered me his deepest sympathy. Little did I know what lion's den I was entering. The meeting was meant to be about the children, or so the letter said. I could talk about them all day, if required. I was not. The guardian and her colleague after a brief greeting and conversation moved onto what Domestic Violence Intervention Project (DVIP) would I agree to. Once again, I was dumbstruck. When I eventually stuttered a response asking why, the reply was truly magnificent. 'The professionals in Brent have deemed you to be violent'.

I have often mentioned Alice in Wonderland. Lewis Carroll, its author, needs to come back to life and write another book because reality is totally absent where many of these professionals are concerned. In the course of this meeting I decided I had to defend myself. Shock is one thing, survival another. So, I mentioned the false allegation regarding the phantom family dog. This seemed to have an effect on them. I was then sent out of the room because they wished to comply with an equalities directive and presented me with a form to fill in. As a white Irishman, I decided that black or Asian did not apply to me. I ticked the box, and noticed there was no box for a black Irishman to tick. Funny what the mind notices when severely stressed.

I was called back into the room and to my deep joy they were frantically poring over the BDVAP document (Brent Domestic Violence Advocacy Project), the litany of allegations against me. My novelist admirers in Brent had found new fans in Cafcass and this became their accusatory document against me. I firmly stood my ground, stating that some of the allegations were totally false, the rest hugely exaggerated and that I had witness statements to prove it. I was then met with true, stark child endangering gender discrimination. I was rebuked for having procured witness statements. So much for children's welfare and The Paramountcy Principle. Section 1 of the Children Act 1989 states that 'welfare of the child is paramount'. About as relevant at that meeting as noticing no section in their equalities document for black Irish. Discrimination works best when cloaked with the guise of concern was the thought that occurred to me when leaving that brutal experience.

Cafcass are like Brent Council children's section, there have been several official investigations including a Select Committee from the House of Commons and several OFSTED investigations. OFSTED is the official regulatory body acting on behalf of the British Government. Its remit is to set and maintain standards for all schools and public bodies with responsibility for children. On several occasions, OFSTED investigations into Cafcass have described them as *'not good enough'*. House Of Commons Select Committee in 2011 described Cafcass as *'unfit for purpose'* and OFSTED summarised them thus: *'their conclusions are not reasoned'*. A beautiful and accurate use of language if ever there was.

What lessons have been learned from this? Christine Gilbert, the former chief executive of OFSTED, later became the Chief Executive Officer for Brent Council. And Anthony Douglas, Chief Executive Officer of Cafcass, is at the time of writing in 2013 one of the principal advisers to the British Government on proposed revisions to the Children Act. Welfare of the Children is Paramount! (Children Act 1989). God help all children from professionals deliberately misinterpreting this simple language, because the system will not.

My then wife engaged a new solicitor in 2008. I was assured this was bad news as he was notoriously aggressive and a master of sharp practice. I believed that as there was the Solicitors Regulatory Authority, the professional body which oversees the conduct of all solicitors, I had protection from malpractice. At this stage, I have to say I am a slow learner. To the point of stupidity in fact. Several court orders were broken by him which meant I lost heavily during ancillary financial proceedings. A three-day hearing on complex technical matters as a litigant in person, assisted by a very good McKenzie Friend, while crippled with pain as one week later I underwent a hip operation is difficult enough without the huge handicap of solicitor malpractice. I sought leave to appeal when I was discharged from hospital two weeks later.

The appeal hearing was scheduled for half an hour. I lost on a narrow technical point, yet again. Costs were sought by the opposition. They told the Judge 'in the region of £5,000'. Bad enough in itself. Then amazingly the bill arrived. It was for almost £9,000. I protested and said I would bring a complaint before the Solicitors Regulatory Authority (SRA). Nothing happened for several months. Then I was hit again for costs but also an attempt to bankrupt me. Once again, my incredible family and friends came to my assistance. My mother gave me her burial money rather than see me bankrupt. Pride is a strong element in my family. I lodged a complaint with the SRA, who informed me that they do not handle complaints for solicitors when they are acting for the other side. I smelt a large rat here. So, unless you are a client of a solicitor you cannot complain about them? I persisted with my complaint and asked for help from my friend the former senior University Lecturer, now recovering from a breakdown. We then discovered that all complaints against solicitors have to be lodged within six months of the alleged malpractice. Now I understood why the thieving solicitor had waited six months and a day before hitting me with costs, plus attempted bankruptcy and a charge on my house.

Fortunately, my friend had the phenomenal intellect necessary to get my complaint to the Legal Services Ombudsman. And the LSO's verdict was very severe indeed. The Ombudsman formally criticised the Solicitors Regulatory Authority for not accepting my complaint: which obviously stopped all Solicitors from malpractising ever again!

After two dud Ombudsman investigation's I decided to forget about formal complaints. I was still fighting in the family courts for Shared Residence of our three children, as I had been from the beginning. With more three-day hearings looming, major problems with my hip resurfacing, and the need to convert my house from a dump to something remotely habitable for the children to stay overnight, I had far too much to deal with.

Several months later I received a letter from OFSTED. This is the body responsible for all children's services in the UK. They had recently been put in charge of Cafcass. OFSTED wanted to know how I felt about my experiences with Cafcass. I looked at their letter in total disbelief. I had so much to say about the brutal child endangering malpractice of that body I had not got a clue where to start. I had never complained about Cafcass as I had always been told they are answerable to no-one. A formal request on the Government forum "What do they Know?" established that never ever had a Family Court Judge recommended a corrupt Cafcass or Social Worker be reprimanded or retrained. I had decided there was nothing I could do. A major part here was that every time I thought of Cafcass I felt physically sick. And hugely relieved that two quality Judges had been critical of my children's Guardian's work.

I sat down as if in a daze and just put everything on paper to OFSTED. No formal complaint, just several pages of horrible history so that others could be spared from this misery. And then an astonishing thing happened. My letter was lost!

I could not believe it. Brent all over again. But by now I had dragged myself off the floor and was up for the fight. The lost letter galvanised me. I wrote again, and again, to OFSTED. And their wonderful reply was, 'we do not deal with complaints about individual Cafcass officers'.

End of the road you might think. No. Now I was in full battle mode: the same energy I had found when dealing with Brent institutional child endangering malpractice after their kind interview with our then three-year old son had returned. Lessons had been learnt, by me. I sent my letter to OFSTED to Cafcass complaints. And it was lost again! This letter was seriously lacking in geographical ability.

I can only assume that someone on high is exercising great humour here. But by now I realised that good complaints were always lost when received. This meant that Cafcass were afraid. And fear means they had something to hide, so I

persisted. The letter was found and I received what can only be described as an insulting reply. Then I became truly focused and put together the best two-page letter of my life. I set out very clearly where they had done wrong. And I promised Cafcass I would bring this matter before every authority applicable. And I awaited their response, which never arrived. Because it was never sent, as you will read about later.

Earlier on I had complained to the GSCC (General Social Care Council), the body responsible for all registered social workers in the UK. The GSCC told me I would have to get the Registration numbers of the social workers I was complaining about. I wrote to their employer, Brent Council. I was told that Janet Palmer's registration had ceased and the other social worker I had complained about was no longer employed by Brent. I had also established through Freedom of Information that in Brent social workers only last on average for two years and four months. This is yet another direct snub to Lord Laming's recommendation for continuity of personnel after he had investigated Brent in the Victoria Climbie case. This effectively meant that a cabal of middle management hard-line feminists were running Brent children services, hence the link with Brent domestic violence agency discriminating on grounds of gender when providing service. And the dud token man, who was not even a social worker, was nominally in charge and had as much knowledge about vulnerable children's safety as a meerkat has about car insurance: just a front for the public.

You might think that people in charge of children's social services would be experienced social workers. Think again. Dozens are not. Ex-councillors, ex-teachers, ex-headteachers, and ex-educationalists, for example, were made directors of children's services and child protection. The boss of children's services in Haringey at the time of Baby P had no social work background.

A few weeks later I entered CAMHS (children's mental health services) in Brent on a child related matter. And who do you think had entered the building earlier? My good friend the social worker whom I had complained about and the council had earlier denied knowing. She had dutifully signed in with her name and position as a social worker in Brent. She had married and her married name was added to her original name. So technically, when I asked Brent for her registration using the name I knew her as, they exploited the loophole of her name change. I will not name this social worker because I believe she had tried to do the right thing. But she was junior and overruled. The system in Brent was much more interested in getting rid of fathers than focusing on children's safety. Gender ideology tramps over children's welfare as it requires.

I persisted with my complaint to the GSCC. They had a surprise for me. They would not accept my complaint in the manner I had presented it to them. I would have to present it in their format. Which, surprise surprise, was a total dilution of the complaint. I approached the Minister in charge of social services. Their name clearly says they are in charge of social services. They sent me a letter informing me they are not in charge of social services. Another government department is, they told me, so I sent them a letter. And after a long delay, and following reminders, I ended up being sent to several government departments, all of whom denied responsibility. I later found out that it was the policy of the General Social Care Council at that time to refuse to handle complaints. As the nominated government departments who had the responsibility all denied having it, then it was no surprise the GSCC decided they did not need to handle complaints. Who would want to find fault against themselves when the exercise is optional?

Around this time our eldest boy was beginning to show behavioural patterns which reminded me of the pressure he had been under when the divorce proceedings started. I tried to get some assistance for him. I had been told by the children's mother which GP he had been registered with some months earlier after his mum had fallen out with the children's previous GP who had been her business partner. I approached this GP surgery only to be informed the children were not registered there. I requested they double check, which they did, and still no registration of my children. I approached the local Primary Care Trust (PCT) to find out my children's GP: Brent PCT refused to tell me. I had sent them a copy of the Shared Residence Order which demonstrates that I had Parental Responsibility (PR) for the children. I persisted and requested the PCT comply with their statutory duty here. They responded that as I had been deemed a danger to our children they were not obliged to inform me. Under General Medical Council (GMC) guidelines for all GP's there is a very clear paragraph, number 55, which says divorce or separation make no difference to a parent's rights to have access to their children's medical information. The GMC had already refused to inform me and had suggested I approach the PCT some months earlier. So once again I wrote to the PCT and then received their huge procedures bundle, which was utterly useless for anything other than providing insulation in a dog kennel on cold nights. Perhaps of some benefit to a phantom dog, as phantom appears to be the operative term where children's services in London Borough of Brent are concerned.

The Brent PCT unknown to me had at this time taken legal advice regarding my complaint. And the legal advice was that they should provide me with the information as to who was our children's GP. Brent PCT then did what so many corrupt organisations do when they don't like the legal advice received - they sat on it.

I then complained to the Parliamentary and Health Service Ombudsman (PHSO) via my Member of Parliament (MP). And the Parliamentary Ombudsman informed me as the Brent PCT had not replied to my complaint the matter would have to be referred back to Brent PCT. We were on the merry-go-round, but this one was going somewhere. Brent PCT under pressure from the Parliamentary Ombudsman then informed me about six months later who my children's GP was – it was their mother!

When she caught wind of me knowing this, she promptly changed the children's GP to her own GP who refused to comply with the statutory regulations when I approached them.

At this stage, my respect for Ombudsmen was not too great. But, as there was no choice, I referred my complaint via my patient MP back to the Parliamentary Ombudsman: and they did their investigation into Brent PCT. Among the first actions of the Parliamentary Ombudsman was a phone call to the new non-compliant GP practice.

The Parliamentary Ombudsman report upheld my complaint against Brent PCT. He found that their response fell so far short of the applicable standard that it amounted to maladministration. And his recommendations were:

1) Brent PCT should acknowledge the failings identified in this report and apologise to me for the injustice suffered.
2) Brent PCT to pay me the sum of £250 as compensation for the frustration and distress caused to me as a result of the maladministration identified.
3) A copy of the apology and evidence of payment should be sent to the Ombudsman.
4) To ensure continuous improvement, in line with the principles for remedy, he further recommended that

within 3 months the PCT should prepare an action plan that describes what it has done to ensure that it has learnt the lessons from the failings identified in the report and what it has done or plans to do to avoid a recurrence of those failings.

5) Copies of the action plan should be forwarded to Mr McGovern, NHS London and the Care Quality Commission, each of which should be kept regularly updated on progress against the plan. A copy of the action plan should also be sent to the Ombudsman.

It is difficult to describe how I felt when I received this report. I cried like a child, but for a different reason, just as I had when Brent Social Services had informed me they were sabotaging the court ordered holiday contact for the children with me in 2007.

After shall we say, recovery, I phoned the Parliamentary Ombudsman investigator to thank him for his excellent work. I have to say that any conversations I have had with Parliamentary Ombudsman staff and investigators were light years removed from the absurd conversations I had with other pseudo regulatory authorities: simple, concise, effective and to the point. I realised that the truly capable do not need to hide behind spoof management jargon and stilted language. As we were finishing the conversation I expressed regret that Cafcass were not subject to such proper regulation as I had discovered with their report into Brent PCT. His simple response totally stunned me, 'the Parliamentary Ombudsman is the body responsible for all government bodies including Cafcass'.

I found myself looking at the handset of the phone as if it had ten heads. Unbelievable, disbelieving, shocked and totally stunned, probably goes some way to describe how I felt. When I managed to reconnect brain to speak, which took a while, I asked how I should complain against Cafcass. I was told to contact my MP for assistance.

For the record, I never did gain access to my child's medical records. Reason being, this process took so long it worked in the system's favour as he had then reached an age when legally I didn't have to be informed.

Shortly afterwards Brent Primary Care Trust was disbanded. Obviously, my successful PHSO investigation was totally unrelated to this?

You see, how these institutions self-protect so brilliantly is the well established method of disbanding when the heat becomes too much and then reforming under a different name. Just as Cafcass did in 2001 when they dumped the Court Welfare Officer title and became Cafcass, Children and family court advisory support service. What a wonderfully benign title, how could anyone take offence at it?

The Emperors invisible clothes is the title I have for them!

Chapter 3

Cafcass Part 2

Initially Cafcass practitioners had informed me that only Cafcass regulates Cafcass. Which of course is absolutely beautiful, for Cafcass. Laugh if you wish but I decided to change that. Someone once told me I'm like Don Quixote, tilting at windmills. I replied, "the good Don only had single windmills, I have a windfarm to attack." Gee up good donkey, we have many enemies to attack.

Once again, my MP received a letter requesting his assistance. After some time had elapsed, I received a very friendly phone call from an investigator in the Parliamentary Health Service Ombudsman office. They informed me that as I had only completed a formal Stage 1 complaint with Cafcass, the Ombudsman could not become involved until all Cafcass complaints procedures were exhausted. I protested that Cafcass would just run my complaint into the ground, it would suffer an administrative mishap! But the kind lady assured me that Cafcass at Stage 2 are much more capable than at their Stage 1 process.

To help matters this lady on the Ombudsman's behalf had already discussed with Cafcass senior management how to process my complaint. It would be done under the Ombudsman umbrella watch, and a letter to that effect was en-route to my MP and myself.

I had liberty to bring the matter back before the Ombudsman without my MP's assistance if Cafcass did not deal with my concerns properly. I was concerned that good though he is, he may be leant on to drop me if I persisted. Thankfully, Barry Gardiner MP remained resolute.

I now had a formal Stage 2 complaint with Cafcass to deal with, purely thanks to the Ombudsman and my MP. This complaint was being dealt with by a senior Cafcass service manager who had no prior involvement with the case.

I was given a choice of dates to attend a meeting in central London with this lady. Upon arrival, I met a professional woman, a Cafcass Service Manager. Good, I thought to myself, this will get sorted. But I am still a slow learner.

Unfortunately, irrelevant side issues were getting highlighted by this woman and the central complaints were being ignored or marginalised. Characters were being deliberately mixed up. For example, my McKenzie Friend, a former secondary school teacher, had to lodge his entire original case bundle with Cafcass at the Guardians Ad Litem's desk to prove he was not a child rapist. He had obtained Shared Residence after demonstrating this accusation, like so many others, was false.

Cafcass had during my proceedings insisted I cease working with him. The Guardian also insisted over the phone, on three consecutive days just after my hip resurfacing, when I was on four different types of medication due to complications, that I also cease membership of the Shared Parenting Charity, Families Need Fathers. This was where I had met my McKenzie Friend after running out of borrowed money for legal assistance.

In court a few weeks after my operation, instead of dealing with Shared Residence, I had to contend with the Guardian seeking injunctions preventing me from having this McKenzie Friend. I had to partially agree to these injunctions on the understanding that he would provide the Guardian with his entire case bundle in the next few days. This bundle we were assured would be returned forthwith. Two days later he brought his original bundle to the Guardians desk. It was never returned!

My principle complaints to this service manager against Cafcass were that they resolutely refused to accept the fact I had been the children's primary carer for over nine years, despite twenty-nine witness statements in court corroborating this, and not one counter statement was produced as evidence. Also, I was protesting about Cafcass institutional child endangering gender discrimination, for example, their insistence on working with agencies and local authority contractors that discriminate on grounds of gender, the Brent Domestic Violence Agency. The Cafcass service manager assured me that this agency does excellent work. I replied that Hitler made the trains run on time, and that at all times with Cafcass I had felt like a black man approaching the local branch of the Ku Klux Klan for assistance. I had said this in Court and also told this black service manager.

After the above comment, there was a sudden eruption of anger, surprising in intensity. The manager sharply stated she was going to walk out of the meeting. I realised this was a ploy to get me to walk out first, then the complaint would go no further because I had abandoned it. Being polite, I asked if I should leave the door open or shut? 'What do you mean?', was her confused response. I explained that when she left, I would have to either shut the door or leave it open until someone else from Cafcass came to handle my Stage 2. I had learned from Brent Special Amendments 2006 of the Children Act Management Executive meeting in 2008.

The phoney anger left as quickly as it had arrived, after she realised I was calling her bluff. It is just a standard technique used by these professionals to confuse and either subjugate or anger the pesky complainer who is getting too far. Then they control the situation, and the outcome. We were back to professional lady, what a surprise.

A few weeks after the Stage 2 meeting I received the outcome in writing. Cafcass apologised with a letter expressing sympathy for me in various measures, lessons would be learnt (I swear I read that somewhere before) my McKenzie Friend's bundle would be found and returned, and near the end on a certain paragraph in the Guardians report for the 3-day Finding of Fact hearing in February 2008, it clearly stated that the Guardian had reported I was the children's primary carer. Nothing has ever confused me as much as reading that paragraph.

I could not believe I had been so stupid as to have believed and processed my complaint against Cafcass for years on this delusion that it had not been stated. In a complete daze, I grabbed my bicycle and started to cycle to a reservoir where myself and the children had spent so many happy hours. Utterly confused and blind with fury at my own stupidity, I started to cycle off road up the steepest hill I could find. Just at the point where my legs, hip and lungs were in agony it suddenly hit me. Cafcass had falsified the stage 2 report. I suddenly remembered the paragraph numbers as being different.

I fell off the bicycle laughing like an idiot as I had forgotten to continue pedalling. Other park users were giving me a wide berth, madness can be infectious I suppose was their fear. Who wants to see a middle aged man lying down laughing with a bicycle on top of him. I cycled home as fast as possible, suddenly my body was pain free, but my mind still had a small doubt. I raced up to the attic and searched among boxes for the original report. The paragraph mentioned was not in it.

Déjà vu, we're here again, they are all corrupt… and several similar expressions came to mind. And huge relief that I was not, as I had initially believed, wrong.

I settled down and read the Stage 2 report carefully, then formally requested a Stage 3 report to deal with what had so studiously been ignored and lied about in Stage 2. I now had the false report from Stage 2 as added ammunition. One week after I had sent my formal request for Stage 3, I received a response stating that a senior consultant from Cafcass and another consultant from the NSPCC were available to deal with my complaint. I was stunned. Had Cafcass decided to organise the Stage 3 panel before they had sent me the Stage 2 response, just in case it did not get rid of me? Either that, or these incredibly busy consultants have a lot of spare time on their hands for the likes of me.

So onwards to Stage 3, and once again I borrowed someone with a brain, although this time not my good friend the former senior university lecturer. He was too busy living in his barricaded kitchen trying to avoid imaginary government assassins seeking to kill him. Words fail me when trying to describe what was done to this man who only sought to remain in his children's lives and attempted to get the local services to do their job properly. I have learnt from his mistakes in assuming there is integrity among child professionals, and I owe him a great deal. Perhaps some-day he will recover and I will be able to explain to him, I don't know, so many things that need to be said, will probably never be said, as he is now too damaged.

Stage 3 was at a large imposing building in Croydon, South London. The Germans had bombed Croydon heavily during the war: I had a feeling they hadn't completed the job after I left the Stage 3 meeting. At Stage 3 your complaint will not be dealt with: it is solely to sort out the procedural matters in the handling of your complaint. I was a bit like a bull in a bullfight, he is so weakened and tortured before facing the matador, there will only be one outcome.

We were introduced to the two consultants. Immediately I recognised the type of Cafcass consultant I was dealing with. I had met his brethren in Brent some years earlier at the management review. However, this man was sharper, god damn he was unbelievably quick in administrative nuances. It was like hand fishing with your hands tied behind your back and wearing gloves. I was really struggling to deal with him. Part of my problem with the Cafcass complaints procedure, is the fact it is revised every two years. Their beautiful revolving door system and my complaint actually spread over three of these. Bureaucracy and administrative procedures were doing good here, but not for me. He could hop from one procedural block to another like a fly.

I remembered the first meeting at a Cafcass office in central London almost four years earlier, how they were so focused on their pre-determined objectives and contemptuous of my concerns for the children. I also recalled the Brent Executive Management panel and their unbelievable sophistication at twisting and diverting what the independent former senior social worker was so effectively saying to them. Best of all I remembered the comment from my wonderful friend on the day in early 2008, when he said Brent Social Services and Council were facilitating and promoting false allegations depending on gender. Finally, at last, I could get in close for a real fight with one of these professional eels. I'd had a steep learning curve over the past four years.

Then the surprise, he says my complaint is invalid because I had not formally requested a Stage 2 investigation by Cafcass after their dismissive response to me in 2010. Once again credit to the independent consultant from the NSPCC, just like the previous independent in Brent, he knew his onions. He established that my letter of response to Cafcass that outlined their mistakes and assurance of further action demonstrated I had continued my complaint. But the Cafcass consultant argued fiercely that I had not used the formal words 'Stage 2.' He argued ferociously on that point and I realised I might be going home with my tail between my legs if he succeeded. But the NSPCC consultant very cleverly pointed out that it was not up to me to use the words Stage 2 formally. As an ordinary member of the public how would I know what the correct wording for Cafcass complaints are? Rather, it is the responsibility of Cafcass to provide me with this knowledge when I complained to them. Bingo, game on, and suddenly the eel was not so fast.

So, slowly, nicely and steadily I took him apart. I started with the false paragraph in their Stage 2 report. A nice concrete issue, bypassing all his procedural and administrative niceties. But the NSPCC guy insisted this was not for today, today was just for technical overview of handling. I could only complain about conduct, not content. I insisted that content is proof of conduct, one without the other is meaningless. The false paragraph was in the game. Then comedy, the Cafcass consultant had not read Cafcass own reports, he said. So, is he incompetent or lazy? Neither, it is a standard tactic to gain time, to read again and come up with a better excuse. Once again, we had the administrative error excuse. How convenient these administrative errors always suit the professionals when there is a complaint against them. So now we really had game on.

One of my opening comments was the varieties of truth as an excuse for regulators to avoid responsibility. Now we had Cafcass using all of these contextual interpretation excuses, what was written was not what was meant, what was meant was not what was written, the well-practised merry-go-round was spinning. So, I turned his merry go round upside down to stop him and myself from getting dizzy. I simply said that the Guardian is a professional officer of the court, and as such is educated, trained, and well paid at public expense to present a professional report where she writes what she means, where she is duty bound to reflect reality as much as possible for the assistance of the court.

The bigger picture here regarding Cafcass insisting on working with agencies and local authorities and Cafcass DVIP/DVPP that discriminate on grounds of gender was not allowed for consideration here. The gentleman from the NSPCC was very insistent on this. We had a huge section of institutional malpractice procedurally barred from discussion. Similar to Brent Council cherry picking what part of a complaint will be dealt with by higher regulation. The equivalent of a bank robber who having received the parking ticket while robbing the bank, choosing when caught, to only have the illegal parking ticket dealt with by a court. Power corrupts when such options exist.

Now we had Cafcass man doing the innocent bystander act. The Guardian is only a reporter, of no real authority, just a passer-by asked to write about a snapshot of a family when confrontation exists. I pointed out the section where family court judges have to give serious weight to Cafcass and Guardian reports and are not allowed to stray from them without giving good legal reason. At this stage, we were head-to-head. I insisted that an Officer of the court who deliberately omits vital evidence from a report, thereby seeking to mislead a court and predetermine the outcome, is guilty of perjury.

Perjury is a criminal offence punishable by imprisonment and that would also apply to management who colluded and protected the perjurer, such as himself. Cafcass man was seriously rattled and insisted this was not a matter for this hearing.

Then I flattened him. I agreed it was not a matter for this hearing, it would be a matter for a criminal law judge on judicial review and the evidence and notes from this hearing would feature. Like the scene in the Wizard of Oz, where the wicked witch dissolves after getting splashed with water, we had Cafcass consultant folding up like a flat pancake.

The meeting then became procedural with the NSPCC dealing with outstanding issues. Cafcass man was sitting slumped, his previous aggressive and effective verbosity replaced with short utterances that sometimes had to be repeated for us to hear. The NSPCC consultant sent his report to the CEO of Cafcass, Anthony Douglas, OBE and myself. A few days later I received a short letter from Mr Douglas which contained many apologies and of course, lessons would be learnt.

I smelt a rat. I believed that this abject display of apology was a tactic to prevent the real issues from proper scrutiny. I brought the outstanding issues back before the PHSO for their consideration. There was the deliberate omission regarding my nine years of rearing children and I also sought to have Cafcass barred from working with agencies and corrupt local authorities that discriminate on grounds of gender when providing children's services.

Plus, Cafcass own DVIP/DVPP gendered practice, not much use to have everyone in these agencies forever quoting the Children Act 1989, 'Welfare of the Child is Paramount', and then barring half of all children's parents from access to services. My McKenzie Friend had still not received his case bundle back from Cafcass over two years after personally delivering it by hand to the Guardians desk in the presence of security. The cleaner must have taken it away?

A few weeks later I received the verdict from the NSPCC consultant. To put it mildly, I was not happy. I contacted the PHSO investigator who was eager to bring this matter to a PHSO panel. This panel was convened and no doubt deliberated at length, I assume. I was not present nor asked, no notes were ever delivered to me from this panel so I don't know what was said or discussed. But I do know the outcome.

The PHSO ruled that Cafcass should improve their procedures when handling sensitive legal documents. And it noted that Cafcass had returned the bundle to my McKenzie Friend.

At the time of writing this he has yet to receive his bundle back from Cafcass. When I approached our children's GP seeking help for our eldest I was told that as he was now of an age to make his own decision, I could not see his medical records.

I hope that others can learn from my work. If you consider reading this to be heavy going and too intense, just consider the circumstances and what I had to go through to get to these outcomes. Before you dismiss me ask yourself this, do you know of anyone else with so many Ombudsman Investigations to their credit? If you do, please introduce me to that person so I can learn more.

Chapter 4

Cafcass Part 3

It is impossible to accurately describe how unbelievably biased and disastrous for protecting children Cafcass are. By now my ex wife had been diagnosed with bi-polar illness. I as a quality fool and eternal optimist assumed this would help and feature in my youngest son having been alienated from me when I sought to get the family court and Cafcass to enforce their own order. Guess what, it was significant by omission. So much for 'Welfare of the child is Paramount.' But as you will discover, social workers in the UK have a fantastic protectionist body.

The recurring joke that is Cafcass featured negatively yet again in our children's proceedings. In late 2013, I made an application to the family court for enforcement regarding our youngest child, then aged nine. From previous experience with his older brother I recognised good old fashioned parental alienation at work and did the best I could in the circumstance. Any child will be worn down by a resident parent of unlimited hostility and especially where there are documented mental health issues diagnosed. I'm not the parent diagnosed as having mental health issues nor the child, but sometimes when dealing with these agencies I have a much better understanding of mental health.

I made my application, went to court on due date some months later and met a Cafcass officer whose office at that time was on the fifth floor of the Central London Family

Court building in High Holborn. Which was one floor above where the court hearing was. Obviously, I have to observe the rules on confidentiality as otherwise I'm liable to contempt proceedings. And Cafcass would no doubt love to get me into their clutches and silenced via contempt proceedings which far too often is a protective measure to protect institutional malpractice. A very handy tool indeed for those who wish to have immunity from public scrutiny.

Suffice to say that yet again Cafcass caused unbelievable delay, hilarious if one had sufficient sense of humour. They were so bad the court had to order Cafcass to accept a court order several months later. The Cafcass officer, a different one from before, actually managed to be worse than the hopelessly useless Guardian which had been appointed in 2007. Only Cafcass can have such a monopoly on hopeless staff.

The next Cafcass officer appointed was so useless for the child that not alone did I persuade the court to dump her and Cafcass from the case, I also managed to obtain yet another successful PHSO investigation into Cafcass. This time I was awarded a small sum of money as token compensation for my suffering from Cafcass malpractice plus lessons would be learnt etc, etc. The sum was eye watering, £100. I will live happily ever after on the interest from such a large amount.

Cafcass caused huge delay, deliberately fostered parental alienation by such delay and once again did all they could to portray me as a violent monster. It was as if the three-day Finding of Fact hearing in February 2008 had never taken place. Just the usual Cafcass regurgitation of false and exaggerated evidence with their usual spoofology pseudo research used which is common practice with them when they try to solidify false allegations. I believe Cafcass were deliberately contemptuous of the court and I have often felt that.

After Cafcass were ejected a year later after several hearings the National Youth Advisory Service (NYAS) were brought in. They are not as overtly hostile against fathers as Cafcass. They are however equally useless which is hardly a surprise as they are contracted to Cafcass. If you are confused by how many successful Ombudsman investigation I have to my credit here is the answer.

Until 2015 I had four Ombudsman Investigations to my credit, Local Government Ombudsman, Legal Services Ombudsman, and two Parliamentary and Health Service Ombudsman investigations into Brent Primary Care Trust and Cafcass. In 2015, I managed a second successful PHSO investigation into Cafcass, so now I have two PHSO against Cafcass. To put that in context in 2016 I was informed off the record by a deputy manager within Cafcass that there was only one successful PHSO against Cafcass in 2015. Was it mine?

What really really annoys me is that there are so many highly educated fathers within society who have seen their children being further damaged by institutional Cafcass malpractice. And what do they do about it? A big NOTHING. You will, if you have read this far be aware of my background and education, which is broadly working class. Yet I have five Ombudsman investigations to my credit, plus twice managed to present to the European Parliament Petitions Commission on its motion Systemic Failings in UK Family Court System.

My case is not unusual, this malpractice which the children and I suffered is standard malpractice within UK family court system. From experience, I consider 25% of Cafcass officers and social workers do wish and try to do a decent job. I believe 50% just work to rule, go with the flow, perhaps they were once in the 25% who tried. 25% I consider grossly incompetent regarding the children, but very determined to remove dad from the picture. Virtually every father and child who is within the system is subject to what me and our children were subjected to. I sense unique uselessness among many modern father's and it is very disappointing to witness.

There is however one father who seriously sorted a Cafcass officer. She falsely accused him of sexually touching his daughter during a contact session observed by her and reported him to the police which led to his arrest. But he managed to turn the tables on her.

Suzi Smith from Cafcass was later arrested herself and confessed under police questioning to having made a false accusation against Mr Coupland. Like so many fathers involved in the family court process and as happens so often to fathers who challenge the mother, he was put through the wringer by Cafcass. Mr Coupland had been his daughter's primary carer since shortly after she was born. It was during a disputed Residence Proceedings six years later that Ms Smith who was 'really really angry' Mr Coupland had complained about her work and Ms Smith then falsely accused him of sexually abusing his six year old daughter.

Ms Smith was sacked by Cafcass six months later and Mr Coupland received an £86,000 payout from Cafcass. Brilliant work by him. But this case now gets really interesting. Ms Smith who is a registered social worker was brought before the replacement for the General Social Care Council which used to uniformly dump complaints in the bin, as I found out. And the replacement for the GSCC is the Health Care and Professions Council, and you decide how effective they are.

On 4/1/14 the HCPC deliberated on the matter of Suzi Smith. Now please suspend all forms of reality when you read their judgment. The HCPC found that Ms Smith despite falsely accusing Mr Coupland of sexually abusing his daughter during contact she had observed 'had not acted dishonestly'. What corruption of logic and language was at play here. She received a caution and many years later was still working with children. Of course, you may not wish to believe me, so here is the proof.

40. The Panel has already found that Mrs Smith did not act dishonestly in making what she has admitted is an inaccurate record. Mrs Smith clarified to the Panel that she did not make the inaccurate entry because she was angry with Father A, rather she made it while she was angry and therefore distracted and unfocussed. The distinction is important because if the Panel was satisfied that Mrs Smith had deliberately made a false entry as some sort of punishment on Father A, that would be a very serious situation indeed. The Panel notes that this is not part of the HCPC allegation and, in any event, having had the benefit of hearing Mrs Smith give evidence and the opportunity to ask her questions, the Panel does not find that she made the inaccurate record deliberately with the intention of getting Father A into trouble.

Susan Smith - HCPC - Health and Care Professions Council ...

www.hcpc-uk.co.uk/complaints/hearings/index.asp?id=4917&month=11...H

Location: Health and Care Professions Council, Park House, 184 Kennington Park Road, London, SE11 4BU. Panel: Conduct and Competence Committee.

Perhaps now you better understand the term I used earlier 'Unregulators.'

Jonathan Coupland's £86k payout after falsely accused of abusing ...

www.dailymail.co.uk/.../Custody-battle-fathers-86-000-payout-social-worker-falsely-...

21 Apr 2014 - **Jonathan Coupland,** 53, from Spalding, Lincolnshire, was ... Sacked: **Suzi Smith** was sacked from **Cafcass** for falsely accusing Mr Coupland.

Chapter 5

Local Children Safeguarding Board

I have difficulty finding words to adequately describe how utterly useless at protecting vulnerable children the 'Local Children Safeguarding Boards' are. That is until you realise they are not very concerned with protecting children. Their primary concern is crude gender politics and dad demonization. Who can now say the state should have more involvement in families until it is massively reformed.

What a beautiful title. Innocent children protected from the cradle to adulthood. Say it slowly and savour it, Local Children Safeguarding Board. I mean, when every Local Authority has a Local Children Safeguarding Board what could possibly go wrong? From cradle to maturity, the benign protective arm of the LCSB is there to protect all children. Obviously staffed by professionals and in charge of all child professionals in their area, the cocoon of protection is complete for children.

Section 13 of the Children Act 2004 requires each local authority to establish a Local Safeguarding Children Board (LSCB) for their area and specifies the organisations and individuals (other than the local authority) that should be represented on LSCBs.

<u>WARNING:</u>

If ever you feel the need to read the Serious Case Review for the child Daniel Pelka, make certain there is a large field with trees nearby. I walked to one and kicked several trees halfway through reading the SCR. Especially important if you have lost contact with a child because of child professional malpractice, which is far too often standard practice.

To protect trees and your feet from considerable pain I will summarise. Daniel Pelka was a lovely blonde haired little boy who was hated by his murderous mother and equally murderous stepfather. The couple had two other children from different fathers who were not maltreated in the manner Daniel was. Daniel's father had tried to stay in his child's life and when Daniels mother threatened the father with a knife he slapped her hand. She then obtained an injunction against him, for violence!

There were numerous child professional interventions in his young life. The school noted Daniel was always hungry and stole from other children's lunch boxes. Being a sensible school, they ensured the children's lunch boxes were better secured. It was then noted Daniel was stealing food from the bins.

At no stage did any child professional ask the child if he was hungry.

The sentence above was difficult to write because of the anger it brings up in me. How in the 21st century, in one of the most prosperous countries in the world, with the most expensive child services and public education system did such utter insanity take place? But wait, it gets better.

No child professional or teacher was found to be at fault.

In fact, the outcome was the child professionals in Coventry were given a much larger budget of five point six million pounds to recruit more social workers. Ref: Guardian Newspaper 21st March 2014.

There is no funding in the world capable of protecting children from such unbelievable malpractice. I would argue that increasing the funding for these pseudo professionals is fuelling more malpractice.

Although I hesitate to state the bleeding obvious, why did the school not think of feeding him when he was stealing from lunch boxes and bins? Perhaps I'm too simple for this world.

Teachers, health professionals, social workers and police officers treated 4-year-old, Daniel Pelka, as if he was invisible, failing to prevent his mother and stepfather from murdering him after a campaign of torture and starvation, an independent report has since found. Ref: BBC, 17th September 2013.

A serious case review published on BBC 17th September 2013 could find no record of any conversation professionals had with Daniel about his home life, his feelings or his relationships with his mother and her male partners.

Daniel's first language was Polish and the report suggested that this could have been a problem. It said: 'Of particular note was that without English as his first language and because of his lack of confidence Daniel's voice was not heard throughout this case'. Ref: SCR, BBC 17th September 2013.

Children's services in Coventry - in the spotlight since 4-year-old Daniel Pelka's death - have been branded 'inadequate' by Ofsted.

Coventry City Council was criticised for a lack of robust management and not seeing vulnerable children fast enough. Managers at the authority said the department would now receive a £5.6m cash boost.

Daniel died in March 2012, after being starved and abused by his mother and her boyfriend. Ofsted's investigation in the wake of his death also stated the effectiveness of the Local Safeguarding Children Board was 'inadequate'.

Daniel Pelka weighed 10 kilos, one and a half stone when he died aged 4.

The stories you need to read, in one handy email

At times, the review concluded, Daniel appeared to have been 'invisible' against the backdrop of his mother's controlling behaviour. Professionals failed to act on 'what they saw in front of them' but accepted parental versions of events.

The report said Daniel's 'traumatic abusive experiences' during the last six months of his life were 'shocking', adding: "He must have felt utterly alone and worthless for much of that time, being the subject of his mother and stepfather's anger and rejection. At times he was treated as inhuman, and the level of helplessness he must have felt in such a terrifying environment would have been overwhelming. The extent of his abuse, however, went undiscovered and unknown to professionals at the time".

1. Review looked at how he was starved and beaten but ignored by authorities
2. Police were called to his home 26 times but failed to ask enough questions
3. Little boy forced to scavenge food from school bins and steal from friends
4. Arrived at school with black eyes, broken arm and looked 'a bundle of bones'
5. Yet 'invisible' boy, 4, was never asked about his tortuous life at home
6. Police, health and social workers did not dare to 'think the unthinkable'

7. Not one person has been disciplined for failing to protect Daniel from harm

By Martin Robinson

Read more: http://www.dailymail.co.uk/news/article-2423264/Four-year-old-Daniel-Pelka-beaten-starved-death-invisible-authorities-missed-chance-chance-save-report-finds.html#ixzz4TVTH722j

Follow us:@MailOnline on Twitter| DailyMail on Facebook

Chapter 6

Brent Local Children Safeguarding Board

You will no doubt be surprised to read that I had a brief run in with the above Apostles of excellence. In December 2013, I was invited in a particular child protection capacity to the Brent LCSB Daniel Pelka Briefing Review. I duly attended to see what lessons were learnt and where I could learn and improve. It was scheduled for ninety minutes. There were four women on the platform, three presenting, one technical assistant and about thirty people attending. Most were senior professionals, and a few amateurs such as myself. And pantomime ensued.

Overall the briefing was informative, OFSTED were behind it (The UK Government Inspection Authority) and we were all told verbally and from slides to think the unthinkable, never accept anything at face value, always look beyond the obvious etc. Excellent advice and pleasantly free of the usual gender politics. The more senior lady presented herself as head honcho of Brent LCSB and the 'Wikipedia' of Brent Social Services, another mature short haired lady and two others, one of whom seemed to be the technical supervisor for computer slides.

However, this is Brent. The child centred professionalism quickly came to an end. The head honcho's sidekick intervened to present after about seventy minutes. And she had a horse to flog. This poor old nag, much abused within Brent is called Domestic Violence. Never heard of him running at the Grand National or Aintree but he has astonishing running ability within Brent children's services. As we discovered, once he breaks into a gallop, there's no stopping him.

We were all informed by short hair that DV played a major part in the life of Daniel Pelka's mother. In fact, did we know that one in three women were victims and survivors of domestic abuse? We should keep an eye out for these female victims in our daily and professional lives. No mention whatsoever that men and fathers are quite often victims of domestic abuse, or that the one in three number is from bogus research, but then we are in Brent. I decided this horse needed a bit of reining in.

I raised my not very delicate hand and asked if I could ask four questions. Wikipedia herself was delighted to have me ask four questions. Initially!

The four questions were preceded by a short introduction:

"There was an approximately eighty-minute presentation on the above. I kept hearing that lessons will be learnt, think the unthinkable, and that one in three women are victims of domestic abuse and violence which has severe impact on vulnerable children".

Q, Does the LCSB panel know if Daniel Pelka's biological father approached Brent PCT tomorrow asking for his child's GP details, would they be provided to him?

After quick discussion among the panel, the answer was...

A. Don't know.

Q. Are all of Brent's services available to Daniel Pelka's father if he were to approach them today if he had concerns about his son's safety?

More intense discussion and a few angry looks my way.

A. Don't know.

By now I had decided these clowns appeared to have unlimited ignorance.

Q, Does the LCSB know who Sir James Munby is?

This time I was brusquely told my questions were unhelpful. But I politely insisted.

A. Don't know.

Q. Does the LCSB know who Sir Michael Wilshaw is?

A. Don't know, although the technical lady assisting the panel did hazard a guess.

Now before you suspend disbelief entirely, consider this. You have a few pages earlier read about Daniel Pelka. The above briefing was ordered by OFSTED to be delivered to all child protection agencies by LCSB in each area.

As you can see their joint knowledge was very comprehensive, in total gendered ignorance that is. Mummy can do no wrong, only Daddy can be bad to children. No comedy script could hope to remotely approach Brent LCSB for satire. It is a total citadel of child endangering gender discrimination. And you can take a wild guess at the snake eyes I was getting from the LCSB panel as the questions progressed. I swear I heard hissing in my direction from them.

The meeting was then abruptly finished and many of us went for a coffee break. All the local experts gave me a wide berth but to their credit two women from the audience wanted to have a chat with me. The self-appointed Wikipedia of Brent Social Services approached me with a piece of paper, her hand was shaking with anger. Apparently, my mini popularity was unsettling for her and her professional colleagues. She demanded I give her the answers to the questions I had asked. Being a very polite man, I smiled my brightest smile and assured her I would agree to her request.

My answers are in Italics.

Q. Does the LCSB panel know if Daniel Pelka's biological father approached Brent PCT tomorrow asking for his child's GP details, would they be provided to him?

A. Brent PCT automatically refuse to inform Fathers post-divorce or separation of their children's GP details. The Parliamentary and Health Service Ombudsman investigation into Brent PCT in my name of September 2011 is proof of this. This is available to interested parties.

Q. Are all of Brent's services available to Daniel Pelka's father if he were to approach them today if he had concerns about his son's safety?

A. A letter I obtained under Freedom of Information act from Brent in 2009, greatly assisted by Mr Barry Gardiner MP Brent North, clearly states that Brent's Domestic Violence service in constitution and practice does not help male victims of domestic abuse or violence.

The British Crime Survey, Home Office Statistics England and Wales 2010/11 published February 2012 states that male victims are '35%-50% of victims from female perpetuated assaults'. The Equalities Commission in 2008 reported that where shared care is the norm females provide fifteen minutes more childcare per day than males. According to the last UK census there are approximately 230,000 official house husbands in the UK. All children deserve the protection of both parents, Brent clearly discriminate here.

3. Q, Does the LCSB know who Sir James Munby is?

A. Sir James Munby, President of The Family Courts, recently described Brent Social Services as 'lamentable'. Family Law Week, London Borough of Brent 2013, EWCA CIV 926. Could not have described it better myself. The Brent LCSB is set up under Section 14 of the 2004 Children Act.

Q. Does the LCSB know who Sir Michael Wilshaw is?

A. Sir Michael Wilshaw, OFSTED Chief Inspector in October 2013 in a widely reported interview stated that 'Child Protection is manifestly and palpably weak, Local Children Safeguarding Boards are not worthy of the name'.

All in all, a nice little result considering I only went there en route to a more important meeting and to comply with an obligation.

For a few day's I did nothing about this matter. Then I decided, what the hell, don't let them get away again. I wrote a short letter of complaint 90% of which you have already seen. And it got lost. Oh dear, some work still has to be done here. Some lessons to be learnt!

I persevered and got the huge distance of...nowhere. I sent a copy of my complaint to various bods within Brent including the new Councillor responsible for children's services, Councillor Michael Pavey. And credit to him he aimed a boot up some backsides. I received assurances of a full and complete response etc, you know the story by now. I got a wonderfully full and complete response, eventually, a lengthy epistle of worthlessness. And also, I was criticised by the Director for expecting members of the Brent LCSB to have the answers to the questions which I had asked. Apparently, they are not expected to possess such intelligence. I decided I needed to up the ante and sent my letter of complaint to my new best friend, Sir Michael Wilshaw, Chair Inspector of OFSTED, the headman himself, he who had been so coruscating about the palpable uselessness of LCSB nationally when he addressed a news conference at length two months earlier on the release of Daniel Pelka briefing.

Sir Michael does not waste time. Three days later I had a response from his office and instruction from him to the London head of OFSTED to assist me. And this lady assured me my concerns would be priority when OFSTED would later do an investigation into Brent Children's Services.

Despite all the warnings from me and OFSTED, when Brent Children's Services were investigated several months later by OFSTED they were found to be inadequate in child protection. The local paper, *The Brent and Kilburn Times,* in October 2015 described it as a 'damning verdict'. The local authority insisted they 'only' needed to improve in certain areas.

And I presume Daniel Pelka was 'only' peckish.

Chapter 7

Duluth Model Wheel, Power and Control. Failings

There are many fathers and people in society who believe they are equal before the law and in-service provision from local authorities. The wheel of misfortune below is standard operating mechanism for social services, domestic violence agencies, local authorities and indeed the wider 'male demonisation' so regularly featured in the media. So fathers, grow a pair or be forever subjugated to second class citizenship and absent parenting.

The single greatest tool ever devised to demonise and subjugate all men and especially Fathers. The wheel below and the following text is taken from the Duluth Model website in December 2016. (www.theduluthmodel.org)

The Power and Control Wheel. The outer ring reads PHYSICAL · VIOLENCE · SEXUAL at both the top and bottom. The central hub reads POWER AND CONTROL, surrounded by eight segments:

USING COERCION AND THREATS — Making and/or threats to do something to hurt her · threating to leave her, to commit suicide, to report her to welfare · making her drop charges · making her do illegal things.

USING INTIMIDATION — Making her afraid by using looks, actions, gestures · smashing things · destroying her property · abusing pets · displaying weapons

USING EMOTIONAL ABUSE — Putting her down · making her feel bad about herself · calling her names · making her think she's crazy · play mind games · humiliating her · making her feel guilty.

USING ISOLATION — Controlling what she does, who she sees and talks to, what she reads, where she goes · limiting her outside involvement · using jealousy to justify actions.

MINIMIZING, DENYING AND BLAMING — Making light of the abuse and not taking her concerns about it seriously · saying the abuse didn't happen · shifting responsibility for abusive behavior · saying she caused it.

USING CHILDREN — Making her feel guilty about the children · using the children to relay messages

USING MALE PREVILEGE — Treating her like a servant · making all the big decisions · acting like the "master of the castle" · being the one to define men's and women's roles

USING ECONOMY ABUSE — Preventing her from getting or keeping a job · making her ask for money · giving her an allowance · taking her money · not letting her know about or have access to family income.

WHAT IS THE DULUTH MODEL?

Since the early 1980s, Duluth, a city in northern Minnesota, has been an innovator of ways to hold batterers accountable and keep victim's safe. The 'Duluth Model' is an ever-evolving way of thinking about how a community works together to end domestic violence.

A community using the Duluth Model approach:

Has taken the blame off the victim and placed the accountability for abuse on the offender.

Has shared policies and procedures for holding offenders accountable and keeping victim's safe across all agencies in the criminal and civil justice systems from 911 to the courts.

Prioritizes the voices and experiences of women who experience battering in the creation of those policies and procedures.

Believes that battering is a pattern of actions used to intentionally control or dominate an intimate partner and actively works to change societal conditions that support men's use of tactics of power and control over women.

Offers change opportunities for offenders through court-ordered educational groups for batterers.

Has ongoing discussions between criminal and civil justice agencies, community members and victims to close gaps and improve the community's response to battering.

How does your community respond to the problem of domestic violence?

Learn more about what you can do.

This photograph is of the largest and most prominent poster which is placed in the central reception area of Wembley Central Police station and it was taken on 28/12/2016. This poster and many others in a similar vein are dotted all around the reception area. We can quickly see that those two bastions of gender discrimination in provision of service are prominent, Brent Domestic Violence Advocacy Project and

National Domestic Violence Helpline. So, not much had changed since 2007 within Brent regarding domestic violence. The Asian Women's Resource Centre and Brent Women's Aid are also prominently featured. The two Police telephone numbers follow the policy of proactive arrests regarding Domestic Violence, exactly as required in the Duluth Model. There is not one phone number there that exercises gender neutrality. Neither is there one phone number for male victims of domestic abuse. Which number do male victims phone?

The office of National Statistics and The British Crime Survey published February 2012 consistently show that DV is approximately 55% male perpetrators and 45% female perpetrators. Furthermore, most children are killed by either their *mother acting alone or with a new boyfriend.*

71% of children killed by one parent are killed by their mothers

The following graph was produced by Mark B Rosenthal, 23 July 2008. His source figures are taken from the U.S. Department of Health & Human Services (DHHS).

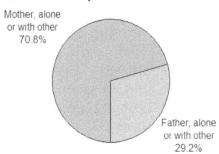

Children Killed by One Parent: 2001-2006

Mother, alone or with other 70.8%

Father, alone or with other 29.2%

Source: U.S. DHHS *Child Maltreatment* reports 2001-2006

The DHHS is in the US, not the UK. The NSPCC used to have a similar figure on their website but that seems to have disappeared. The DHHS found that 70.8% of the children killed were by either the mother acting alone or with others. 29.2% of children killed were by the father either alone or with others. So statistically women, on their own or with others, kill over twice as many children as men. Children are safer with their fathers than their mothers. Yet the entire focus of all domestic violence agencies within the UK I ever came across is on removing the father from caring for his children at the request of the mother. Can someone please tell how the Welfare Of The Child Is Paramount within this scenario?

All the domestic violence agencies funded by UK national and local government that I have ever come across use the Duluth Model wheel and especially the Male Privilege section. This especially applies where M.A.R.A.C process is concerned in implementation by social services, C.A.M.H.S, and most importantly our friends in Cafcass whose DVIP/DVPP programmes are applied ONLY to men. Cafcass do not accept as a matter of policy that women or mothers are capable of domestic violence. Rather they insist, and have repeatedly stated to me and many other fathers, that where a woman is violent it is only out of terror, because a man usually has such physical advantage. Hence Cafcass domestic violence programmes for women are only for VICTIMS. Credit to Brian Maloney, Chair of Cambridge FNF, for eliciting this information from Cafcass via the government website that their Domestic Violence programmes are only for male perpetrators.

https://www.whatdotheyknow.com/request/last_year_how_ many_women_were_re?nocache=incoming-866159#incoming- 866159

Perhaps Cafcass staff and personnel need to be introduced to the tender mercies of Myra Hindley, Rose West, Daniel Pelka's mother, Samira Lupide, who killed her two children in a women's refuge so she could 'hurt him' referring to their father, and nurse Beverly Allit who killed 5 children and attempted to kill three more while working as a nurse. The problem is when institutional child endangering sexism is the entire DNA of an organisation the only way to correct it is by the removal of funding and retraining. But I'm not holding my breath.

The Duluth model wheel is also the underpinning for the extraordinarily well funded and UK Government backed, End Violence Against Women and Girls - VAWG. The gender vigilantes hate men so much it extends to their hatred of all male children also. Where does the expression 'Every Child Matters, No Child Left Behind' in large Government programmes have any relevance in the face of such blatant child endangering misandry.

The situation in the UK for most fathers who encounter problems with the mother of their children is that she has virtually unlimited power because of her gender and the eagerness of so many state agencies to intervene at her request and on her behalf. Most of these agencies exercise or closely follow the Duluth approach. This means the father is remarkably powerless as the mother and children have full state protection and he is without even a pretence of adherence to any concept of justice or child welfare, immediately labelled and treated as a domestic terrorist. Guilty by gender is the overall rule. And no father can be innocent once accused.

So please tell me the difference between a man suffering domestic violence from a female partner who enters this or indeed virtually any police station within the UK in 2016, seeking police assistance, and a black man during the Jim Crow era in the southern states of America between 1865 and late 1970s? Until men and society insist on equality of opportunity before the law, this discrimination will not just continue, it will increase. The price of freedom is eternal vigilance.

Possibly the biggest obstacle to societal and system improvement for better protection of children are what I call 'Poundland Chauvinists.' Men doing the cheap hero bit eager to demonstrate how 'gallant' they are in defending all those vulnerable little ladies who need the protection of pennysworth Sir Galahads. Easily manipulated and incapable of providing the necessary protection which children so badly need.

Before any man or father laughs too much at the above scene ask yourself one simple question. What is the situation regarding domestic violence as applied by the local authority and police in the area you live in? Find out what is done in practice and if it discriminates on grounds of gender ask yourself this simple question, are you fit to be a parent knowing you are a second-class citizen and unable to protect either your children or yourself because of local institutional gender discrimination?

In 2020 during the Covid -19 lockdown, Domestic Violence agencies really went to work. For example the Met police NW London guidelines on DV to partner agencies April 9th contained only 2 phone numbers, the National Domestic Violence helpline and Respect. I respectfully pointed out that organisations who discriminate on grounds of gender are not helpful for society. A revised list was sent out, which included Mens Advice Line and an LGBT number. Men's Advice Line is run by Respect, their DVPP programmes are for male perpetrators of DV to my knowledge. Funny thing is, I thought the police were supposed to deal with crime! So where is the help for heterosexual males, half of society!

Chapter 8

Gender Discrimination and Back Door Social Engineering in UK Family Court System

From the above chapters and basic general knowledge, you will be aware that fathers involved in the UK Family Law system are viewed as somewhere between a second-class citizen and irrelevant, with only a very few exceptions. This discrimination is steadily increasing. And why not, who is prepared to fight it!

The real genius of the system within the UK is to always present itself as being purely child focused, with each case determined on its own merits to arrive at the best possible outcome for the children. This self-serving mantra is virtually unassailable. Further genius is how the myriad father removal agencies throughout local and national government hide behind statements such as, 'of course we support dads being involved with their children, where safe to do so'. Men are repeatedly portrayed as violent monsters and women and mothers are always the victims. The demonisation of men and fathers is now virtually an obligation in the UK.

To highlight how child endangering this is, consider this together with the U.S DHHS material above (2001-6), the majority of injuries and deaths for children are committed by the mother either acting alone or with others. *Child Maltreatment in the UK*, a report published by the NSPCC, showed 49% of children abused in the home were abused by mothers and 40% by their father/stepfathers, (Cawson P, Wattam C, Brooker S, & Kelly G, 2000.)

A second report, *Child Maltreatment in the Family,* showed that 65% of total child abuse (neglect, sexual, emotional and physical) is perpetrated by mothers and only 8% by fathers, (Cawson P, 2002). This study is the experience of a national sample of young people by the NSPCC.

For those who really wish to learn how we got to this situation there is in my experience only one book that truly explains the current situation in searing and very accurate detail. Written by Nick Langford, one of the former best brains within Fathers for Justice. Its title is '*An Exercise in Absolute Futility*'. The title is taken from a comment by the now President of the Family Division Sir James Munby. It was the comment the then, Lord Justice Munby, uttered when having to deal with a case of an 'unimpeachable father' who had over one hundred hearings and having 82 orders from the family courts ordering contact, yet had never had a relationship with his child.

In what walk of life apart from some sort of crazed nihilism would such lunacy be accepted? Munby had assured all upon becoming President of the Family Division that such matters would be a thing of the past. Having met the man, I believe he meant and means well. Problem is, he is virtually in a minority of one.

This quite hopeless system is rooted in systemic gender discrimination. If you don't wish to accept that then you are a central part of the problem. If you believe that for the general good of society and children the mother should have significant advantage in proceedings, then you are sexist and not child focused. Would you care to revisit the Daniel Pelka Serious Case Review?

The problem is when a culture of 'mother can do no wrong' and 'only fathers are unsafe with children' becomes widespread and entrenched.

Like so many organisations and Governments, who have to be accountable, they find a handy way around it. This is the way of the gender vigilantes who are not just dominant in local service provision, they _are_ the local service provision. By gender vigilantes I mean the Marxist feminists who detest men and especially fathers: they are misandric. These unregulated, unaccountable individuals and agencies have an astonishing choke hold throughout the initial provision and delivery of service. Below is some information copied from Erin Pizzey's site entitled: Honest-Ribbon.org.

The work and words featured below come from William Collins' website: September 17, 2016 (http://mra-uk.co.uk) You are here: Home/Domestic Violence Funding/UK Domestic Violence.Domestic

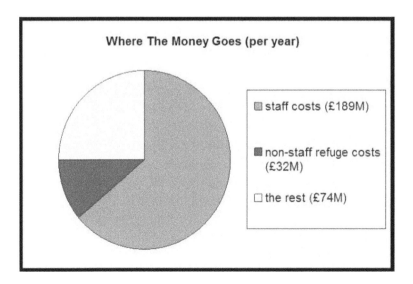

UK Domestic Violence Charities' Finances, 2015

'The data presented above was collated between June and December 2015. Several hundreds of different charities are involved, and, as is shown here, public funding is in the order of £295 million annually.'

'Questions are already beginning to orbit around the Domestic Violence sector. Vera Baird, the Police and Crime Commissioner for Northumbria, was initially to be investigated in 2015 for using her position to donate £500,000 to a DV charity, '*Victims First Northumbria*'. Vera Baird just happens to be a Director. We were assured that, "*A Ministry of Justice spokesman confirmed it would investigate the circumstances to conclude whether any conflict of interest rules had been broken*". Days later, minds were changed. Perhaps an investigation by the MoJ might have been less than fully reassuring given that there is another similar charity, 'Advocacy After Fatal Domestic Abuse', of which Vera Baird is a Patron which is funded by....wait for it....the Ministry of Justice – as well as the Home Office and Thames Valley Police.'

'Women's Aid is not one Company but a Federation of many. The Federation is divided into four, one for each of the four nations of the UK. It is not easy to compile a definitive list of Women's Aid Federation (WAF) affiliated charities, nor even their number. There is a web site called uk refuge online which might be helpful in this respect but it is intended for industry members only and the current author has no access. (In passing I note that the maintenance of this central registry alone was granted an *additional* £131,000 by the government in July 2015).'

'Sources differ as to how many WAF-affiliated Charities there are, but an estimate based on various web sites indicates the following numbers,

- Women's Aid Federation of England is the sole national coordinating body for the England-wide network of over 370 local domestic violence organisations, providing over 500 refuges, outreach, advocacy and children's support services.
- Scottish Women's Aid site lists 46 federated WAF charities in Scotland
- Welsh Women's Aid site lists 26 federated WAF charities in Wales
- Women's Aid Federation Northern Ireland lists 9 separate area charities.'

'This leads to an estimate of 451 WAF affiliated Charities in the UK. This will not include other DV support organisations which are not directly WAF affiliated. Hence the total number of DV charities in the UK may exceed 451, possibly markedly. However, for the present purposes it will be assumed that 451 is a reasonable working estimate for the number of UK DV charities.'

'In July 2015 the Budget announced a £3.2 million funding boost to, *"support victims of domestic abuse and ensure offenders are prosecuted"*. This announcement built on the £10 million funding for refuges announced in March 2015. It is worth noting that this latter press release was entitled, "£10 million support for *women* facing the threat of domestic violence", and the text referred to "marking International Women's Day". Polly Neate, Chief Executive at Women's Aid, reacted to this announcement saying, "We warmly welcome the news that specialist domestic violence refuges in 148 local areas will receive additional funding. *Women* and their children across the country will benefit from this."

'The July press release also stated that this builds on "steps taken by the government to end domestic violence, support victims and ensure offenders are prosecuted. These include:

£40 million for Violence Against *Women and Girls* support services and specialist helplines."

'Despite these being large sums of money, we will see below that the total public funding of DV charities is far greater, mostly coming from local authorities.'

'It is not the primary purpose of this review to discuss the gendered nature of the existing DV support arrangements. However, it is pertinent in passing to make the following brief observations.'

'Despite the proud claim of the July 2015 announcement that the budget funding would *"ensure no victim of domestic abuse is turned away from help,"* the foremost English helpline for male victims of domestic abuse, Mankind Initiative, receives none of the above government funding. Indeed, it receives no public funding of any kind. Thus far it has operated on a shoe string and on private charitable donations alone. It requires a mere £45,000 per year to maintain its operation at current levels. We will see below that this is loose change compared with the vast expenditure by the <u>women's DV support services.</u>'

Compliments to William Collins on the above piece and now my take on the subject.

Large funding of highly politicised domestic violence agencies strangles children's opportunities to have a meaningful relationship with both of their parents and wider families post-divorce and separation. This directly leads to the UK having the worst outcomes and expectations for children within the Organisation for Economic Co-operation and Development O.E.C.D countries and hopelessly behind other developed nations according to UNICEF 2007.

For example, Refuge which along with Women's Aid runs the National Domestic Violence Helpline gives this advice to mothers:

Do I have to let my ex see our children?

- Unless the child contact has been decided by a court (see below), you do not have to let your ex see any children you share together. If you feel under pressure to allow your ex-partner contact, call the National Domestic Abuse Helpline so we can talk through your options and connect you with specialist services. You can also seek advice from a family law solicitor. Try to find one with experience in domestic abuse.

Here one can clearly see that if the father seeks to co parent the children, Refuge deem this a Domestic Violence issue and offer appropriate signposting to it's chosen partners. Is it any wonder the UK has the worst outcomes for children post-divorce or separation?

I know of several instances where fathers and their children have spent many months and sometimes years meeting in contact centres once or twice a month. Sometimes the costs are several hundred pounds per month. The highest that I know of is £750 per month. Then the mother just makes more and more allegations utilising these agencies and eventually the father has to give up because the child is just being used as a pawn by the mother and this becomes too upsetting for the children and their father. What is particularly deplorable is the father may be completely cleared of all allegations in the family court eventually, and then the court decides the child has been too damaged by the above process and there should be 'indirect' contact only. For this I curse the courts for their child endangering.

By now you have read the chapters about the M.A.R.A.C. process, Cafcass, Duluth Model, Local Children Safeguarding Boards, and Unregulators. During 2013 there were great hopes among many within Shared Parenting that the UK government was going to bring in a Presumption of Shared Parenting with some element of time provision.

Newspaper headlines led to several dads approaching me assuming they just had to make an application to the family court and they would automatically have 50-50 shared parenting rights as the starting point. In fact, the man who advised the Government, Mr Norgrove, had recommended such in his interim report. In his final report, it was deleted. For proper detail and understanding of how this came about read Nick Langford's book, *An Exercise in Absolute Futility*.

To my mind there have been six significant and, taken together, crucial factors brought to bear since April 2014 when there were the revisions to the Children Act 1989.

In the following order, they are:

1. A Presumption of Shared Parenting in Law
2. Legal aid and gender advantage for females
3. Wishes and Feelings of the Child
4. Coercive Control Act December 2015
5. Istanbul Convention
6. Changes to cross–examination in Family Courts

1. A Presumption of Shared Parenting in Law with actually no time allocation. So, a letter once a year from a father to a child counts as Shared Parenting Presumption having been met.

Family Law Week, 2014, Anna Heenen: Family Law Solicitor. *Section 11*
    'There has been a lot of discussion about shared parenting in the media but the Act does not introduce a presumption of

shared parenting. Instead, s 11 of the Act, entitled "Welfare of the child: parental involvement", introduces a presumption of continued parental involvement into the welfare checklist in s 1 Children Act 1989.(2B) **In subsection (2A) "involvement" means involvement of some kind, either direct or indirect, but not any particular division of a child's time.'**

2. Legal aid and gender advantage for females.

Actually, Legal Aid provision in the family courts was altered so effectively only women who alleged domestic abuse could receive legal aid. Anyone reading the following would think that the government is being gender neutral. However, most of the agencies quoted below are not independent and will only accept evidence from females. The following is taken from the government website (https://www.gov.uk/legal-aid/domestic-abuse-or-violence)

What counts as evidence

You'll usually need to show that you or your children were at risk of harm from an ex-partner.

You can ask for evidence from:

o   the courts
o   the police
o   a multi-agency risk assessment conference (MARAC)
o   social services
o   a health professional, e.g. a doctor, nurse, midwife, psychologist or health visitor
o   a refuge manager
o   a domestic violence support service
o   your bank, e.g. credit card accounts, loan documents and statements
o   your employer, or education or training provider
o   the provider of any benefits you've received

The entire understanding as to what domestic abuse is was heavily modified to give huge extra advantage to females (see Chapter 13). Effectively a woman in a relationship has carte blanch to say whatever she likes about her husband or partner and he will be processed.

'Controlling behaviour' is now taken as domestic abuse and it is perceived by the domestic violence agencies, social services and Cafcass that only a man can be controlling.

3. Wishes and Feelings of the Child.

When I heard Simon Hughes, then MP for Bermondsey and Minister for Justice in the coalition 2010-2015, announce to the Family Justice Young People's Board that the *'wishes and feelings of the child shall be taken into greater consideration'* I remember shouting at the television. Straightaway he was giving the green light to parents, nearly always mothers, who seek to alienate the child from the other parent. Still, what can be expected from a man who when campaigning to become an MP in Bermondsey during the 80's happily had his team denounce and distribute leaflets decrying that his opponent Peter Tatchell is homosexual. Peter Tatchell openly was and is. Years later Hughes came out and announced he had been a homosexual for years. Here is an excerpt from the Bermondsey section of wikipedia

'Hughes was first elected to Parliament in the Bermondsey by-election of 24 February 1983. The by-election was described by Gay News as "the dirtiest and most notorious by-election in British political history" because of the slurs against the character of the Labour candidate and gay rights campaigner Peter Tatchell by various opposition campaigners. The Liberal Campaign leaflet described the election as "a straight choice" between Simon Hughes and the Labour candidate. Hughes won the seat with 57.7% of the vote.'

'Hughes apologised for the campaign in 2006, during the same few days revealing his own <u>homosexual</u> experiences, and confirming that he is <u>bisexual</u> after being outed by <u>The Sun</u> newspaper.[3] He told the BBC's <u>Newsnight</u> programme: 'I hope that there will never be that sort of campaign again. I have never been comfortable about the whole of that campaign, as Peter knows, and I said that to him in the past... Where there were things that were inappropriate or wrong, I apologise for that.'[4]

Hypocrisy stinks big time.

4. <u>Coercive and Control Act December 2015</u>.

Karen Bradley, then Minister of State for Preventing Abuse, Exploitation and Crime, announced this act was to protect female victims of domestic violence. The following quotes were taken on 22 June 2017 from the government website:

https://www.gov.uk/government/news/80-million-to-stop-violence-against-women-and-girls

Karen Bradley:

"No one should live in fear of domestic abuse, which is why this government has made ending violence against women and girls a priority.
'Through our strategy we are making preventing violence against women and girls everyone's business. It is vital government, the police, local authorities and service providers work together to help women get out of dangerous situations early, and stop perpetrators from moving from one victim to the next'.

Communities Minister Baroness Williams of Trafford said:

'*Nobody should have to face domestic abuse which is why we are determined to do more to eradicate violence against women and girls.*'

International Development Secretary Justine Greening said:

'*One in three women worldwide are beaten or go through sexual violence in their lifetime. That is totally unacceptable, and Britain is leading the global effort to bring an end to violence against women and girls.*'

The government's new coercive or controlling behaviour offence means victims who experience the type of behaviour that stops short of serious physical violence, but amounts to extreme psychological and emotional abuse, can bring their perpetrators to justice. The offence carries a maximum of 5 years' imprisonment, a fine or both.

It is obvious that the Minister, and the country's leading female politicians, request all local authorities and government services to only look at violence against women and girls in their interpretation and implementation. You may have noticed that there is a hardly accidental gender omission in the above new law and the advice to all government agencies and services. As there are generally considered only two genders in society, and one gender is completely omitted from the above, it therefore follows that the missing gender has to be the sole perpetrator. Apparently, all little boys in nappies are guilty by gender and cannot be considered victims of abuse.

5. Istanbul Convention

This is not yet law but is widespread practice among UK agencies attached to the Family Courts.

What is the Istanbul Convention? The "Istanbul Convention" is a Council of Europe convention on preventing and combating violence against women and domestic violence. The Convention was adopted by the Council of Europe on 7 April 2011 and it came into force on 1 August 2014. The UK signed the Convention on 8 June 2012.

From The Council of Europe website in January 2017:

'The Council of Europe Convention on preventing and combating violence against women and domestic violence *is based on the understanding that violence against women is a form of gender-based violence that is committed against women because they are women. It is the obligation of the state to fully address it in all its forms and to take measures to prevent violence against women, protect its victims and prosecute the perpetrators. Failure to do so would make it the responsibility of the state. The convention leaves no doubt: there can be no real equality between women and men if women experience gender-based violence on a large-scale and state agencies and institutions turn a blind eye.'* **Like number 4 above, here we have another example of highly gendered politics dominating the narrative. Look what happened to Philip Davies MP when he tried to make this bill gender neutral.**

Conservative MP tries to derail bill protecting women against violence ...

https://www.theguardian.com › Lifestyle › Conservatives
1.

16 Dec 2016 - *'Philip Davies, an anti-feminist, accused by Labour and Lib Dems has spoken for more than an hour in the House of Commons to try to derail a bill to protect women against violence... to ratify the Istanbul convention on tackling and preventing violence against women'.*

One question, what about violence against men by women?

6. Changes to cross-examination in the Family Courts

In the UK, the domestic violence laws and implementation has long since moved past being a shield of protection for women allegedly facing domestic abuse, undoubtedly necessary in some instances, to being a weapon of choice by parental alienating mothers. What man in a difficult relationship can reasonably counter the force of the state and the malevolence of the mother when an abusive partner (of which there are lots) threatens him with her virtually unlimited powers courtesy of the state accessed via the state-funded domestic violence agencies and local authority provision of them.

On 9 January 2017, 3.38pm, Column 25, Hansard reports the following:

Oliver Heald, the Minister of Courts and Justice,

'This sort of cross-examination is illegal in the criminal courts, and I am determined to see it banned in family courts, too.

Basically, a father within this process will not be allowed to cross-examine the alleger on the most crucial issues of his life i.e. the right to have proper involvement with his children. Forgive me, and possibly yourself, for being in a spot of confusion here but I have always been under the misapprehension that the duty of a court is to establish guilt and innocence. The above comments are not very heartening for those who believe innocent until proven guilty, the right to a fair trial or the right to a family life. Both guilt and innocence are too often determined by gender in this system. The rest is just process.

Chapter 9

William Collins Expose of Women's Aid Propaganda

This is a very heavy-duty section, incredible detail and phenomenal accuracy. The author 'William Collins' regularly blogs on the systemic failings and crass propaganda from the myriad vested interests especially 'Women's Aid.' I deeply appreciate the kind permission of 'William Collins' in allowing me to present a considerably shorter version of his piece. His work here is from Serious Case Reviews and Coroners reports re child homicide and how 'Women's Aid' have so selectively portrayed fathers as violent child murdering beasts while deliberately overlooking the whole picture which surprise surprise, totally contradicts their propaganda.

Thanks to William Collins, author of: **'The Illustrated Empathy Gap,**

'challenging public incredulity on the disadvantages faced by men and boys' for allowing me to borrow this excellent chapter directly. The discerning reader will note that Mr Collins has a better grasp of statistical reports than I do.

330 Child Homicides verses 19 Child Homicides

In the 7 years 2009 to 2015 there were 330 children culpably killed in the UK whose deaths have been subject to Serious Case Reviews by the child protection authorities (excluding suicides). Below I present a review of information gleaned from these Serious Case Reviews (SCRs). This serves two purposes. Firstly, as I and others have noted <u>elsewhere</u>, identification of the perpetrators of child homicides in the UK is subject to considerable obfuscation. This review of the SCRs serves to provide some information on perpetration by mothers, fathers, the mother's partner, and other people.

The second purpose, and the initial motivation for this review, is to provide a response to the recent Women's Aid report "*<u>Child First: Nineteen Child Homicides</u>*". This report is discussed further in the text below. In brief, it trawled 10 years of SCR data in order to identify a carefully selected dozen cases of men killing their children whilst on 'contact' visits. These carefully selected cases are used in *Nineteen Child Homicides* to spuriously justify calls for further restrictions on fathers being granted contact with their children. This Women's Aid report is staggeringly dishonest. This statement is justified by the findings of the more complete review of SCRs presented below.

Women's Aid are dedicated to promulgating a partisan account. For example, just two months before the publication of *Nineteen Child Homicides* a mother who was separating from her partner stabbed to death her two young daughters whilst resident in one of their refuges (see Section 10, Samira Lupidi, below). There was no mention of this in *Nineteen Child Homicides*. Nor was there any mention of the two cases (identified in the review below) of mothers killing their children while *they* were on 'contact' visits, the father having been granted residency – the gender-reverse of the specially selected cases in *Nineteen Child Homicides*. Given the relative rarity of men being granted a residence order, these cases alone are sufficient to discredit the entire narrative of *Nineteen Child Homicides*

330 Child Homicides – Contents

1. *"Child First: Nineteen Child Homicides"* Report

In January 2016, Women's Aid launched a campaign called "Child First". This campaign is underpinned by a report produced by Women's Aid entitled *"Child First: Nineteen Child Homicides"*. The organisation writes,

We have launched the Child First campaign to stop avoidable child deaths as a result of unsafe child contact with dangerous perpetrators of domestic violence.

They request that the public should,

Help us stop avoidable child deaths and make sure children are put first in the family courts.

These objectives are entirely laudable. However, the thesis of this review is that these statements are actually a smoke screen concealing the true objectives of the *Child First* campaign. The pernicious nature of this subterfuge is that the above objectives will not be well served by the campaign's recommendations.

Women's Aid claim that their campaign report, *Nineteen Child Homicides,*

"Highlights the tragic stories of 19 children and 2 women in 12 families that were killed by perpetrators of domestic abuse in circumstances related to unsafe child contact within a ten-year period. It's possible that these deaths could have been prevented if the domestic abuse had been considered as an ongoing risk factor."

Polly Neate, CEO of Women's Aid, in the Foreword to *Nineteen Child Homicides* writes, *"whatever the stated requirements on the family courts, there is a deeply embedded culture that pushes for contact with fathers at all costs."* And later in the report we read,

The 'pro-contact' approach taken by the family justice system has seemingly overtaken the need for any contact orders to put the child's best interests first.

The cultural assumption in the family justice system that contact with both parents is the most beneficial outcome for a child is perpetuated by a public conception of the family

courts as being biased against fathers applying for contact. There is no evidence to suggest this is the case. Research shows that the majority of non-resident parents achieve the type of contact and the amount of contact they seek.

A refutation of these reality-reversing remarks would take us too far from our present purpose and must be a task for another day. However, these remarks usefully expose the true intent of the *Child First* campaign. It is not to put the children first, as claimed, but to further assist mothers in their custody battles against fathers, and to encourage the courts to prohibit all contact by fathers in more cases.

Polly Neate further writes,

While it is impossible to prevent every killing of a child, when the risks are known no other consideration should be more important – yet there is evidence here that other considerations were rated more highly.

True, but this admirable sentiment can take on a very different interpretation from that intended by Polly Neate. A more complete examination of the same evidence base as used by Women's Aid shows that mothers are responsible for more deaths of children than are fathers and male partners combined. (This will be demonstrated later.)

Nineteen Child Homicides refers to various Key Themes, including,

- The importance of recognising domestic abuse as harm to children.
- Professional understanding of the power and control dynamics of domestic abuse.
- Supporting non-abusive parents and challenging abusive parents.

It is hardly a secret that the Women's Aid interpretation of the "power and control dynamics of domestic abuse" is simply that it is men who are the violent abusers and women who are their victims.

The key fact, which will be demonstrated below, is that more mothers are responsible for the deaths of children than are fathers and other male partners combined. But this key fact is precisely what Women's Aid will never encourage exposing to public view.

Moreover, the *Child First* campaign focuses on children killed by their father whilst on contact visits. A further key fact which Women's Aid fails to advertise is that there are also cases where residence orders have been granted to the father and the child is subsequently killed by the mother whilst on contact visit to her. *This Child First campaign by Women's Aid received huge publicity in the mainstream media.*

The Women's Aid campaign makes various Recommendations, addressed to the Government, the family court judiciary and CAFCASS. The chief of these is the call for an independent, national oversight into the implementation of *Practice Direction 12J – Child Arrangement and Contact Orders: Domestic Violence and Harm.* The direction which any change in practice would take, if Women's Aid had their way, is clear and reinforces the true purpose of their Campaign: frustration of fathers' contact with their children.

The cases reported in *Nineteen Child Homicides* were identified using the Serious Case Reviews (SCRs). Here we conduct a more comprehensive review based on this same source of information.

The message of the present review is simple: children should be protected from harm whether the harm is likely to come from the mother or the father or another person. The *Child First* campaign's exclusive concentration on the risk posed by certain fathers is misplaced since the empirical evidence is that mothers pose the greater risk.

2. Selection of Cases in *Nineteen Child Homicides*

Nineteen Child Homicides makes the following statement,

In this study Women's Aid aimed to identify those cases where a child had been killed by a perpetrator of domestic abuse in circumstances relating to child contact (formally or informally arranged).

The selection of cases was done on the following criteria,

- *a child had been killed*
- *the perpetrator was the child's parent and had perpetrated domestic abuse against the other parent*
- *the parents were separated and child contact had been arranged informally or formally*

The report continues (I have removed section 3)

4. Review of the Serious Case Reviews

The basis of the review reported here is the database of Serious Case Reviews (SCRs).

The SCRs relating to children may be found in the <u>NSPCC's on-line library</u>. All the SCRs for the seven years 2009 to 2015, inclusive, have been reviewed, confining attention to only those cases which involved child deaths.

The SCRs are reviewed by year, but note that this refers to the year when the SCR was published, not the year of the death(s).

The deaths were often the previous year, and sometimes several years earlier.

The report continues (I have removed section 5)

6. Identification of Perpetrators

For the purposes of this exercise, cases have been categorised according to the following perpetrator classes,

- Mother as perpetrator;
- Father as perpetrator;
- Mother's partner as perpetrator (where the partner is not the biological father);
- Joint perpetration by mother and father;
- Joint perpetration by mother and partner;
- Other perpetrators;
- No culpability or perpetration could not be determined.

The methodology adopted is described in more detail in the Appendix.

7. Single mothers

Table 3 breaks down the data differently, in particular it identifies single mothers as perpetrators.

Table 2a

Summary of Statistics Obtained from Serious Case Reviews of Child Deaths

The data in the Table refer to the number of cases. The data in brackets are the number of children killed where different.

Item	2009	2010	2011	2012
Total child homicides#	90	56	47	67
Number of child suicides or overdoses	18	23	11	8
Number of SCRs involving child deaths excluding suicides/overdoses	78	54	39	28
Perpetrator was mother	16	17(19)	11(12)	9
Perpetrator was father	16(19)	5(6)	9(10)	7(8)
Perpetrator was partner	3	4	2	4
Perp mother plus father	11	3	3(4)	1
Perp mother plus partner	4	4	1	0
Perpetrator was someone else	9	1	6	2
Suicide* of mother	1	1	1	3
Suicide* of father	0	0	1	2
Perpetrator not determined	19	20	7	5

*Including attempts #Approximate only, relates to April-to-March (ONS data)

Table 2b

Summary of Statistics Obtained from Serious Case Reviews of Child Deaths

The data in the Table refer to the number of cases. The data in brackets are the number of children killed where different.

Item	2013	2014	2015	TOTAL 2009-2015
Total child homicides[#]				
Number of child suicides or overdoses	11	5	10	85
Number of SCRs involving child deaths excluding suicides/ overdoses	38	34	35	306
Perpetrator was mother	7(8)	10(14)	15(17)	85(95)
Perpetrator was father	7(9)	8	3	55(63)
Perpetrator was partner	2	2	3	20
Perp mother plus father	9	3(8)	5	35(41)
Perp mother plus partner	3	2	2	16
Perpetrator was someone else	3	2	1	24
Suicide* of mother	0	2	2	9
Suicide* of father	3	2	1	9
Perpetrator not determined	7	7	6	71

*Including attempts   #Approximate only, relates to April-to-March (ONS data)

Table 3: Mothers as Perpetrators: Single Mothers versus Cohabiting Mothers and Percentage of Cases Involving Mothers as Perpetrators[@]

year	Single Mother	Cohabiting Mother	Mother with Father or Partner	Father or Partner	Other Person	Mother involved in % of cases[@]
2015	12	3(5)	7	6	1	76%
2014	7(10)	3(4)	5(10)	10	2	58%
2013	6(7)	1	12	9(11)	3	59%
2012	6	3	1	11(12)	2	43%
2011	7(8)	4	4(5)	11(12)	6	47%
2010	15(16)	2(3)	7	9(10)	1	71%
2009	8	8	15	19(22)	9	53%
TOTAL	61(67)	24(28)	51(57)	75(83)	24	58%

[@] Percentage of cases for which a perpetrator has been assigned which involve the mother as the perpetrator or one of the perpetrators

The report continues (I have removed section 8)

9. Cases of mothers killing while on contact

As a by-product of our review of the SCRs, two cases were found relating to a child killed by the mother whilst on contact visit to the mother, the father being the resident parent, i.e., the gender-reverse of the cases considered by *Nineteen Child Homicides*. These cases relate to 2014 and 2015 and are described briefly below.

April 2015 – Lancashire LSCB – Child N

Given the relative rarity of residence being granted to fathers, and hence the rarity of mothers being the parent involved in contact orders, it is noteworthy that two cases like those above have been found in 7 years of data – compared to just 12 cases of fathers killing children whilst 'on contact' in 10 years of data.

Nineteen Child Homicides selected cases by requiring that the perpetrator had a history of partner abuse against the other parent. The cases identified above illustrate how this criterion works to spuriously select only fathers as perpetrators, contrary to the facts. This ideological approach elides the danger that mothers can also present to their children.

10 *The Samira Lupidi Case*

The Samira Lupidi case does not involve killing whilst 'on contact', but it does involve a mother killing her children during a break-up from the children's father. Lupidi stabbed to death her daughters, 17-month-old Jasmine and three-year-old Evelyn. Incredibly the murders took place whilst Lupidi was resident in a women's refuge in Bradford, West Yorkshire. She was found guilty of murder and sentenced to 24 years. The claim was made that Lupidi was suffering from "a complete misinterpretation of reality", having falsely accused her 31-year-old partner of domestic violence. One wonders if this is the same sort of complete misinterpretation of reality from which false accusers generally suffer.

The fact that Women's Aid can publish *Nineteen Child Homicides* just two months after this mother murdered her two children in one of their own refuges – motivated by the sort of revenge which they are implying is the sole province of fathers – tells you all you need to know about their standards of honesty.

11 *Mothers killing children after the father was subject to a non-molestation order or a criminal accusation*

A number of cases have been identified in which mothers were responsible for the deaths of children after the father had been removed by a non-molestation order, or by virtue of a criminal accusation. In these cases one wonders if the right person had been separated from the child. They are as follows,

November 2014 – Torbay – C42

Death of 2 siblings and their mother. Child A and his mother died on the 12 July 2013 following a fall. The body of Child B was found later that same day at their home address. The inquest into the deaths found that the mother took her own life and that Child A was unlawfully killed. An open verdict was recorded in respect of Child B. Children were living with their mother following a short period in foster care whilst their father was charged with the assault of their mother.

April 2014 – Devon – CN08

Death of a 2½-year-old boy. Mother admitted to killing the child; she was convicted of manslaughter and received a hospital order. Mother had been detained under the Mental

Health Act for a period in 2011. A history of domestic abuse reported against the father had led to a Restraining Order against the father being in place at the time of the incident.

November 2013 – Bradford – Hamzah Khan

Death of a 4-year-old boy in December 2009, as a result of chronic neglect. Hamzah's body was discovered by police during a search of the family home. (The child had been dead for two years and this fact had been covered up). Mother was convicted of manslaughter and child cruelty in October 2013. Maternal history of chronic alcohol dependency; depression; social isolation; domestic abuse; and reluctance to engage with services, including registering children for health and education services. Father was made the subject of a non- molestation order in 2008 following an arrest for assault against mother.

12. Cases of single fathers killing children

There were no such cases in the 306 SCRs involving child deaths reviewed.

This is in contrast to the 61 identified single mothers being responsible for 67 child deaths.

Of course, there are far fewer children living with single fathers than with single mothers. Estimates are that single fathers account for between 5% and 10% of single parents. Hence 3 to 7 cases of single male carers being responsible for child deaths might have been expected from the SCRs reviewed on a purely random basis. The fact that none have been identified may be of some significance.

13. Informal Observations on the SCRs

The author is not a professional in this field and has had no previous exposure to SCRs of any sort. As such he can bring an outsider's perspective to bear.

At this point we echo the words of Polly Neate, but with a very different intended meaning,

While it is impossible to prevent every killing of a child, when the risks are known no other consideration should be more important – yet there is evidence here that other considerations were rated more highly.

14. Conclusions

If the SCRs are indicative of all child killings, then the findings of our review suggest that,

- One or both parents are culpable in the killing of at least 65% of children – and probably a much greater percentage if culpability could be assigned in every case.
- Mothers' male partners, where not the father, are culpable for ~11% of child killings. This might be a somewhat larger percentage if culpability could be assigned in every case.
- Where culpability was established, children were killed by someone other than their parents or the mother's male partner in only ~7% of cases.
- Where culpability is established, the mother is the lone perpetrator in 36% of cases and either alone or a co-perpetrator in over half of cases (58%).
- Mothers are more likely to be responsible for a child death than fathers and male partners combined.
- Single mothers are the demographic most likely to be responsible for the deaths of children (61 cases versus 55 cases of fathers as sole perpetrators).
- No cases of single fathers killing children were identified in the 306 SCRs reviewed.

Armed with these observations let us return to the objectives of the *Child First* campaign. Firstly, to… *stop avoidable child deaths and make sure children are put first in the family courts.*

Contrary to the claims of the *Child First* campaign this objective will not be met by further restrictions on child contact by fathers – for the simple reason that it is mothers who are responsible for most child deaths – and single mothers in particular. When all the available data is used – as opposed to the specially selected 12 cases presented in *Nineteen Child Homicides* – the *Child First* campaign's recommendations are seen to be the opposite of putting the safety of children first.

And secondly, in respect of the plea that... *no parent should have to be told that their child has been harmed in an act of revenge or rage* we have seen in Section 9 that mothers are just as capable of such destructive behaviour as fathers. The 12 cases presented in *Nineteen Child Homicides* were specially selected to give a false impression – a misinterpretation of reality.

The *Child First* campaign by Women's Aid is profoundly dishonest.

Chapter 10

Father Hunger: '*An Exercise In Absolute Futility*' by Nick Langford

Once again, I turn to someone of an infinitely better intellect than myself, namely Nick Langford, author of a book of the above title. It describes better than any text I know of the deep damage done to children and society of the systemic failings of the Family Courts and associated myriad one-dimensional services.

The following is selected pieces of Chapter 28 of the above book by Nick Langford. I strongly recommend that anyone who wants to have the macro-picture of systemic failings in the UK family courts and government services for children to please read this book, or at least go to the exinjuria.wordpress blog and have a look at the individual chapters.

'The welfare system entrenched in the last decade of Labour government has had two pernicious effects: it has encouraged people not to work; and it has encouraged women and girls to stay single when they have children, because single mothers receive more in benefits than mothers who are married.

Result? Our children grow up trapped in the benefit system. They see benefit dependency as a "lifestyle": the best one available, other than becoming a criminal.

They have their aspirations destroyed – which makes crime, with its false but persuasive promise of instant riches, very alluring.'

Shaun Bailey[1]

'There are powerful links between fatherlessness and gang culture. Teenagers are joining gangs at a younger age and indulging in more violent behaviour. Lone teenagers without supportive adults in their lives fail at school and feel on the outside of society; they cling together for mutual support, forming loose collectives; the membership of a gang gives them a sense of belonging they cannot find anywhere else.[2] One gang member quoted in a report on social breakdown put it succinctly, 'He said that the anger created by family breakdown "messes children up", which encourages them to get involved in violence and gangs'.[3] In brief: 'Young boys join gangs because they are afraid'.[4]

Fatherless homes provide rich pickings for those who recruit for gang membership, whilst strong family involvement protects young people against becoming ensnared. Many fewer gang members than non-gang members live with both biological parents.[5] Maureen Lynch, founder of the charity Mothers Against Guns says, 'Family values have gone, young people involved in gun crime come from deprived, broken

---

[1] Bailey, S. (2010, June 17). Welfare dependency and lack of discipline are turning black boys into criminals. *Sunday Telegraph*.
[2] Duffy, M. P., & Gillig, S. E. (2004). *Teen Gangs: a global view*. London: Greenwood Press.
[3] Centre for Social Justice. (2008). *Breakthrough London: ending the costs of social breakdown*. London: Centre for Social Justice.
[4] Sergeant, H. (2007, August 19). Gangs, alas, are offering what boys need. *Sunday Times*.
[5] Li, X., Stanton, B., Pack, R., Harris, C., Cottrell, L., & Burns, J. (2002, December). Risk and Protective Factors Associated With Gang Involvement Among Urban African-American Adolescents. *Youth & Society, 34*(2), 172-194.

112

homes and more often than not have been excluded from school. The rise in gun crime is due to the frustration, desperation and jealousy that these young people feel, compounded by the increased availability of guns'.[6] Psychologically these youths have failed to develop attachments to others – normally their parents – which would enable them to see other persons as fellow psychological entities. Youths who grow up without paternal support and discipline are far more likely to get drawn into gang culture, just as they are far more likely to be caught up in drugs – another factor in gang culture – and violent crime. Under the bravado and 'attitude', they are just frightened children,

They don't know what it's like when you come from a family that didn't have a father there to guide you in the right path. They don't know what it's like when there is nothing to eat when you come home from school. They don't know how it feels when your mother tells you that you need to quit school to get a job, because there ain't enough money for food.

It is probable that fatherlessness played a large part in the August 2011 riots: according to Labour MP David Lammy, of 19 youths arrested, only two had involved fathers.[7] Simon Marcus, founder of the London Boxing Academy Community Project and one of the report's authors, subsequently blew the whistle on the politically-correct ideology espoused by his colleagues,

I sensed the discomfort in the room as they spoke about absent fathers, family breakdown and the extent to which an over-generous welfare system had become part

---

[6] Op. Cit. Duffy, M. P., & Gillig, S. E. (2004).
[7] Corner, L., & Normanton, K. (2013, March 23). Young, black and prod to be a father. *The Guardian.*

of the problem. In many riot-hit communities, social services professionals spoke of 'parent-carers' and 'significant others', while most children spoke of families, mums and dads. There sometimes seemed an iron curtain between the politically correct local government elite and the people they are meant to work for.[8]

The racial and gender stereotyping is profoundly offensive and damaging to black fathers. A study by *Black Britain* showed that black fathers were struggling to fulfil their roles as reliable, mature and 'present' fathers, but were often defeated by restrictive legal rights, constant criticism and a lack of recognition.[9] Shaun Bailey, a Conservative candidate in the 2010 General Election and a special advisor on youth and crime to the Prime Minister until he was forced out in 2013, blamed the promotion in the black community of sex without responsibility, he said that the Labour Government had failed to promote the married two-parent family 'in an attempt to be cool and not make people feel bad'.[10] Camila Batmanghelidjh, founder of the now disbanded Kids' Company, laid the blame on black women, because of their cruelty to men,

I also think that actually the mothers are hugely responsible, because they have created a culture where they can get rid of the adolescent boy; they can get rid of the male partner; they can survive on their own. Often people think it is the males who are the culprits, the irresponsible people who actually come along and make these girls pregnant and walk out, and they underestimate

---

[8] Marcus, S. (2012, May 12). Minority Report: As a member of the Riots, Communities and Victims Panel, I believe that we failed to address the deeper causes of last summer's violence. *The Spectator*.

[9] Black Britain. (2005). *Young black fathers tell the truth about their struggle*. Retrieved from Black Britain.

[10] Op. Cit. House of Commons Home Affairs Committee. (2007).

the level of rejection and cruelty from the females towards the males. I actually think the males are vulnerable. It starts the minute the adolescent boy looks slightly like a male and behaves like a male and often the mother wants that young male banished from the house and a hate relationship often develops. I really think we underestimate the vulnerabilities of young black men.[11]

Decima Francis, founder of the From Boyhood to Manhood Foundation, expressed the tragic effects of these attitudes, 'at the moment our men are like bees. Once they reproduce they are of no use and they are dying, and our young black men are dying. They are having strokes at 28'.[12] Paul Skerret of Black Men and Fatherhood said that it is to government policy that we must look, and to the legal system which—

continually aids in the destruction of families, with its ludicrous orders. A lot of these men are battling in the courts to see their children.[13]

For Shaun Bailey, the solution to the problem was clear: 'support for marriage... I put it down to Government policy robbing adults of responsibility'.[14] Similarly Neil Solo of the *Babyfather Alliance* said,

In our experience, talking with African Caribbean fathers, overwhelmingly the majority want contact and are frustrated in that generally by the operation of the law which would imply that mothers and women are the primary caregivers and also understanding that

---

[11] Ibid.
[12] Ibid.
[13] Black Britain. (2006, November). *Black fatherhood group hits back at attack on black parents.* Retrieved from Black Britain.
[14] Op. Cit. House of Commons Home Affairs Committee. (2007).

difficulties post-relationship will make the father visiting and building a relationship with the child somewhat more difficult. I would say that by and large in our experience, talking with fathers, the majority want that contact.[15]

The result of this fatherlessness is a condition many referred to as 'father-hunger',

There are boys and young men who without the protection and guidance of fathers struggle each day to figure out what it means to be a man, improvising for themselves expedient and too often violent and self-destructive codes of manhood.[16]

One example shows why black families were losing the fight. In March 2007, the Labour Government commissioned an investigation into the over-representation of black youths in the criminal justice system. Black youths were disproportionately represented as both the perpetrators and victims of violent crime. According to figures released by the Metropolitan Police in June 2010, although only 12% of the London population was black, they were the suspects in 54% of street crimes, 59% of robberies and 67% of gun crimes.[17] The result of the investigation was published in July.[18] In October, the Government responded.[19] What is

---

[15] Ibid.

[16] Ibid.

[17] Alderson, A. (2010, June 26). Violent inner-city crime, the figures, and a question of race. *Sunday Telegraph*.

[18] House of Commons Home Affairs Committee. (2007). *Young Black People and the Criminal Justice System, Second Report of Session 2006–07*. London: Stationery Office.

[19] Ministry of Justice. (2007). *The Government's Response to the House of Commons Home Affairs Select Committee Report: Young Black People and the Criminal Justice System*. London: Stationery Office.

heart-breaking about the report and the Government's response is the manner in which any reference to the influence of family breakdown on crime was progressively removed. The raw data showed clearly and unequivocally the effects of family breakdown and fatherlessness,

> *These young men are crying out for fathers... They are looking for that affirmation, they are looking for that identity; they are looking for that role model. They do not find it in the home and they go out and meet a group of men or young boys who are involved in devious activities; they find affirmation.*[20]
>
> *We understand the lack of effective father involvement promotes in young people a condition they have called "father hunger". African Caribbean children unable to forge a father child closeness experience a trauma, leaving them vulnerable to peer pressure and external influences.*[21]

Father-hunger leads inexorably to antisocial behaviour and to gang membership,

> *Critically this study implies, families and children who experience father hunger are more vulnerable to influences, action and behaviour resulting in anti-social behaviour, as perpetrators, suspects and victims.*[22]

Whereas the presence of a father prevents this,

---

[20] House of Commons Home Affairs Committee. (2007). *Young Black People and the Criminal Justice System, Second Report of Session 2006–07 Volume II Oral and written evidence* . London: Stationery Office.
[21] Ibid.
[22] Ibid.

The point being, children from a married, two-parent family, like it or not, do better: less time in jail; less time in hospital; more time in school; greater careers. That is a fact.[23]

What we have found out there is that fathers are extremely important in many areas, such as raising self-esteem, building self-worth in children that can help to make them more resilient against the more destructive aspects of youth culture.[24]

There is little doubt about the causes of this situation,

You gave licence to young girls to go out and get pregnant so that they can leave their family home, because you gave them flats and money and furniture, but you did a very dangerous thing in that you said that the young men, their partners, were not allowed to live there or be there, and then you talk about fatherless children.[25]

But father-hunger can be assuaged,

By the time the Government produced its response every reference to fathers had been expunged: the F-word did not appear once. Instead the response was replete with the mentoring concept, and agreed to establish 'a national role model programme for black boys and young black men'. Predictably, however, the Government refused to create a database to monitor the methods and effectiveness of different mentoring organisations. In September 2007, it set up its own mentoring programme (the *Mentoring and Befriending Foundation*), though crucially this was dedicated to 'peer

---

[23] Ibid.
[24] Ibid.
[25] Ibid.

mentoring' – that is, mentors of the same age as the mentee – and was not designed or equipped to compensate for the loss of a father.

Traditionally, inspirational male teachers have provided vital role models for fatherless children, but such opportunities are becoming rarer. Only a quarter of Britain's teachers are men,[26] and most of them work in secondary schools;[27] of these, 11% no longer work in the classroom.[28] Male teachers make up only 12% of primary school teachers, and a quarter of primary schools (and six secondary schools) have no male teachers at all.[29] In state-run nurseries, the situation is even worse and in 2011 there were a mere forty-eight male staff across the nation.[30] Much of this is down to naked prejudice; one of them described the prejudices which kept men out of his profession,

> *Even in my first week at the children's centre I encouraged anxiety from a parent who was reluctant to leave their three-year-old in my care because I am a male within a female-dominated environment.*[31]

In 2016, would-be Conservative leader Andrea Leadsom demonstrated the repellent nature of this prejudice in a Times interview,

---

[26] Department for Education. (2016). *School Workforce in England: November 2015.*

[27] Ibid.

[28] General Teaching Council for England. (2010). *Annual digest of statistics 2009-10.*

[29] Paton, G. (2013, February 5). Teaching in primary schools 'still seen as a woman's job'. *The Telegraph.*

[30] Paton, G. (2009, September 25). Male teachers shun primary schools. *The Telegraph.*

[31] Garner, R. (2010, September 3). Now just one man aged under 25 works in a state nursery school. *The Independent.*

*most of us don't employ men as nannies, most of us
don't. Now, you can call that sexist; I call that cautious
and very sensible when you look at the stats. Your odds
are stacked against you if you employ a man. We know
paedophiles are attracted to working with children. I'm
sorry, but they're the facts'.*[32]

The Shadow education Secretary, Lucy Powell, retorted, 'she
should know as well as I know that not only are men just as
capable of doing childcare jobs but we should want to
encourage more men into those jobs as they can bring other
benefits'.[33]

Half of children between 5 and 11 have no contact at all with
male teachers, and in some inner-city areas 70% of children
have no father. For a man to enter the teaching profession,
and particularly the teaching of young children, is to put his
head on a block. At all times, he must watch his back and be
on the alert for accusers; should he inadvertently touch a child
or be alone in a room with one he makes himself vulnerable to
false charges, or a hidden report. He has entered a career
which many women regard as their rightful domain and one a
man wishes to enter only if his intentions are reprehensible.
He may well find he is the only male in the school, and will
have no one with whom to share his concerns. A survey by
the Association of Teachers and Lecturers revealed that a false
allegation had been made against more than one teacher in
four.[34] Only 5% of these resulted in a conviction, and the
majority of those falsely accused were men.

---

[32] Coates, S., & Sylvester, R. (2016, July 15). Leadsom: male carers might
be paedophiles. *The Times.*
[33] Spanswick, E. (2016, July 15). *'Outrageous and out-of-step': Andrea
Leadsom suggests male childcarers might be paedophiles.* Retrieved from
www.daynurseries.co.uk.
[34] Association of Teachers and Lecturers. (2009, October 26). Press release:
One in four school staff have faced a false allegation from a pupil.

It is little wonder there is still a gender gap in education, though Michael Gove's exam reforms narrowed it somewhat. GCSE results for 2016 showed that 8.9% more girls than boys achieved grade C or higher, up from 8.4% in 2015.[35] Less widely reported was the fact that 43% more girls were awarded the top A* grade.[36] In A Level results just 0.3% more girls achieved the top grades (A*, A and B) than boys.[37] This figure hides the fact that 23.2% more girls than boys took the exam.[38]

A shocking 40% of boys enter secondary schools unable to read or write, compared with 25% of girls.[39] They are then labelled as having special educational needs (SEN) in order to cover up poor teaching and attract extra funding; twice as many boys than girls are classed as SEN, representing one boy in six.[40]

Traditionally, more men than women went to university; equality was achieved in the early 1990s, but by mid-January 2016, 37.7% more women than men had applied for university.[41] Amongst applicants who Girls learn they are

---

[35] Busby, E. (2016, August 25). GCSE results: gender gap widens as girls pull further ahead. *Times Educational Supplement*.
[36] Ibid.
[37] Crerar, P., & Edmonds, L. (2016, August 18). A Level Results Day 2016: gap between boys and girls for top grades is lowest in 10 years. *Evening Standard*.
[38] Data Reporters. (2016, August 19). *What do 2016's A-Level results tell us about gender equality in education?* Retrieved from www.datareporters. com.
[39] Ratcliffe, R. (2013, January 29). The gender gap at universities: where are all the men? *The Guardian*.
[40] Department for Education. (2016). *Special educational needs in England: January 2016*.
[41] Hillman, N., & Robinson, N. (2016). *Boys to Men: The underachievement of young men in higher education - and how to start tackling it*. Oxford: Higher Education Policy Institute.

cleverer than boys by the age of four[42] and there is evidence that such prejudice derives directly from female teachers who commend stereotypically feminine behaviour and disparage normal boyish conduct; women teachers mark girls' work more favourably than that of boys.[43]

Nine times as many boys as girls are diagnosed as having ADHD,[44] a condition for which there is no blood test, no scientific basis and which is defined by behaviours such as fidgeting, running about or a failure to concentrate. It may well be that normal masculinity has been turned into an illness – treated in 2014 by 922,200 prescriptions for Ritalin,[45] a potentially life-threatening drug with an effect similar to amphetamines – when in reality the problem is a combination of fatherlessness, junk-food nutrition, female teachers who cannot cope with normal male behaviour, and a culture which chooses to enforce standards of conventional behaviour through medication rather than discipline. In France, there are almost no diagnoses of ADHD. Shortly before his death in 2009, Leon Eisenberg, 'the father of ADHD', admitted it was a fictitious, hypothetical disorder, a social construct; Edward C. Hamlyn, a founding member of the Royal College of General Practitioners, called it 'a fraud intended to justify starting children on a life of drug addiction'. Boys raised without fathers and without male role models are left

---

[42] Hartley, B. L., & Sutton, R. M. (2010). A Stereotype Threat Account of Boys' Academic Underachievement. *Journal of Child Development, 84*(5), 1716-1733.

[43] Hartley, B., & Sutton, R. (2010). Children's development of stereotypical gender-related expectations about academic engagement and consequences for performance. *British Educational Research Association (BERA) Conference*. Warwick.

[44] American Psychiatric Association. (2000). *Diagnostic and Statistical Manual of Mental Disorders DSM-IV-TR Fourth Edition*. Arlington: American Psychiatric Publishing.

[45] Boffey, D. (2015, August 15). Prescriptions for Ritalin and other ADHD drugs double in a decade. *The Guardian*.

floundering, easy prey to those who would exploit them or lead them into lives of terrorism, crime, gangs or drugs. If this were the result of war or disease it would be heart-breaking; that it is the product of deliberate policy is monstrous. While there is a pusillanimous refusal even to use the word 'father' in public debate and the word 'family' is redefined to denote a household from which the father has been removed, there is little hope for these children or for our ravaged society. These destructive trends will persist: boys will continue to underperform at school and be outnumbered by girls at university and in the workplace. Girls will shun these boys who have neither qualifications nor prospects and continue to have babies without fathers, trusting to the liberality of the state, and so the whole sorry cycle will perpetuate itself.'

Deepest thanks to Nick Langford for the above chapter.

Chapter 11

UK Government Increasing Discrimination Against Fathers and Children

This chapter is for the benefit of those who like myself are 'educationally challenged' when it comes to understanding matters. In particular I seek to demonstrate how this quite absurd system is steadily becoming much worse for children and fathers.

In chapter nine you will have read of the six significant changes which disadvantage fathers and their children since 2014, though technically L.A.S.P.O (Legal Aid, Sentencing and Punishment of Offenders Act 2012) was introduced in 2012 but was implemented in April 2013. You may ask what have I got to add to chapter 12. The answer is too much.

As I write this in January 2017, Labour's shadow minister for domestic violence, **Sarah Champion,** was once **arrested and** cautioned over a bust-up with her husband after hitting him causing actual bodily harm. I will leave you to form your own opinion on the impartial professionalism of such champions of domestic violence. Mike Buchanan, former Conservative Party consultant, said: '*Sarah Champion should stand down. If this was a male politician, it would be inconceivable that they could remain in this position having admitted that they have a caution for domestic violence.*'

Another relevant example is Gloria De Piero. She is a Labour Party MP and current shadow Justice Minister. Previously she was Shadow Minister for Women and Equalities.

Ms Piero was selected from an All Women shortlist and very narrowly won. While Shadow Minister for Women and Equalities she very heavily campaigned on the ending Violence Against Women and Girls bandwagon (VAWG). No mention of course of ending violence against that half of children which is male. In her second election, her Liberal opposite number was suddenly subject to allegations of domestic abuse and her majority increased. Aged 15 she posed topless for 'spending money' and yet Ms Piero has contempt for Rebekah Wade who, when she was the editor of the Sun newspaper, kept its page 3 topless models. One rule for me and another for everyone else it appears.

The reason why I have started with these two female Labour Shadow Ministers is to demonstrate the complete contempt they hold for men and fathers who are victims of domestic violence.

The Labour Party, which was unquestionably the greatest social movement of the 20th Century, is now basically a single gender issue party. Jeremy Corbyn, it's leader, was extremely critical of Philip Davies MP when Mr Davies made a presentation in 2016 to the International Conference on Men's Issues (ICMI London 2016 organised by Mike Buchanan, leader of the political party 'Justice for Men and Boys (J4MB) and the women who love them'). In this very accurate presentation using, almost exclusively, information from the House Of Commons Library, Mr Davies carefully explained that much of the alleged women's equality movement is of the *'have your cake and eat it variety'* where differential sentencing of prisoners by gender is concerned.

The Minister for Women and Equality, Women's Aid, all publicly funded domestic violence agencies, Cafcass, Family Law Solicitors and Barristers who harvest the *female victim only* domestic violence industry, are only the obvious tip of the iceberg.

The much greater enemy of shared parenting operates within the government shadows. Feminist academia using standpoint research from select and pre-determined groups perpetuate the myth that contact between children and fathers is dangerous to the children. For example, the NSPCC campaigned vigorously against shared parenting during the Norgrove report pre-April 2014. The NSPCC, to my mind, is now as anti-shared parenting as Cafcass. This venerable and much respected children's charity with a Royal Charter to protect children from abuse happily used Jimmy Saville to assist it in revenue collection.

During Lord Laming's inquiry into Victoria Climbie both Brent and the NSPCC supplied 'altered' documents, which under pressure were later 'corrected'. Haringey Children's department 'lost' vital documents behind a filing cabinet.

The next paragraph 2.26 is copied directly from Lord Laming's published findings. Just please bear in mind that despite the most expensive, highly publicised investigation ever into malpractice among children's services and charities in the UK, Brent, Haringey and the NSPCC misrepresented, were disingenuous and blatantly tried to sabotage the investigation. To my knowledge not one of the individuals concerned were sacked, lost their pensions, or saw any sanction made against them.

2.26 'This work was made particularly difficult because of the late supply of some relevant material by some of the Interested Parties, and by others. For example, Brent council was late providing some documents and at times I felt material was drip-fed to us. Similarly, at one stage I was unhappy with the NSPCC's provision of documents. Documents which were supposedly lost were suddenly discovered, and on one occasion it was only during witness examinations that it became clear that documents had been given to the Inquiry in an edited form.'

The reason why I include the above section from Lord Laming's inquiry into Brent and the NSPCC is to demonstrate that within this disorganised morass of confusion hard-nosed anti-father gender vigilantes such as the domestic violence agencies and similar have a field day. They offer their services to these hopeless departments, hide behind their charitable status and suddenly they are the OFFICIAL Lead Domestic Violence Partner and they effectively decide what happens where children are concerned. And in their minds fathers have no place unless the mother believes he *should*, post-divorce or separation. In a class of two dads are second and last.

I had never read the Lord Laming report about Brent until 2010. Suddenly all their child endangering malpractice made sense. Discovering their continued habit of 'losing' documents etc, I determined that as a department they brought lying into disrepute. Judging by Brent's -Local Children's Safeguarding Board's incompetence in their Daniel Pelka briefing in December 2013 (chapter 6) not much has changed.

When Saville died and all the allegations suddenly appeared the NSPCC were put in joint charge of the investigation into Saville's alleged abuse. For years thousands of vulnerable children, mostly young girls in care, were being exploited by various, usually Asian, gangs of men, in Preston, Oxford, Rochdale, Rotherham, Doncaster and Sheffield. Basically, everywhere there were children in care across Northern England. And we are led to believe that NOT ONE of these children or their parents EVER contacted the NSPCC or BBC Childline, which has now been run by the NSPCC since 2006. Political correctness in these local authorities and police forces apparently prevented proper investigation of the most serious complaints because the perpetrators were Asian. It appears that the toxic element of feminism, cultural Marxism and political correctness are all bedfellows.

The following is taken from Allison Pearson's article in The Telegraph of 27 August 2014:

'The Labour Party, in particular, is mired in shame over "cultural sensitivity" in Rotherham. Especially, cynics might point out, a sensitivity to the culture of Muslims whose votes they don't want to lose. Denis MacShane, MP for Rotherham from 1994 to 2012, actually admitted to the BBC's World At One that "there was a culture of not wanting to rock the multicultural community boat, if I may put it like that. Perhaps, yes, as a true Guardian reader and liberal Leftie, I suppose I didn't want to raise that too hard." Much better to hang on to your impeccable liberal credentials than save a few girls from being raped, eh, Denis?'

In Professor Jay's 'Independent inquiry into child sexual exploitation (CSE) in Rotherham,', she says:

'there was a widespread perception that messages conveyed by some senior people in the Council and also the Police, were to 'downplay' the ethnic dimensions of CSE. Unsurprisingly, frontline staff appeared to be confused as to what they were supposed to say and do and what would be interpreted as 'racist'. From a political perspective, the approach of avoiding public discussion of the issues was ill judged.'

In fact, there are documented cases where some of the children's fathers went to their local police stations complaining about what was happening to their children. The innocent fathers were arrested! Concerned dads wanting to protect their children are unwanted by vast swathes of the UK government. Arresting them, silences them!

It is of course important to understand that during the years these abuses were taking place on children placed under Rotherham Social Services they, the Rotherham social workers, were exercising Impartial Professionalism at all times!

While up to 1400 girls were being attacked and raped in Rotherham the social services thought it was more important to remove children from experienced foster parents because those parents were members of the political party UKIP. On September 7th 2017, it was reported in London's Metro newspaper that after 6 reports into Rotherham council failings on the above that '*no one was to blame.*'

UKIP couple have foster children removed from care - BBC News

www.bbc.co.uk/news/uk-20474120

So, during the years vulnerable children, nearly all girls were being groomed, molested, raped and sometimes impregnated, the local services in Rotherham, Police, Local Authority and Social Workers were arresting fathers who were attempting to protect their children and experienced foster carers had children removed from them because they were registered members of a perfectly legal political party, whose manifesto promoted Shared Parenting!

While all these abuses were being perpetrated against vulnerable children, nearly all girls, and apparently nobody ever told the NSPCC about it, during December 2012 the NSPCC spent much time and money with a train poster campaign depicting children being abused by violent fathers as a very successful funding campaign. Strangely none of the NSPCC poster campaigns to my knowledge ever depicted an abusive mother, though one did depict an alcoholic mother. I complained strongly as did others against this blatant anti-father propaganda by the NSPCC with some success. It stopped.

In 2015, I was offered an opportunity by the NSPCC/Social Care Institute for Excellence '*Serious Case Review Learning into Practice*' project to attend a seminar. At last I thought, these people are getting serious about eradicating malpractice and working towards improved services for children. I dutifully filled in the application form and shortly afterwards was accepted. I was delighted to discover my campaigning to remove systemic malpractice was getting noticed and looking forward to attending along with other professionals who sought to improve the system.

My optimism was quickly extinguished some weeks later. I was 'disinvited'. First time ever in my life I have been invited, and then 'disinvited' to anything. Their reason for 'disinviting' me was truly genius. Talk about raking the bottom of the barrel for an excuse, would you care to hazard a guess as to why I was 'disinvited'? Please do, and I guarantee you it will not be as good as the actual excuse used by the NSPCC/SCIE.

The formal excuse they used was, 'I lack sufficient diversity'.

Among the people invited and not 'disinvited' were Children's social care services, both local authority and private sector, and from a long list also included were my close friends Cafcass and Local Safeguarding Children Board (LSCB) Academics and students were also invited. But the dude with 4 Ombudsman Investigations at that time plus kick-starting an OFSTED investigation into LSCB was 'disinvited' because he lacked diversity. If a middle aged, bald and bearded Irishman, with nine years-experience as a house husband and at that time four Ombudsman investigations into child endangering malpractice, plus Ofsted into Brent LCSB, lacks sufficient diversity, one hesitates to consider the constitutional diversity of those who possessed sufficient diversity for attendance. Draw your own conclusions from this 'disinvite'.

The NSPCC and many of the organisations named above may claim they are not a part of government and the UK government may claim it does not have direct control over these organisations. Yet whenever I attended the All Party Parliamentary Group sessions in the House of Lords, these are the bodies the UK Government takes advice from. From my half dozen attendances there, they were the principal bodies the government invited to speak.

In 2013 the NSPCC lobbied Parliament in its opposition to Shared Parenting. The paragraph below is from Nick Langford's, *'Exercise in Absolute Futility'*, 2015.

The final elimination of any beneficial impact the clause might have had was achieved by an alliance of anti-shared parenting organisations including Coram and the NSPCC, perversely calling itself the Shared Parenting Consortium, which successfully lobbied to ensure that the presumption did not imply any division of time, thus ensuring their favoured group would retain the lion's share of parenting time.

In 2013, I sent a letter to the Minister of State for Crime Prevention outlining my concerns about comments he had made about domestic violence and abuse. I received a comprehensive response from the Home Office. After the usual thanks for bringing my concerns and the Minister being very busy and matters of domestic violence are taken very seriously etc, the following gems were also included:

'Domestic violence and abuse is a terrible crime and the Government is determined to do all it can to tackle domestic violence and bring those who are perpetrators to justice. Our approach is set out in our strategy, "Call to End Violence Against Women and Girls' which was published in November 2010, together with a supporting Action Plan. A revised version of the Action Plan was published in March 2013 and contains a hundred actions across government departments.'

In the next few paragraphs I'm told the Government takes the issue of male victims extremely seriously. And it has a plan for how to deal with this:

'As the Government recognises that men can be victims of domestic violence and abuse it has ring-fenced £40 million funding for victims of domestic and sexual violence and abuse to support local domestic and sexual violence support services, rape support centres, the national domestic violence helplines, and the stalking helplines for all victims of domestic and sexual violence and abuse, regardless of their gender. I note your comments about the lack of support you received from the National Domestic Violence helpline. I hope you will appreciate that I am unable to comment on individual circumstances'.

There is serious high satire contained within this latter. The UK Government is very concerned about male victims of domestic abuse as set out in their strategy in November 2010, 'Call to End Violence Against Women and Girls'.

To add further insult to injury as proof of UK Government increasing discrimination against men and fathers it was discovered that the Crown Prosecution Service (CPS) was recording domestic violence against men statistics under 'Violence Against Women and Girls' statistics. (The Guardian, 7 September 2016. William Collins initially exposed this in July 2015.

Further evidence of the UK Government determined to appease the VAWG lobby can be seen in the truly horrible Mark Pearson case. The Crown Prosecution Service charged a totally innocent commuter called Mark Pearson with sexual assault of a female. He was accused of having penetrated her while walking to his train at Waterloo Station. Despite holding a bag in one hand and a newspaper in the other, no witnesses, no forensic evidence, CCTV on him the entire time, and the victim (sic) not having identified him in a police line-up, the case was still brought by the now heavily politicised CPS. The absurd case was quickly dismissed by a jury. Despite this Mark Pearson was widely named and shamed because of the allegation. His accuser had anonymity. It transpired that the CCTV of the images had been slowed down deliberately by half a second per frame, thus rendering it technically possible for the crime to have occurred. (Rob Waugh for Metro.co.uk, 8 Feb 2016)

The anti-shared parenting agencies use these highly falsified statistics to portray all men as violent monsters who should never be allowed near their children, unless of course the mother allows it. You also have local authorities such as Brent whose chosen partner for dealing with domestic violence, the B.D.V.A.P, *only accept evidence from female survivors of domestic abuse. In the Brent magazine issue 154 Winter 2017, Brent announced it had received £300,00 from the Home Office to break the cycle of 'domestic violence by men against women.'*

This deliberate statistical misinterpretation is why men are portrayed as violent monsters and all women as vulnerable victims is so horrifying. So-few are doing anything about this blatant discrimination which quickly answers why it continues and increases. Ideology and funding are wonderful bedfellows. Denigration was ever the handmaiden of discrimination.

Comedians probably often wish for material as laughable as the above. Furthermore, the government gives £40 million extra to local agencies and the National Domestic Violence helpline, the very same agencies which discriminate on grounds of gender where service is required. To add insult to injury despite acknowledging my complaint that the National Domestic Violence helpline refused to support me because of my gender, the Minister of State for Crime Prevention claims he cannot comment on individual circumstances.The brilliant TV satire show of the 80's, 'Yes Minister', would have received many laughs if this fellow had been a script writer. Language is totally corrupted with this doublespeak. What's worse is that children and society are deeply damaged by the implementation of such gendered policies.

As an example of the BBC exercising a negative image of fathers consider this programme on Parental Alienation on the Victoria Derbyshire show in November 2016. Three people were featured who had suffered parental alienation, with one parent alienating the child from the second parent. Two of the three examples shown were where fathers had alienated a child from its mother. There was a break in the programme and when it restarted one of the two dads doing the alienating was shown again. Any uninformed neutral viewer would believe fathers are the primary alienators of vulnerable children. With the programme drawing to an end Victoria Derbyshire rather shamefacedly read a few emails which had been sent to her show while live. She read one which said fathers also suffer from parental alienation. By far the vast majority of alienated parents are fathers yet the BBC on this occasion managed to depict fathers as the primary cause of parental alienation.

Another example of 'dad' demonisation by the BBC is apparent from Chloe Tilley, the BBC presenter who stood in for Victoria Derbyshire in February 2017. There were concerns raised by the NSPCC about how many calls they get from children living with alcoholic and drug dependent parents. Joy of joys, the BBC found three children with fathers who had been either alcoholics or illegal drug takers. To cap it these children were with these parents for weekend contact post-divorce.

We had an extended comment by an MP who as a child suffered from an alcoholic father. I have huge sympathy for the enormous pain these innocent children suffered because of these parents and indeed any child living with such a parent. But the complete absence of discussion about alcoholic/drug addicted mothers seriously stretches credibility in believing the BBC according to their charter to exercise 'balance'. I wonder if all this is a coincidence when there was so much false publicity at that time initiated by Women's Aid about children being killed while being with their father for court ordered contact?

I'm very aware that the most affected fathers, and indeed mothers, where care proceedings occur are from the lower economic class. The vast majority have neither the money nor the connections to protect either their children or themselves against crude back door social engineering by the state. As a person reared in Ireland I detest the expression 'working class' and how it is so snidely used by the mainstream media and political commentators pontificating at length about the failings of this class. The Labour party long ago abandoned the working-class man except when it comes to election time. Gender politics are now it's main interest.

The Liberal party with the notable exception of former MP Greg Mulholland appear to absolutely detest the working-class male. The Conservative party which promised to drastically change and improve Family Law proceedings once in power abandoned that idea to such an extent that David Cameron on Father's Day 2011 made headlines by his denunciation of fathers in his 'feckless fathers' diatribe.

For decades, the Central London Branch of 'Families Need Fathers' used to organise and pay for a 'Father's Day' boat trip on the Thames for fathers and their children. I had attended some of these along with my children and they were immensely enjoyable. Grandparents and wider family members often attended; it cost adults £6 and children £3. Most of the costs was met by CLB. Face painters, story tellers, trick balloonists, children's magicians, Harry Potter lookalike etc were all arranged. The boat had large double decks enclosed and everyone always enjoyed the experience mainly because the children were so happy. Some fathers who had no contact with their children used to attend as it reminded them of their own children playing happily.

On this particular Father's Day in 2011 while cruising along the Thames I was handed a copy of the Sunday Telegraph. By now I was the chief organiser of this event but had as usual excellent assistance from CLB committee, especially on the day. Imagine how I felt reading this disgusting article about 'feckless' fathers from the new Prime Minister whose party had made so many promises about reforming the systemic failings in the family courts. While reading I paused for breath and looked outside to see of all things the Houses of Parliament, a joke of timing if ever there was. I knew then that Cameron had reneged on his promise to improve the UK family court system, and did so in a particularly vile manner.

That was the last ever Father's Day boat trip CLB arranged. The cost to our branch attendees was £1,165 for that day alone as we heavily subsidised the event. At the next committee meeting we were unanimous that never again in the current circumstance would we badger quite so often impoverished attendees for funds and then be insulted by the Prime Minister for doing so. Thanks for nothing David. They removed legal aid from all but those where domestic abuse allegations featured (in practice only women receive) and, hey ho, you quickly ended up with a much worse situation.

People should ask themselves why the UK has the worst outcomes for children in the so called developed world. Institutional child endangering misandry allied to vested interests is the answer.

"If one half of society is so deeply discriminated against then all of society is damaged. You cannot poison half a well." (Elizabeth Hobson, Liberty Belle).

Chapter 12

Legal Aid and Domestic Violence in the Family Courts

Once again, I turn to the brilliant work of William Collins. And I thank him for giving me permission to use selected extracts from his excellent work on the gendered abuse of Legal Aid.

http://mra-uk.co.uk/?p=1525

It is well known that the family courts are a meat grinder for men (yes, and sometimes for women, but mostly for men). Here I examine an aspect of recent history to expose one important mechanism of this meat grinder: the role played by allegations of domestic violence, and in particular its connection with access to legal aid. As usual on mra-uk, you will find that this post is driven by data, not opinion. I gratefully acknowledge certain individuals as the source, via FOI, of some of the data quoted.

Readers will be inclined to think that I am a bitter man with a chip on my shoulder and a history of being harshly treated by the family courts. Not so. I have been married for 34 years, never divorced and have no personal experience whatsoever of the family courts or child custody issues. Nor has anyone in my extended family, not my parents, nor my wife's parents, nor our two sons, nor our respective siblings or their offspring. I am disinterested other than as directed by the facts.

Contents *(click on links to go to that Section)*

1. Public and Private Law and LASPO

Legal aid is usually subject to <u>means testing</u>. However, there is again an exception. The LAA <u>waives the means test</u> in the case of applications for legal aid for an order for protection from domestic violence or forced marriage.

2. The Domestic Violence Gateway

The "domestic violence (DV) gateway" is the term used to describe the route by which legal aid may be claimed in private law cases where domestic violence is alleged.

In criminal cases one thinks of legal aid as being provided to the defendant in order that he may have professional legal representation to facilitate his defence. Oddly, in the case of the DV gateway, it is the person making the accusation who receives the legal aid, not the accused. This has led to a pernicious situation arising in respect of the accused potentially having no professional representation or assistance to facilitate his defence against an accuser who *is* so represented (see Section 11 below).

In 2015 a parliamentary Justice Select Committee held an inquiry into the impact of changes to civil legal aid under LASPO. In its submission to the inquiry the MoJ summarised the types of <u>evidence needed to activate the DV gateway</u> as follows,

1. a conviction, police caution, or ongoing criminal proceedings for a domestic violence offence;

- a protective injunction;
- an undertaking given in court (where no equivalent undertaking was given by the applicant);
- a letter from the Chair of a Multi-Agency Risk Assessment Conference (MARAC);
- a finding of fact in court of domestic violence;
- a letter from a defined health professional (which includes a doctor, nurse health visitor or midwife);
- evidence from social services of domestic violence; and,
- evidence from a domestic violence support organisation of a stay in a refuge.

Evidence, except for convictions, was subject to a 2-year time limit prior to April 2016.

The system was reviewed in early 2013 and new regulations were brought into force in April 2014 which extended the types of evidence accepted to include,

1. police bail for a domestic violence offence;

- a bindover for a domestic violence offence;
- Domestic Violence Protection Notice/ Domestic Violence Protection Order;

- evidence of someone being turned away from a refuge because of a lack of available accommodation;
- medical evidence expanded to include evidence from practitioner psychologists; and,
- evidence of a referral to a domestic violence support service by a health professional.

A further review led to more changes which came into force in April 2016, the most significant of which was the extension of the evidence period from 2 years to 5 years.

It would take us too far from our present purpose to critique the security of these sources of so-called 'evidence', tempting though it is to do so. I make just a couple of observations,

1. It does not take an acute legal mind to distinguish between applying to a refuge and objective evidence of another person's guilt. And the impartiality of some of the parties who are granted the power to create 'evidence' is, to put it mildly, questionable.

   - Following an allegation of domestic violence, it is common practice for a man's solicitor to advise that he sign an "undertaking", as in item (iii), stating that he will not threaten, harass, intimidate or pester his ex (or other such wording as appropriate). This is advised on the grounds that the alternative is a more high-risk strategy involving asking a judge to make a ruling on the matter, which may end up with the man being ruled as a DV perpetrator. Solicitors may convince a man to go down the "undertaking" route on the grounds that there is no admission that his ex's allegations are true. What the man is likely to be unaware of is that, by doing so, he has just provided his wife with legal aid to deploy against him.

The *coup de grace* is this additional ruling,

Legal aid is also available for proceedings which provide protection from domestic violence, such as protective injunctions, without the need to provide evidence of domestic violence.

Consequently, an application for a protective injunction following from an allegation of domestic violence will be funded by legal aid, without means testing and without any need for evidence. Upon such an injunction being granted, the injunction itself then provides 'evidence' for the granting of further legal aid in the private family law proceedings, e.g., over child arrangements. To the lay person this seems like a well-funded mechanism for creating 'evidence' out of thin air.

What could go wrong?

3. LASPO and the Allocation of Legal Aid by Sex

The immediate answer to that question is provided by Figure 1. This shows the breakdown by sex of legal aid applications and awards in private family law. Clearly the introduction of LASPO has driven a huge reduction in the relative availability of legal aid to men in private law cases. Prior to LASPO the split was roughly 40%/60% to men and women respectively. Post-LASPO it is now 15%/85%. That LASPO is the cause of this change is entirely unambiguous.

Figure 1 Legal Aid Provision in Private Family Law by Sex of Applicant (Data provided by LAA Statistics, 21/10/16, private communication to FNF-BPM) *Click to enlarge delete*

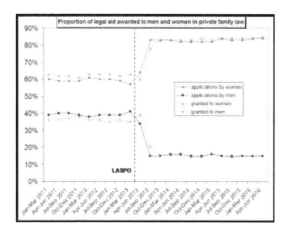

Figure 2 shows how the number of legal aid applications, and awards, using the domestic violence gateway has surged in the four years since LASPO. There are now 3 to 4 times as many applications, and awards, for legal aid citing DV as their basis than there were in mid-2013.

Figure 2 Data from "Legal Aid Statistics: July to September 2016" Tables 6.8 and 6.9 would need to make most Figures bigger to be legible

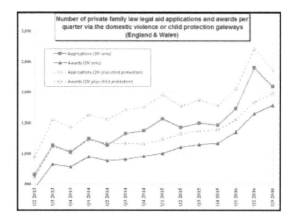

Before examining the statistics of DV allegations in family law in more detail, is there an explanation of Figure 2 other than it being evidence of abuse of the system via false allegations? Two questions may have arisen in the reader's mind in this context,

1. Could Figure 2 be a consequence simply of the increasing number of divorces?

    *   Could Figure 2 be a consequence of the increasing incidence of DV generally?

The answer to both these questions is no, as we see next.

4. Divorce Rate and DV Rate

Evidence that the answers to the above questions are indeed 'no' is provided by Figures 3 and 4. Figure 3a shows that the number of divorce petitions has, in fact, reduced since LASPO. Indeed, Figure 3a seems to suggest that LASPO itself might have reduced the number of divorces, though there has been a downward trend for some time, as shown by Figure 3b, so this may be illusory.

Figure 3a

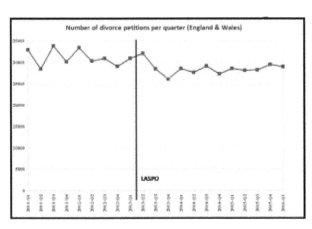

Figure 3b Annual rate of divorces (England & Wales)

The Crime Surveys for England & Wales (CSEW) are generally believed to be the best indicators of the incidence of domestic violence. Figure 4 shows the percentage of people reporting DV in the preceding year. The rate of DV has been falling, not increasing (despite the impression you might get from the media).

Hence, the dramatic increase in the applications for legal aid via the DV gateway, Figure 2, is *in spite of* a falling divorce rate and a falling DV rate in the population as a whole.

Suspicion that Figure 2 is driven by an increasing rate of false allegations can only deepen.

5. Numbers of Injunctions for DV

Injunctions for DV ordered by the family courts are of two types: non-molestation orders (NMOs) and occupation orders. The latter relates specifically to who is allowed to reside in the home in question (regardless of ownership) and may also prohibit the respondent (the person against whom the injunction is taken) from entering a specified area in the vicinity of the home. Non-molestation orders are to protect victims of domestic abuse and the specific terms of the order vary. Typically, the injunction will seek to stop the abuser from being violent towards the victim(s), either physically or by threatening and intimidating. Commonly the order will prohibit the respondent from communicating in any way with the person who obtained the Order against them.

Substantially more NMOs are awarded than occupation orders.

Both types of injunction may be made either *ex parte* or 'on notice'. The former relates to an order made by the court at the request of the applicant but without the respondent being present, or even initially aware of the order until he is informed later

Over England and Wales as a whole, averaging over the nine quarters before LASPO and the 12 quarters after LASPO, the number of NMOs awarded increased by 20%. We will see below that even greater percentage increases in awarding NMOs are apparent in some parts of the country.

To recap: the rate at which DV related injunctions were issued increased after this became a route to the acquisition of legal aid.

Figure 5 (Data taken from <u>Family Court Statistics Quarterly,</u>
<u>July to September 2016</u>, Table 14)

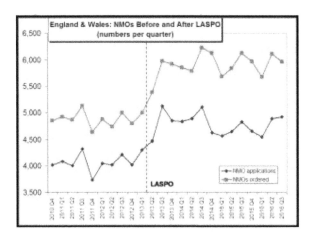

Figure 6 (Data taken from <u>Family Court Statistics Quarterly,</u>
<u>July to September 2016</u>, Table 14)

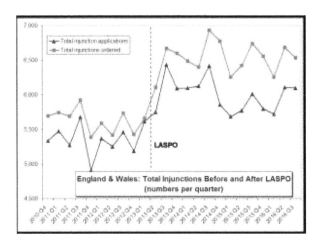

6. Proportion of Family Cases Involving DV

The same source of data which provides Figures 5 and 6, the
<u>Family Court Statistics Quarterly, July to September 2016</u>,
also provides the total number of cases under the Children Act

in private family law in England & Wales (see Table 1 of this reference). Data are given for both the number of cases starting and the number completing. Dividing the number of DV injunctions by the number of private law 'children act' cases plus DV cases provides the proportion of all relevant cases in which DV injunctions are requested/granted. The results are plotted in Figures 7a and 7b which show,

Figure 7a (starting position)

1. NMO applications as % of total children act private law plus DV cases started;

   - Total injunction applications as % of total children act private law plus DV cases started;
   - NMO applications as % of total children act private law cases started;
   - Total injunction applications as % of total children act private law cases started.

Figure 7b (final position)

1. NMOs granted as % of total children act private law plus DV cases completed;

   - Total injunctions granted as % of total children act private law plus DV cases completed;
   - NMOs granted as % of total children act private law cases completed;
   - Total injunctions granted as % of total children act private law cases completed.

Also shown on Figures 7 are some Welsh data obtained from CAFCASS Cymru.

Figure 7a clearly shows the effect of LASPO in increasing the percentage of cases in which applications are made for DV injunction orders.

It is worth pausing to contemplate just how staggering are Figures 7. Roughly half of all these cases – essentially child arrangements cases – involve allegations of domestic violence.

Is this really credible?

Figure 7a

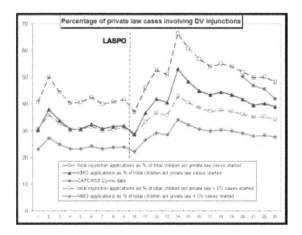

Figure 7b

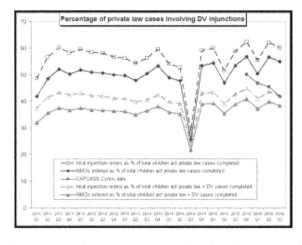

NB: the blip in Figure 7b at 2014 Q3 is attributed in the source reference to an audit by HMCTS of all open private law cases in that quarter.

The 2015 parliamentary Justice Select Committee inquiry into the impact of changes to civil legal aid under LASPO made the following remarkable observation, adding emphasis by using bold text,

"*We note with concern the evidence from the Rights of Women survey suggesting 39% of women who were victims of domestic violence had none of the forms of evidence required to qualify for legal aid. Any failure to ensure that victims of domestic violence can access legal aid means the Government is not achieving its declared objectives.*"

7. False Allegations Before LASPO?

Let us pause our examination of the effects of LASPO for a moment to consider more closely what Figures 7 imply. Contrast Figures 7 with Figure 4, the incidence of DV in the population as a whole. In recent years some 6% of women report being a victim of DV in the preceding year. This contrasts with around 50% claiming DV during family court child hearings. The former figure is 'per year'. Before April 2016 the DV gateway explicitly required that DV incidents must be within two years of the date of application to be considered. (Whilst this was extended to 5 years in April 2016, all but the last quarter or two of data quoted here relates to the earlier period). The percentage of women experiencing DV over a two-year period will not be double 6% because some incidents will involve the same victim. However, it will not exceed 12%.

8. NMOs by Sex of Applicant

So far it has been tacitly assumed that allegations of DV, and hence NMOs, are overwhelmingly dominated by female accusers and alleged male perpetrators. This is true, as illustrated by Figure 8 which shows how NMOs granted split by sex. Men constitute only 5% – 7% of applicants. [I have not seen a breakdown by sex of alleged abuser. However, it is likely that same-sex cases account for only a very small proportion of the total, recalling that the data relate predominantly to child arrangement cases].

Figure 8 (Data obtained from MOJ via FOI enquiry by FNF)

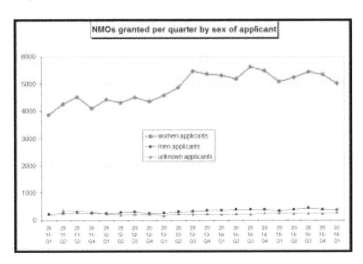

9. What Path Through the Gateway?

In Section 2 the many ways were listed by which 'evidence' sufficient to be granted legal aid may be acquired via an allegation of DV. Even the least critical person will note that many of these options do not constitute evidence in any meaningful sense. For example, "evidence from a domestic violence support organisation of a stay in a refuge". It is well known that the refuge charities will automatically believe a woman alleging abuse. In the context of providing refuge facilities this may be a perfectly reasonable policy. However, automatic acceptance of a woman's allegation hardly constitutes validation.

Another of the paths through the gateway listed in Section 2 is the granting of a protective injunction. It was noted that an application for a protective injunction following from an allegation of domestic violence will be funded by legal aid, without means testing and without any need for evidence. Upon such an injunction being granted, the injunction itself then provides 'evidence' for the granting of further legal aid to the alleged victim in the private family law proceedings, e.g., over child arrangements. This remarkable facility is rather like being able to pick yourself up by your own bootlaces. So how frequently is this particular path through the gateway used? The answer is: more than any other route.

Figure 9 shows how many legal aid awards were granted by evidence offered. Note that more than one item of evidence might be offered, so the sum of the curves in Figure 9 will slightly over-estimate the total number of legal aid awards. The injunction order route (dominated by NMOs) is the most frequently deployed route – and this is increasing steeply in frequency now. This is hardly surprising in view of how readily it accommodates the false accuser.

Table 1 gives the data for 2016 Q2 as the percentage for each path through the gateway. Note how small a percentage is accounted for by the more robust evidence, e.g., ongoing criminal proceedings for DV, or a prior conviction for DV, or a "finding of fact" of DV. The latter, which is the only pathway which actually examines the accusation itself, accounts for just 0.6% of cases.

It really is hard to believe. Or, rather, it isn't. Not anymore.

Figure 9 (Data obtained from MOJ via FOI enquiry by FNF)

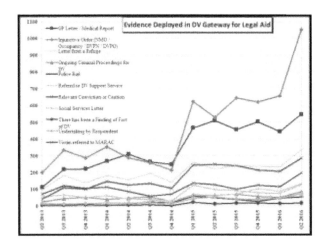

Table 1: Different paths through the DV gateway

DV Gateway 'Evidence' for Legal Aid	Percentage of cases deploying this type of evidence (2016 Q2 data)
Evidence of financial abuse	0.1%
GP Letter / Medical Report	18.8%
Injunctive Order (NMO / Occupancy Order, etc)	36.1%
Letter from a Refuge	11.5%
Ongoing Criminal Proceedings for DV	3.0%
Police Bail	1.9%
Referral to DV Support Service	4.6%
Relevant Conviction or Caution	6.8%
Social Services Letter	4.3%
There has been a Finding of Fact of DV	0.6%
Undertaking by Respondent	2.5%
Victim referred to MARAC*	9.8%

*multi-agency risk assessment conference

10. Numbers of NMOs by Region

Table 2: Changes in Quarterly Numbers of NMOs Between Periods (a) and (b) by Major Region [Period (a) is the 9 quarters prior to LASPO; Period (b) is the 12 quarters after LASPO].

Region	Mean in Period (a)	Mean in Period (b)	Percentage Increase
Midlands	663	1206	82%
North West	525	655	25%
South East	951	1181	24%
South West	488	574	18%
England & Wales	4,884	5859	20%

11. NMOs Issued by specific Designated Family Justice Areas (DFJA)

Dozens of individual courts (DFJAs) have issued substantially more NMOs since LASPO. Here I give just a few examples. Figures 14 and 15 are the chief culprits in the Midlands, whilst Figure 16 is the worst in London, namely Barnet. The increases are given in numerical form in Table 3.

Table 3: Changes in Quarterly Numbers of NMOs Between Periods (a) and (b) for Example DFJAs in the Midlands Region or London [Period (a) is the 9 quarters prior to LASPO; Period (b) is the 12 quarters after LASPO].

Region	Mean in Period (a)	Mean in Period (b)	Percentage Increase
Telford	13.8	30.4	121%
Stoke On Trent	37.0	72.4	96%
Birmingham+Solihull	128.0	416	225%
Derby	11.6	50.3	336%

Region	Mean in Period (a)	Mean in Period (b)	Percentage Increase
Leicestershire	39.8	88.3	122%
Northampton	54.9	86.8	58%
Wolverhampton	38.2	147.0	284%
Milton Keynes	38.4	53.3	39%
Barnet	25.0	58.3	133%

12. Abusers Cross-Examining Victims

Taking into account all the above information, what is a typical situation in the family courts? A mother makes an accusation of domestic violence and receives legal aid, whilst the man she has accused gets no legal aid and, being non-too rich, is obliged to manage his own defence. Enter the lurid headlines such as <u>Revealed: how family courts allow abusers to torment their victims</u>. We read that *"violent and abusive men are being allowed to confront and cross-examine their former partners in secretive court hearings that fail to protect women who are victims of abuse"*.

Well, yes, quite possibly – in some cases. But the majority of these men cannot legally be called perpetrators of domestic violence, only alleged perpetrators, and the loaded terms "victim" and "survivor" are equally unproved in most cases (as is clear from Table 1). So, these men, having done nothing wrong in many cases, and having been denied the legal aid that their accuser has received, are now being criticised for attempting their own defence.

13. Conclusions

LASPO withdrew legal aid from private family law cases, unless allegations such as domestic violence were raised. The 'evidence' required to support obtaining legal aid via a DV accusation is defined by a gateway as wide as the Grand Canyon. Since LASPO the number of grants of legal aid obtained via the DV gateway has been climbing steadily, despite falling rates of DV in the general public. Who would have guessed?

The most popular route to obtaining legal aid in such cases is via a non-molestation order (NMO). The process is so accommodating that it might as well have a sign attached "false accusers welcome". An application for an NMO will be funded by legal aid, without means testing and without any need for evidence. Upon an NMO being granted, the NMO itself then provides 'evidence' for the granting of further legal aid in the private family law proceedings, e.g., over child arrangements. One can readily understand the temptation a woman would feel to avail herself of this opportunity, especially when her predominant emotional state is to punish, or merely outdo, her ex.

LASPO has led to a substantial increase in the volume of NMOs which is evident in the overall statistics for the Midlands, the North-West of England, the South-West of England and the South-East of England. Over England and Wales as a whole, the number of NMOs has increased by 20% post-LASPO and this change occurs unambiguously at the time of LASPO. By far the greatest increase in volume of NMOs post-LASPO is found in the Midlands (82%).

The data strongly suggest that *most* DV allegations in private family law are false.

For those who despair about the situation regarding the abuse of domestic violence as a vehicle of choice to remove fathers from their children's lives, fear not, help is on the way via Cafcass, Women's Aid and Amber Rudd, Home Secretary. Cafcass, at an Open Board meeting on 27 January 2017, have stated that they are doing joint research with Women's Aid to better understand what is happening where there are allegations of domestic violence in family court cases about child contact. So, Cafcass, the state appointed agency to advise the family courts, have apparently suspended all pretence at gender neutrality when it comes to statistical evidence. To further cheer you up the Home Secretary, Amber Rudd, announced on 5 July 2017 that 40 projects will share around £17 million to end violence against women and girls. Obviously, she is only Home Secretary for half the population.

Chapter 13

The Four Pillars of Failure

These are my own conclusions based on experience. They are listed in order of ascending with number 4 being the biggest pillar. For those especially men's rights activists and dads who have lost so terribly in this system who wish to attack me regarding no 4, I have one simple question? How about shutting up as to how unfair the system is and how horrible I am for pointing this out and actually doing something about it. Face up to it, don't facebook about it. The time is now, the person is you.

1. Outdated Patriarchal Judiciary
2. Unregulated unaccountable anti-dad misandric services
3. Professional anti-father personnel
4. Modern men, especially fathers

1. Outdated Patriarchal Judiciary

Most senior judges are male and come from an upper-class background. Many who have ruled on cases which became case law were born either before or during WW2 and the 1950s. There were totally different, almost Edwardian, social structures in those days. Many were privately educated and quite often nannies and au pairs did a lot of the child minding before junior was sent to boarding school.

Their fathers were semi-detached at best, quite often abroad helping run the empire or working long hours in the city, law firms, insurance companies, business, medicine, armed forces, etc. Plus, during both World Wars many fathers were conscripted and spent years away from their families with millions dying while fighting for their country. This obviously meant that children were seeing much less of their fathers. Father provided the finance, usually quite well, mother cared for or organised the care.

An excellent example of this antiquated chivalrous mindset was provided by retired family law solicitor John Bolch writing on the Marilyn Stowe Family Law blog. I have copied his most outstanding sentences against fathers in my reply which I now show. The blog was entitled, 'Myths About Fatherhood', John Bolch February 13th. 2017.

Obviously, Mr Bolch was not feeling the love of Valentine's Day approaching when he wrote this article which contained the following sentences,

'The myth, though, in this 'golden past' argument is that back in those rose-tinted days fathers played a greater role in their children's upbringing. They did not. I grew up in a world where parenting was almost the exclusive preserve of mothers, and fathers only played a peripheral role. For example, despite having three children my father never changed a nappy in his life, and I doubt that many of his contemporaries did either.'

My response was:

'I'm 58 and grew up in rural Ireland. Every father I ever knew looked after their children and sometimes the child appeared to follow the father everywhere while farming. Who changed the children's nappies when the mother was two weeks in hospital far away giving birth to another? Being away from the house was an absolute treat for a child in the days before

TV, videos and computer games etc. I have often thought John Bolch has an antiquated chivalry about him. No wonder you became a family law Solicitor, perfect occupation for your mindset. Enjoy your pension.'

Of course, most childcare until the 1970's was done by the mothers, and in the circumstances, many were absolutely incredible. My own mother and many of her generation have contempt for much of modern feminism because it too often belittles women and especially labels them as victims. These women performed heroically with genuine poverty and very limited material resources. Contrast that with the huge labour-saving machines taken for granted nowadays in domestic use. For example, have you ever tried washing clothes by hand, after carrying the water and then heating it which meant carrying the coal, turf, wood? Doing all this while looking after far larger families than is common today. Those women are the ones to be admired and also their modern counterparts who work to earn a living while also rearing children as part of a family, not the current drivers of hatred against men and boys who live off the state or anti-male agencies and universities while claiming victimhood and exercise horrendous misandry against men and boys. Some benefit to society or children they are!

Many women of my mother's generation correctly saw the damage it would do to children if mothers were forced into work. The fathers who were not farmers usually worked fifty or sixty hours per week including travelling time. Culturally many mothers saw their role as matriarch supreme and resolutely denied fathers infant care as that was perceived to be their sole territory. Different times; different roles.

Now look at the changed circumstances when so often both parents are working. The Equalities Commission in 2008 did research on childcare and found that when both parents are working, all things considered, the time parents spent minding the children only varied by fifteen minutes between the sexes. I strongly believe that young children should be brought to and from school by a parent of either gender, their myriad issues and questions dealt with, and mobile phones switched off for at least one hour after collecting the child. This is the child's time with their parent, and the parent's duty is to provide it if possible.

Go to any primary school in the UK today and very likely 25% or more of the parents doing the collecting or dropping off is the father. There has been a huge increase in mothers within the workforce between the 1950s and 2017. I am confident many, especially older male senior judges, have probably never brought their children to or from school let alone cook for them apart from a very few occasions. Plus, there is the very strong desire to 'protect' the mother which in modern society is nothing more than outdated chauvinism. White Knight to the imaginary rescue!

Many fathers believe that where there are myriad lurid false allegations against a dad he is better off in front of a female judge. From personal experience, I agree with this viewpoint. Female judges don't buy into the vulnerable mum quite so much: they see through the spoof far better. Also, they are not so possessed of the 'White Knight' delusion which so handicaps many male judges' thinking.

Much as lay magistrates are dismissed as being incapable of dealing with the complexities of family courts and associated legalese, I have to say some lay magistrates are well ahead of the dud judges of either gender who so bedevil children's relationships with their fathers. Judicial mediocrity too often rules: children lose.

2. Unregulated unaccountable anti-dad and men misandric gender vigilantes throughout the system especially at Local Authority level.

I have explained the M.A.R.A.C (Multi Agency Risk Assessment Conference) process earlier, also the Duluth Model and derivates, which are standard practice throughout the UK. Local authorities in particular are where the most virulent anti-father agencies are.

Domestic violence agencies in local services have a free hand to exercise as much child endangering misandry as they wish. What I call gender vigilantes rule the roost here, totally. If you want to complain about them bear this in mind: despite my relative success so far with complaining *NOT ONCE* has any regulatory body accepted or ruled on Brent Council and Cafcass (through their domestic violence courses) exercising total gender discrimination in service provision regarding domestic violence.

Add to the above all the unregulated domestic violence agencies, newspaper columnists, television programmes and feminist academics doing endless 'standpoint' research from selected audiences. Then consider reception areas in Police Stations, GP surgeries, hospital waiting rooms, static advertising on billboards, bus stops, train stations, buses, and female members of parliament - especially Labour. Christ, even the Jehovah Witnesses got in on the act in their publication, 'Watchtower', April 2013, by portraying men as sole perpetrators of domestic abuse. I promptly wrote them a letter accusing them of blasphemy by misrepresenting the integrity of the word of Jehovah. Someone took it very seriously: he sent me a five-page response.

3. Professional anti-father personnel and agencies

By this I mean the Legal Aid Provision which includes all solicitors and barristers who so assiduously cultivate the domestic violence man-monster, woman-victim, agenda. Most domestic violence agencies are advised on their unique interpretation of domestic violence laws by solicitors and barristers eager to harvest the generous domestic violence funding. If in doubt read some of the following Law Works training given by Dr Bianca Jackson, a barrister and doctor of law, who advises domestic violence agencies and lawyers with, shall we say, interpretation and advice on implementation.

Dr Bianca Jackson, Family Law Barrister, Coram Chambers

I attended one of these training lectures given by Dr Bianca Jackson. The advice was portrayed as being gender neutral, though she sadly had a cough when saying that men can also be victims of domestic violence. In case of any doubt this picture below dominated the power point presentation, which I have copied from her website.

163

From the above photograph, which is the photograph that dominated the presentation, you decide on the gender neutrality of the image. I felt like the black man who accidentally ended up being exposed when asked to sign his name when he was dressed in KKK white robes and hood at a Klan rally in the Mel Brooks film, Blazing Saddles.

According to Dr Jackson, who also advises solicitors on how to interpret the law on domestic violence, including the wonderful new Coercive and Control Act 2015, any time a man disagrees with a woman in an intimate partner relationship he is being violent to her.

Add to the above, the social workers within the UK, their training, the family therapists attached to the NHS at local level, the innumerable psychologists and the family professionals ensconced within the system. If you still insist these are all proper professionals, and therefore expert witnesses with deep knowledge of their subject and regular professional development, have a little look at this link.

Case dismissed against author of damning expert witness report ...
https://www.lawgazette.co.uk/news/case-dismissed-against... **expert**.../5055691.article

The author of this damning expert witness report, Professor Jane Ireland, had been commissioned by the Family Justice Council to look into the quality of expert witnesses in the family courts:

'A disciplinary panel has dismissed allegations against the author of a damning study on the quality of expert witnesses in the family courts which had raised questions over the conduct of her research.

She was accused of reaching conclusions that were not justified by the data and of threatening fellow psychologists with legal action if they did not withdraw complaints about her research.'

But the panel yesterday dismissed the case against Ireland, finding that she had no case to answer in respect of all but one of the allegations. After hearing evidence from Ireland, the panel rejected the remaining allegation, dismissing the entire case against her.

Ireland welcomed the decision, stating: 'I have already been and remain deeply committed to high quality and raising standards in the profession.' Her report, 'Evaluating Expert Witness Psychological Reports: Exploring Quality', was funded by the Family Justice Council and was highly influential when it was published. It found that two-thirds of expert witnesses in family courts were 'poor' and that one-fifth of the authors of reports had no proper qualifications.

Dear tax-paying reader, just consider what you are paying for. Two thirds of these 'expert witnesses' are 'poor' and one fifth of the authors of reports used in the family courts had no proper qualifications. I consider this to be a professional scam.

In May 2019, the UK Government announced a Family Justice Review Panel on how the courts protect children and parents from domestic violence. The panel consisted of the following:

- Melissa Case & Nicola Hewer, Director of Family and Criminal Justice Policy, MOJ (Chair)
- Professor Liz Trinder, University of Exeter
- Professor Rosemary Hunter FAcSS, University of Kent
- Professor Mandy Burton, University of Leicester
- Mr Justice Stephen Cobb, Judiciary
- District Judge Katherine Suh, Judiciary

- Nicki Norman, Acting Co-Chief Executive, Women's Aid
- Dierdre Fottrell QC & Lorraine Cavanagh QC (joint representatives), Association of Lawyers for Children
- Isabelle Trowler, Chief Social Worker for England (Children & Families)

Nine women and 1 man, Mr Justice Stephen Cobb, a former director of 'Gingerbread' an association for single parent families. Mr Justice Cobb has recommended that C79 enforcement applications should be abolished! The vast majority of Gingerbread is female. Just consider if you will for a moment the gender constitution of the above panel. Now consider the groupthink!

4. Modern Men and Fathers.

In my mind by far the biggest pillar of failure in the UK system today are modern men and fathers. This makes me unpopular for saying so, but I'm not worried about personal popularity, I'm only interested in improving outcomes for children post-divorce and separation.

I have often said that modern men in the UK are the greatest failures as men and fathers since fish left the sea. The reasoning is quite simple. They are neither capable nor allowed to protect their children let alone themselves once trouble hits their marriage or relationship. Of course, many men will shout at me and say they have done this or done that for their children, always provided for the family home, etc, did their share of the childminding and the housework. So, what?

All the mother has to do usually is make *ANY* allegation of abuse to the local agencies and they will eagerly assist in booting the father from the family home and out of his children's lives. This is heavily funded and promoted by the state. In other words, men bearing the much greater share of the tax burden are unintentionally paying the state to discriminate against them and prevent them from having a meaningful continuing relationship with their children. There are exceptions of course, but this is the system within the UK, as I will explain further in later chapters.

The hundreds of newcomers I see every year demanding something must be done about this sick situation are forgetting one vital part. Like myself they did absolutely nothing about the institutionally biased situation *until* it hit them: what is worse, 99.9% will do nothing about improving the situation *after* they find out.

I have come to the conclusion that modern men who encounter this state sponsored opposition re co-parenting their children post-divorce or separation are the equivalent of Aboriginal warriors who were cast out from their tribes. These warriors could easily live off the land, in fact this is how they had always lived. But the shame and emotional damage inflicted upon them meant they lost the will to continue. Many died within a week or so of being cast out. A major stabilising factor for men is protecting and providing for their women and children. Take that away and what have you left, a hollowed out shell of a man who is either booted out or runs away as quickly as possible far too often for the sake of his sanity. He has been 'cast out.'

The same uselessness applied to me, but at least I'm trying in my small way to remove the institutional malpractice from the system. So many men agonise over understanding the situation, try to analyse why this is so, and believe if they understood it they could deal effectively with it. The problem is so many men fight the system so ineffectively they actually strengthen the system. They keep bleating about their rights but don't understand they have none – the rights are with the child.

Their fantasies of equality are a huge handicap. The real problem is the genius of a system that is amongst the worst in the developed world and yet always manages to present itself as being solely concerned with the welfare of the child being paramount. By now that is well past being a sick joke and long overdue dismantling and improvement is needed. Political pressure allied to budget removal is the only solution.

There are very simple reasons why men cannot understand the situation: chivalry, ego and self-denial. The male desire to protect women and children is an enormous handicap and, post-feminism, hilariously obsolete in the main. In fact, I look upon it as 'outdated chauvinism'. It is of course a total godsend to the personnel and agencies determined to remove fathers from their families.

Hard line feminists have quite brilliantly outmanoeuvred male thinking in this business of family breakdown. Most men believe in equality but also want to care and protect women and children: that is nature. The hard-line gender vigilantes who set so much of the agenda have a superb double strategy. Within the family court system, they ruthlessly exploit the abused female victim approach and straight away the man is labelled and on the defensive. The second part of that quite brilliant double strategy is to forever claim they are equal to men but patriarchy suppresses them outside of the family courts.

For example, in November 2016, I watched a House of Lords debate on women in the workplace. Many expensively dressed and bejewelled ladies from the Lords were demanding more women be on the board of FTSE listed companies, more women in politics, etc. Patriarchy at fault for everything, it appears.

Some wanted legally imposed gender targets to be set to accomplish this. Yet in the UK on that day, most political parties are led by women based on ability. For the record, they are: Theresa May, leader of the Conservative party and Prime Minister; Nicola Sturgeon, Leader of the Scottish Nationalists and First Minister; Leanne Wood, leader of Plaid Cymru in Wales; Scottish Conservatives Ruth Davidson; Scottish Labour Keiza Dugdale; Democratic Unionist Party in Northern Ireland, Arlene Foster and, lest we forget the reigning Monarch over everyone for the past sixty-three or so years, Queen Elizabeth. It would appear these wealthy Baronesses never have enough. They also of course flogged that faithful nag domestic abuse and violence by men against women, conveniently ignoring the official statistics. The usual 'we want everything' approach. Surely in the interest of equality women would like to get to the top on ability, as many obviously have, rather than gender targets!

Not one of them demanded that, post-divorce or separation, fathers who have court ordered parenting with their children be assisted to enforce it to enable working mothers and career women to more successfully pursue their career. From initial service provision at local authority level to the House of Lords itself, there is now an unholy war against fathers.

We are forced to the conclusion that the Family Courts are averse to enforcing contact. This is the biggest failure in the system: they don't even enforce their own orders. Despite the clear evidence that huge numbers of orders are ignored, fewer than 2% of resident parents defaulting on contact orders face any penalty.

In what other walk of life would court orders be so blatantly broken and in less than 2% enforcement apply? I have long believed that fathers paying £215 to the family court for the price of an enforcement application are quite often victims in a fraudulent exercise.

The average man believes in justice, systems, methodology, accountability, his inherent right to justice and a fair trial within the UK. In this he is delusional at the present time and the system is increasingly becoming worse. Erin Pizzey has often commented that the Marxist Feminists targeted the family unit and she and many others, including myself, have to admit they have been phenomenally successful.

It is relatively easy to be successful when the enemy is weak and becoming weaker by refusing to protect either their children or themselves. Or in this case, when men determinedly keep their heads in the sand. Which is why in fact the delusion so many fathers have in believing they have 'parity of esteem' is best described as 'parody of esteem'.

As an example of how much worse this demonization of fathers is, consider this. In 2016/17 the Brent section of M.O.P.A.C (Mayors Office Police and Crime) gave £8,000 and in 2017/18 £20,000 to a charity called Tender to educate boys in Brent schools on how to 'break the cycle of violence by not abusing women.' Girls would be separately educated on how to 'recognise the signs of potential domestic abuse.' This is happening in the borough where the worst educated and most likely to be victims of violence boys are now subject to 'toxic masculinity indoctrination.' And of course, all girls have no agency and can only be victims. What damage to vulnerable children will this do! And the directors of Tender have been trained by.....Women's Aid under ....Duluth and their Respect model. Only one other person on the panel objected to the extraordinary bypass of proper procedures which enabled so many thousands to be misdirected. And that year not one penny from Brent M.O P.A.C was given to support youth centres which were being closed. Unfortunately, malpractice is standard practice within so much of Brent.

As an example of casual abuse of procedure and agencies self-protecting, and despite me being a panel member of Brent MOPAC, it took 20 months and many letters from my very good MP Barry Gardiner to establish how many tens of thousands Brent MOPAC had given to such a misandric charity. The correspondence alone lasted 15 months, before that I had been blocked from asking for 6 months.

Every now and again the media and politicians get excited about homelessness and start demanding, always of the party in power, that they must do something about it. Where do they think all the fathers who are subjected to non-molestation orders etc go to? The Savoy!! Not likely, too many end up on the streets within a few months. Nothing is more sickening that listening to politicians wind-bagging, insisting they are going to 'end the cycle of violence against women,' and on other occasions screech about how horrible the situation is when there are so many homeless sleepers, of which roughly 95% are men. Which is to within a decimal point the same number of fathers in the family courts who are non-resident parents.

Am I being too obtuse perhaps if I ask this question, 'on balance of probability, is there a link between those two figures'? The male suicide rate in the UK has gone up from 4,630 in 2013 to 4,910 in 2015. Could I be further obtuse and enquire is there a link between revised LASPO and male suicide increase?

The increasing number of women who are beginning to stand up for true equality, better outcomes for children and fathers post-divorce and separation will be the determining factor in eventual outcome. It reminds me of the amusing sign I've often seen in Ireland, 'Do you want to speak to the man of the house or the boss?'

Chapter 14

Follow Up by Family Courts against Parental Alienation of Children After Court

None.

Chapter 15

Klaus Zinser, myself and Brussels

In 2014 an opportunity arose to present to the European Parliament Petitions Commission on it's motion, 'Systemic Failings in UK Family Court System.' So, an Irishman and a German decided this required our presence. After all, most great comedy acts are duos!

I have always tried to like Brussel sprouts, my mother used to cook them every year for the family Christmas dinner. It is a good idea to eat and appear to enjoy whatever your mother cooks, especially if she is Irish.

Added to this, I've always had a strong survival instinct. Years ago, sprouts used to taste like diesel, but according to the BBC Countryfile farming programme, that has since been designed out of them.

So, with that in mind, it's fair to say the call to Brussels was not exactly the stuff of wild dreams or something to get too emotional about. As a long-standing motorcyclist and a childhood lover of Western movies, I never once heard the expression 'ride to Brussels'. *Go West* has a much more emotional pull than 'ride to Brussels' ever could. Even the cowboys rode west, never to Brussels.

Nevertheless, in 2014, this cowboy decided the call to Brussels had to be answered. Not so much to visit the home of sprouts, but rather, a visit to the European Parliament which is headquartered in the Belgian capital.

By this stage in my journey through the UK family court system, my resume included four Ombudsman Investigations, two of which were Parliamentary and Health Service Ombudsman and I was getting absolutely nowhere with dud MPs in UK Parliament. Terror of the feminist lobby had all the men shaking at their knees apart from a brave few, George Galloway and Philip Davies in particular. But I did not know how to process the leap from UK to Brussels. And then I met Klaus Zinser.

I'm an Irishman and as you may have assumed, I have a lack of respect for authority. Klaus is a German and has total respect for authority and systems. So not much in common there. He comes from the bottom south-west of Germany, Mercedes country, where they pride themselves on excellence in engineering and all that teutonic perfection. I come from a mountainous area called Glangevlin in north-west Ireland, basically no man's land, astride three county borders and an international border. According to Wikipedia we are known for poitin making, illegal Irish whiskey. We have many sheep and rumour, ahem, has it, that some of these sheep possess passports and there is a subsidy from Brussels under Common Agricultural Policy which apparently means some sheep are cross border tourists – double subsidies, allegedly. You see by now, Brussels meant more than just my mother's sprouts.

Mercedes man and mountain man decided that the UK family court's systemic failings, should be brought to the attention of the European Parliament. And furthermore, this unlikely duo were going to address this parliament while it was sitting. Perfectly logical - and we did a bloody good job.

In the end Laurel and Hardy went to Brussels, twice. One has to make an impact on new friends.

In this day and age people can take great offence when stereotypes are used to describe certain character traits they possess, but I'm sure my pal, Klaus, will agree, he is, a stereotypical German. Honest as the day, a technocrat and yet a deep belief in humanity and systems working properly for the benefit of society. He had never been cautioned charged or convicted for anything in his life, a totally law-abiding citizen as I write this in 2017. Christ, he is even concerned about the environment. Behind that technocratic exterior lies a very warm hearted, caring human being. And his principal concern is for his child. And when he ran out of money and options, he came to the door of last resort, mine.

One could say, if talking in cliches, that Klaus and I are like chalk and cheese when it comes to the way we view the world in many areas. I consider most systems in society to have started with good intentions and too often afterwards, be found only to really benefit those who initially designed, then implemented and now allegedly regulate them.

To get results it is necessary to bypass these bureaucratic politically infiltrated systems which are at their worst when allowed to operate in secret. Justice unseen is justice denied, guaranteed in my view. Also, I'm too lazy to be a criminal, so I'm probably half honest by accident.

The next few pages describing what Klaus and myself addressed the European Parliament on are taken from the truly excellent 'The Custody Minefield' website, courtesy of Michael Robinson, owner and author.

The Custody Minefield: Submissions to the EU Parliament on Failings ...

thecustodyminefield.blogspot.com/2014/07/submissions-to-eu-parliament-on.html

1.
2.

5 Jul 2014 - **Vincent McGovern** is Chair of Central and North London Branches of Families Need Fathers, part of the UK's largest shared parenting charity, ...

Saturday, 5 July 2014

Submissions to the EU Parliament on Failings in UK Family Justice

Vincent McGovern is Chair of Central and North London Branches of Families Need Fathers, part of the UK's largest shared parenting charity, and has recently returned from Brussels having presented evidence to the Petitions Commission of the European Parliament in its session concerning failings in the Family Justice Service. He was also supporting a German father, giving evidence to the EU Review related to the efficacy (or lack, thereof) of the <u>Brussels II Revised Regulations</u>.

The German Father's Submission on cross-border Contact Order Enforcement.

In relation to the German father's submissions, allegations involved the UK courts ignoring a contact order signed under

Bis II in another member state and a failure to enforce that agreement. Further, that there was a lack of legal aid for the German father despite the other party having a six figure sum funded by the state. The father intimated there was a breach in equality of arms, and in this, a failure regarding his Article 6 rights to a fair hearing under the human rights legislation. The father invited the EU Parliament to investigate why the UK Courts do not meet their obligations under international agreements, and asked that, if the Commission accepts his evidence that there has been a breach of EU law, they should commence infringement proceedings with the European Court of Justice against the UK Government. The inference was that by not enforcing the order made in another EU state, the court had also infringed on both his child's and his right to family life. The father was critical of the vast sums of money spent on what he considered an ineffective legal process.

Mr McGovern's Submissions on Abuses within the MARAC Process

Mr McGovern also gave evidence related to the processes followed by the UK's Multi Agency Risk Assessment Conference (MARAC) and their being open to abuse. Indeed, he argued that here too, the system fails to uphold the citizen's Article 6 and Article 8 Human Rights. Mr McGovern raises criticism that when allegations are made, the Conference takes hearsay evidence from one party, especially when domestic violence is alleged, without the opportunity for defence or disclosure regarding the nature of allegations made. He went on to explain that the MARAC process is shrouded in secrecy, and he claimed evidence from a Freedom of Information request that evidence is only taken from females, lending the agencies involved open to criticism for gender discrimination. Mr McGovern went on to explain that this gender barrier has resulted in male victims of domestic violence being blocked from having access to local authority services, and children not having been protected from harm, due to the unipolar nature of such investigations.

One major criticism was that the accused is not provided with the evidence used by the MARAC to reach a finding. Following the finding, Social Services will meet both parents, but will only divulge the finding rather than the evidence upon which it was based. Mr McGovern argues that this secrecy and a failure to disclose evidence is a breach of Article 6 of the Human Rights Act.

The verdict of the undefended MARAC inquiry can equip a vexatious litigant with the ammunition to approach the Family Court without notice to the father, and armed with the undefended MARAC findings, the Court will automatically make orders removing the father from both the family home and the children's. Should he breach the orders made, he may face jail.

Mr McGovern has contributed to a number of successful Ombudsman Investigations where findings were made against London Borough of Brent Social Services, Brent Children's and Adolescent Mental Health Services (C.A.M.H.S), the Solicitors Regulatory Authority, Brent Primary Care Trust (a divisional arm of the National Health Service), and the Children's and Family Court Advisory Support Service (Cafcass).

Despite findings against and criticism of these organisations, Mr McGovern argues that the systems and processes undertaken by Multi Agency Risk Assessment Conferences continue to be incompatible with the Human Rights Act, and violate human rights in the UK.

The representations to the EU Parliament come only days after Mr Justice Tyzack criticised teachers and specialists for accepting abuse allegations without question. The judge emphasised that professionals need to keep an open mind, and not take allegations at face value.

TCM Comment

The costs involved in cross-border litigation, and litigation concerning jurisdictional disputes or other aspects of international family law are staggering. It's not uncommon to have a parent asked for a down payment of £30,000 for a leave to remove case, with estimates given of up to £100,000 in legal costs. In the German father's case, the costs for both sides have exceeded £200,000. All this to enforce an existing order.

In relation to the other matters raised by Mr McGovern, aside from the significant harm done to the falsely accused and their children, false allegations draw diminishing resources from support services for genuine victims of abuse. The transparency wanted by Sir James Munby needs to extend beyond the court to the MARAC process. It staggers us that someone can be barred from seeing their children and lose their home, in a closed court, following a closed investigation, where not all evidence is disclosed, and where the accused does not have representation. To my mind, not a system to be proud of, or one which supports transparent and equitable justice. Due to the draconian nature of injunctive orders, we have no doubt that allegations should be heard against the test 'beyond reasonable doubt' rather than upon the 'balance of probability' as happens in the family court. Violence and abuse are criminal matters, should be treated as such, as should the making of false allegations, and heard in the criminal courts.

The court has to take a cautious approach when allegations are made, but there also needs to be greater use of penalties for false allegations. Tyzack's cautionary words need to be heeded. There is gender bias in DV services, but this reflects an attitude in society that violence against men is more acceptable, or even a matter for humour.

If you're sceptical, watch the video below, published by <u>Mankind</u> (and if the thought enters into your mind "he probably asked for it", would you hold the same thought in respect of the woman being abused).

Note:

I will later in a chapter pay tribute on the remarkable work done by Michael Robinson Author and owner of 'The Custody Minefield' and which is of such benefit for so many who find themselves in the UK family court process.

Chapter 16

Preparation for Brussels

Piss poor planning = piss poor performance. The 6 P's rule. Add unlimited optimism and a strong sense of the ridiculous and it is surprising how far one can go, or two! Fortune favours mad fools on occasions.

Klaus had for years been trying to address the European Parliament Petitions Commission, a body which allows citizens to bring grievances about systemic institutional malpractice directly to the European Parliament. Having seen some of his attempts I was not surprised he was so far unsuccessful. Like so many individuals with deep concern who don't know how to separate the emotion from the logic, which is so necessary to get results, especially when dealing with faceless bureaucrats and systems, the more they try, the more emotional and lengthy their attempts become - and also the less chance of success.

This is something I see all the time with unrepresented parents in the family courts of England and Wales. The vast majority are fathers, as mothers have the option of making domestic violence allegations which usually result in them being granted legal aid, which is delivered on a gendered basis (see Chapter 13 on Legal Aid provision).

So as self-appointed expert man, I decided Klaus needed to take a different approach: dump the lengthy emotional statements; reduce it purely to child welfare endangerment; institutional malpractice; plus, the cost to the UK taxpayer and add in the UK family court's contempt for International orders; demonstrate that EU powers and court orders from another EU country, properly registered and seised, can go nowhere in the UK family courts. Demonstrate that the UK treats with contempt internationally binding family orders but are very handy for profiteering by the legal eagles who hover around such matters. And above all, demonstrate that the 'Welfare of The Child', which is the paramount principle within UK Family Law, is a complete nonsense in this case.

Petition No. KZ1229/2013 developed legs. And the Petitions Secretariat decided Klaus had a case good enough to be presented to the Petitions Commission of the European Parliament. When Klaus described me to the Peti Secretariat, as they call themselves, as being the person with the most knowledge of systemic failings within UK family court system based on then fifteen enquiries or so and four Ombudsman Investigations, including two Parliamentary and Health Service Ombudsman, low and behold, I was also invited and we were informed we would both address the session for five minutes each.

Real delusions of ability and bringing about improvement began to flash through my mind. And when the Peti Secretariat informed us that the motion before the Euro Parliament Petitions Commission that day was called Systemic Failings Within UK Family Court System, my delusions of grandeur were of Himalayan proportions.

However, I had to provide security clearance. Hmmmm, something I'm always nervous about. Well, I am an Irishman. Time was short and my clearance had not come through from Peti Secretariat the day before the due date, but I decided Brussels should have the benefit of my presence anyway.

Getting into the European Parliament, gaining access to the auditorium where the Petitions Commission was having its sessions and managing to address them was all something that could be sorted out once I got there. Never say hope does not spring eternal with me.

Klaus, of course being so organised, had no such problems. His security clearance had already been processed and had been allotted a five-minute time to speak. Damn Germans, they always have to be so efficient. And as he was so experienced at travelling from Germany to London for Family Court appearances and being such an efficient dude, he had booked us into a small hotel near the European Parliament. Vorsprung Durch Technik.

We met around 11pm of the night before D-Day and went to Klaus's room at once, because sadly his excellent petition (well I would say that because I mostly wrote it) had been, shall we say, emotionally compromised. We now had rambling, emotional, all over the place, nervous, terrified father. I've come across these circumstances a few too many times, so I decided to apply the cruel to be kind approach. We stayed in his bedroom until 2am until I had him functioning to what I considered an appropriate standard for a man who was going to address the European Parliament in seven hours.

I was on a mission and nothing would change my course. Through pure brutal emotional and psychological bullying, I dragged Klaus wherever was necessary until he was of sufficient standard. I saw an opportunity probably never to be realised again for bringing outside jurisdictional influence upon UK Family Court systemic malpractice and I was not going to let go.

Chapter 17

Inside European Parliament 19.3.14.

It is highly unlikely that anyone ever attempted to address the European Parliament Petitions Commission with as much last minute forced alterations as we had to comply with, and did as well!

Arriving at Euro Parliament building on the morning of Klaus's superb speech, we immediately noticed a lot of people with yellow baseball caps, also petitioning over UK Family Court failings. I also recognised two or three of their leaders as I'd seen them in animated discussion when I travelled on Eurostar the day before. Myself and Klaus were allowed into the public foyer but not through security. All the yellow caps went through security around 9.15am. My earlier confidence was beginning to get a knock. Klaus has several methods of electronic communication and he was shaking them all. Just after 9.30am a wonderful lady came down to security, approached reception and we were led like Mary's little lambs through long corridors until we were seated in the pretty fine auditorium. Klaus was allowed to present first and I noticed we were getting many funny looks from yellow caps.

On the morning of March 19th 2014 Klaus Zinser delivered to the European Parliament Petitions Commission one of the best presentations I have ever witnessed. In a foreign language for him, controlling the real raw emotion of fighting such an oppressive system, just to have court ordered parental involvement in his child's upbringing, he truly demonstrated how a father can fight for his child at the highest level.

Klaus's petition can be seen if you click on Central London Branch Families Need Fathers webpage and the Custody Minefield blog. I was of the understanding that I would also have five minutes to put my points across but it turned into just the one minute, so instead of my carefully prepared five-minute presentation I had to think on the hoof and ad-lib for the moment I was allowed. What I really wanted was to avoid the lengthy application process and hopefully be allowed to submit my prepared statement to the Secretariat and get invited back. I decided that appearing as a not very bright fellow might help to convince the chair if I lifted the entire microphone and base to my mouth and speak too closely into it. Basically, I was appealing to her sense of concern for a clown.

I spoke about how it was, and is, not possible for Klaus to seek enforcement of his international court order within UK family court system because there were only fifty-three successful committal proceedings in 2011 within UK family Court system, (Hansard, column 113, 25 Feb 2012). It worked, and she said I could put my submission into writing. Yippee and yahoo, I was now part of the European Parliament game. Our petition had been accepted: we had not been booted out.

All the yellow baseball caps were parents, mostly foreign, who had been through the heartbreak of seeing their children, with very questionable legality, taken off them and placed into care by UK family courts. The UK has, compared to Europe, a horrendous record of removing children from parents, usually foreign, and placing them within the broadly mercenary state care system. For those who would insist that such is always done for the best interests of the child and after only the most careful judicial consideration, please click on the following link:

Appeal judge slams decision which led to baby being taken from ...
www.dailymail.co.uk/.../It-never-happen-Appeal-judge-slams-cut-paste-decision-fami...

1.

18 Feb 2014 - 'It must never happen again': **Appeal judge slams** 'cut and paste' **decision** in family court which **led** to social workers taking **baby** from parents ...

So, adoptions within the UK were being done at the request of social workers who had not actually seen the children. It was a 'cut and paste' decision. Now, look at your own children. Think of how you would feel if it happened to you and you could do nothing about it.

While I was very briefly addressing the session, Klaus disappeared. I thought, is he sick or something? After some time, he returned and said he wanted me to meet some people. I dutifully followed him out of the chamber and there were some MEPs and special researchers gathered together waiting to speak to me!

Further back there were queues of nervous looking people waiting to speak to the MEPs. Klaus introduced me as being, 'the UK's foremost expert on Systemic Failings within UK Family Court system'. No pressure then! If ever there was a time to deliver, it was here and now. Klaus had only gone and become the best damn lobbyist I had ever seen, and with such social graces to boot.

The two or three MEPs, aided by special researchers, hit me hard with questions initially. I recognised immediately the method. These were highly intelligent, busy people with no patience for spoofers: so, stand and deliver. I recovered and made a few succinct responses. And then I realised I was in over the wall: they considered me legit and we had without question the most fruitful fifteen minutes or so conversation on this business imaginable.

The female Austrian MEP was the lead. It was so invigorating for me to realise how far ahead these MEPs and the EU in general consider the UK to be the black hole of Europe, where children and shared parenting are concerned. Among the expressions beautiful in their clarity and simplicity were the comments including, 'draconian', 'barbaric', 'medieval', and the real beauty, 'toxic 1970's feminist war mindset still within UK'. From the Austrian MEP the most accurate description I have ever heard about systemic failings within UK family court system, 'It is obvious that the welfare of the child is a phrase of convenience for the welfare of professionals within the system in the UK'. Holy Moly! I travelled that distance to hear a non-native English speaker totally describe the UK family court system far better that any pseudo-professional ever has done within the UK.

I handed them copies of what was meant to be my five-minute presentation: basically, what is also written on 'The Custody Minefield' blog in Chapter 16 above. Klaus and I were assured his petition was going to be considered along with my contribution. So, myself and Klaus returned to the chamber to hear what others had to present, after all, by now, we considered ourselves seasoned experts. Some days are too good to be true, until they become better.

Chapter 18

Party after Parliament

I don't think it is necessary to introduce this Chapter. But I would say that the brass neck and taking quick advantage of a situation is something that others could learn from when attempting to remove systemic malpractice.

For some strange reason, the expression 'party after parliament' always reminds me of the phrase 'Lark in the Park'.

Sometimes there is great humour in life, and usually from the most unexpected of sources. While Klaus and I were attempting to negotiate our way out of this enormous building and feeling very pleased with our day, we found ourselves at the bottom of a giant atrium. We could hear some sort of a formal speech and then applause up somewhere near the sky, as far as we were concerned. What followed was that wonderful clink of nice glass and polite laughter, much like my own. Ten minutes later Laurel and Hardy were still going in circles trying to leave the building and the laughter and party sounds from high above were getting much louder. I said to Klaus, "there is a party taking place somewhere near the sky". He agreed and commented that this place is party central in Brussels once work finishes.

I had one of those inspirational moments, a bit like John Belushi in the Blues Brothers. I said to Klaus, "this party needs our presence". Klaus, being a well brought up German, insisted we could not attend as we had not been formally invited. I reminded him of the international custom that wherever a party is taking place anywhere in the world an Irishman is *always* welcome. He thoughtfully replied that he had not heard of such a custom. How sad I thought to myself, I'm stuck with a German gentleman unaware of international social niceties. By now I was determined to check this party out, temptation being overwhelming, you understand. All those glasses clinking, how could I possibly resist? While we were heading up to the top of the atrium, by various confused means, I had a concerned German expressing unhappiness about my desire to attend said party. I considerately confided in him that I knew why Germany had started two world wars, and also lost them. He asked my opinion.

I explained that Germany is very proper and excellent technically in manufacturing and the sciences. He demurred, but agreed. I also explained that Germany believed if neighbouring nations adopted their methods the world would be a better place, a bit like the current EU. He hesitatingly agreed. Then, because it took us ten minutes to climb Everest atrium, I had time to explain that the Germans lost both wars because they didn't know how to deal with the top echelons of the British establishment's ruthlessness. He semi agreed. And then my masterpiece: I thoughtfully explained that if the Germans had an Irish leader they would have won those wars. Klaus being such a law-abiding citizen, explained that an Irishman could not be voted leader in Germany, as their constitution does not allow it. Which explains why they lost twice, I replied. I just love being knowledgeable!

By now the strategic geniuses still within the EU Parliament building had arrived at a party. And I mean a party. Just like all those Ferrer Rocher ads usually seen around Christmas, the Ambassador from Cuilcagh Mountain in North West Ireland felt right at home. Klaus being Klaus was concerned we would be thrown out. I addressed his concerns by asking him rhetorically if I had ever let him down since the last time. He replied "no", but not with total conviction. I cannot think why!

I explained to Klaus my cunning plan, and this one was better than Baldricks from Blackadder any day. The Croatian Government had donated some fine art to the European Parliament which appeared to consist of around eight large paintings on stands, about two metres high or six feet six inches in real measurement. At the rear was what looked like the most beautiful buffet ever imagined with liveried servers, along with many many bottles of wine. Some sparkling water and juices were also on offer, but who cares about them?

The master plan was put into place. Klaus was told to follow my instructions without arguing. We would stride confidently towards two adjacent paintings, which were centrepiece and comment on them. He would speak to me in German about his view of his painting and I would speak to him in Irish giving my view. I figured that any security who could crack that was well entitled to throw us out. We casually approached the paintings, making friendly eye contact and smiling with whoever looked our way. Klaus by now was in operational mode, the gears were engaged with full synchromesh. He duly looked thoughtfully at a painting or two, as I did. I had absolutely no idea what he said, but I know what I said to him. I recited what I remembered of the Lord's Prayer in Irish which is the first line, and also made some comments in Irish about my home area in Ireland, the grass is green, it rains a lot, it can be very cold. All those profound philosophical statements which determine real intelligence.

We then proceeded to the buffet tables and helpfully guided the servers as to what we wanted on our plates. Continuing our discussion about the paintings in the two languages we used excellent body and sign language to assist the servers. The useless deaf instructor at Nelson Mandela's funeral would have been so proud of us. Armed with a plate of food fit for a prince and an excellent looking glass of wine we retired to some seats. If anyone had stopped us my defence was that I am the Glangevlin County Cavan President of the Croatian Art Appreciation Society. You see down the road from my home parish in Ireland is a place called, The Burren, which had just become a Geopark. I was once told it has remarkable geological similarity with an area in Croatia. I have always admired my fine understanding of the finer points of geography.

Now, where was I, oh yes, the food and wine. There is a scene in the children's film Ratatouille when the renowned food critic enters and asks for a dish. Then his reaction and comment afterwards in his newspaper column. Well, once the first forkful was in my gob, I was that food critic. I never knew that taste buds could be so energised, such beauty of food I had never tasted before. I was mesmerised by the quality. So much so that I actually shut up and just ate. Klaus was like a child opening Christmas presents, a slightly disjointed look of disbelief that we were here, the food was so astonishing, and the Croatian white wine matched the food.

After two plates of food and three glasses of wine, these two reserved gentlemen floated out of the EU building, into a large African-themed park nearby. After our experiences how could we go anywhere normal? Klaus made some phone calls and I made one to my parents. My father answered, and as usual, he was working on one of his many, ahem, classic vehicles, some of which are nearly his age. My mother has a different opinion on these vehicles: she might be accurate.

The party does not end there. In 2017/18/19 Klaus was informing me of yet more madness in his case. He had been informed in 2017 that his child was going to be leaving the UK. Klaus attempted to see if such had occurred by visiting the UK. Nothing could be established so he returned to Germany. Later he was once again told his child would be leaving the UK. Klaus once again visited the UK and surprise surprise, found himself being arrested and detained for over 60 hours. A court date was set for some months later, Klaus attended and was duly found guilty of harassment with violence! Klaus appealed to the Crown court and was unsuccessful. Before the Crown court hearing Klaus had discovered that the female Detective Constable in his case had a court case pending against her for shall we say, artistic interpretation in his case. His request for an adjournment was ignored and his appeal was unsuccessful.

Klaus had learned something over the years, and that was conduct, requirement, consequences and remedy. Klaus persevered and eventually the DC was charged and found guilty of perverting the course of justice. She was sentenced to 4 months imprisonment, suspended. You see, the bright lady had stitched Klaus up by claiming he had been guilty of harassment with violence! Klaus wouldn't know how to be violent if he was paid. The detective constable resigned after her sentence was announced and was later dismissed from the force on 15/1/19.

I can only assume, and it is not a defence, that she was so used to dads being stitched up by the agencies attached to the family court that she believed the criminal courts would take the same approach. They did, but the evidence was there to be used by Klaus against her. I have to say, for a stereotypical German who doesn't know when to give up regarding his son, Klaus has my deep admiration.

Many times have I cursed the delay in getting this book published, but one benefit has been the opportunity to present the above regarding Klaus Zinser.

'On 5th October 2018, at Leicester Crown Court, you were convicted of an offence of exercising the power and privileges of a constable improperly, contrary to section 26 {1} of Criminal Justice and Courts Act 2015, the particulars being that between 22nd October 2017 and 25th October 2017, you falsified a custody record knowing that the exercise was improper. You were sentenced to four months imprisonment, suspended for 12 months.'

All I can say re the above is, have a party Klaus, for yourself and all the fathers who love their children and who will not be stitched up by this corrupt former police detective. I wonder, is she now working for a domestic abuse charity?

Chapter 19

Return to European Parliament, 11.11.14.

Having managed to get 'invited back' Klaus and myself did some serious preparation for this one. And once again forced last minute changes alter our plan. But, we got a result. The UK Family Court System would be 'investigated' by the EU. This is the first time this has ever happened and I'm damn glad of the part myself and Klaus played. The small man can shake the big tree!

Klaus and myself were offered the opportunity to return to the European Parliament Petitions Chamber on 11/11/14. Armistice Day I thought to myself, overreaching myself historically somewhat. Being a senior officer of the UK based Shared Parenting Charity, Families Need Fathers, I thought what a wonderful opportunity for the charity to gain some serious recognition internationally and prepare a short paper which I could present to the Petitions Commission.

Sadly, but not surprisingly, despite asking on several occasions via various channels, the Trustees declined my request. Rather they refused to respond, the time worn manner of those who lack ability to do something or the guts to take responsibility.

Being aware of my own lack of, shall we say, academic presentation experience, I sought help from another source. And my deep gratitude to Karen Woodall of the Centre for

Separated Families who at short notice prepared an excellent one- page statement.

Karen is one of, if not *the*, UK's foremost expert on parental alienation and systemic failings within UK Family Court system. She also runs excellent parental alienation workshops and writes a quality blog. She has always seen the need for lifting the UK children's services out of the dark ages, surrounded by an ultra-feminist mindset with innumerable academics propping it up with virtually unlimited standpoint research at taxpayer's expense. What a tragedy for children within the UK, that she along with her husband Nick and their clinic, are not the Government appointed lead organisation for all professionals within the UK family court system.

Particularly noticeable on 11/11/14, the legal advisor for the Commission did all she could to prevent the Commission from investigating Systemic Failings within UK family courts. Absolutely top marks has to go to Rainer Wieland, the EU Children's Commissioner, who brilliantly outmanoeuvred all administrative blocks she placed in the way. If you look at the video-link on the Central London Branch of Fnf's webpage at the bottom you will see the links to myself and Klaus addressing the Petitions Commission. The first six minutes or so are Klaus and I presenting. Once again, my allocated time was taken from me at the last minute so we decided to do a joint presentation on the day. Once again, I had to ad-lib, instead of delivering a carefully prepared speech. And Klaus, as was becoming rather familiar, did a top job of delivering his statement. Full marks to Klaus, this petition was in his name yet he always insisted I have equal time to present which was taken from his time. This man seriously sees the bigger picture regarding the UK Family Court failings.

There then followed many moments of unbelievable boredom as the Secretariat legal adviser did everything she could to run the petition into the ground. On numerous occasions I have sat in family courts in the UK and listened to similar during my work as a McKenzie Friend. Rainer Weiland, the then EU Children's Commissioner, again outmanoeuvred her and by-passed her deliberate restrictions. Two Germans and an Irishman plus the yellow caps had managed to get the EU to investigate Systemic Failings within UK Family Court system. The first time this has ever happened.

The EU paid a friendly visit some months later and met Sir James Munby, President of the Family Division, for tea and biscuits. To their credit Sir James and some other leading judges had already greatly reduced the amount of forced adoptions taking place within the UK. Some estimates have it at a 50% reduction. Although Klaus and I will never be credited officially, around that time the UK family court clarified via correspondence with Strasbourg European Court, the situation regarding Shared Residence orders from abroad and also enforcement of them. The answer is, to nobody's surprise, that a Shared Residence Order from a Brussels II signatory, and *its* enforcement, *is* applicable within the UK. Then in April 2014 Residence and Contact applications and orders ceased to exist within UK family courts. A Pyrrhic victory.

Chapter 20

My Campaigning to remove Institutional Malpractice Within UK Family Court System

Nothing annoys me more than all the facebook warriors and armchair Generals pontificating on social media about 'how biased' the system is. So quite simply 'shut up,' read, and learn how to force improvement.

Having obtained, after much hard work, my five Ombudsman findings in my favour, including three Parliamentary Health Service Ombudsman, and addressed European Parliament Petitions twice, I was curious as to how the various politicians, newspapers, radio shows and television talk shows would treat me. After all, who has done more to expose child endangering institutional malpractice within the deservedly much maligned UK Children and family court system?

Virtually every single one of the seventy newspaper editors and columnists, political commentators and MPs I sent a short letter to has ignored me. The honourable exceptions are Peter Hitchens of the Daily Mail and Jane Moore of the Sun. As for the radio shows, etc, whenever I phoned up when the show was on and they asked me what experience do I have and I mentioned my Ombudsman investigations, guess what, I'm either left hanging or politely thanked. The BBC, where children and fathers are concerned, I long ago renamed the British Biased Corporation.

Paul Apreda, Welsh FNF dynamo, managed to get me an appearance on Sunday Morning Live BBC1 TV in September 2015. From a scheduled twenty-minute slot I found myself having two minutes. I'm told I did okay, but the BBC must have lost my contact details ever since. In 2012 FNF UK got me a few minutes with Vanessa Feltz, presenter of BBC Radio London. I had the grand total of ten seconds preparation. In December 2013, I was interviewed by Rod Liddle for the Sunday Times Online section re the Norgrove Report on Shared Parenting. That interview lasted for about fifteen minutes and went very well. Only problem is, virtually nobody has seen it. So, I'm semi-anonymous.

To their credit some members of Parliament have responded to me despite not being one of their constituents. Most of these are Conservative MPs. And surprisingly a few young female Labour MPs from the North of England. There appears to be more decency up there. As regards Liberal MPs in general, forget them. The Liberal left elite has utter contempt for fathers and shared parenting. One notable exception here is Greg Mulholland, former Liberal MP for Leeds North West. I had the wonderful privilege of watching him destroy Anthony Douglas CEO of Cafcass during an interview about parental alienation in 2016 on the BBC1 Victoria Derbyshire Show.

In this interview Douglas was doing a brilliant job of acknowledging parental alienation and then insisting nothing could be done about it as any corrective action would 'rebound' on the child. Greg Mulholland very directly told Douglas he is being 'disingenuous'.

Just think of it, 'the welfare of the child is paramount' yet the official government department advising the family courts will not as a matter of policy do anything about 'parental alienation' because it will 'rebound' on the child. Douglas and CAFCASS are brilliant at justifying systemic failings by parroting this doublespeak. I know Anthony Douglas has talked about how scarred he is because of unwanted contact with his father or stepfather, I'm not sure which. This same personal belief is now foisted onto generations of vulnerable children because of his personal background. So much for impartial professionalism.

I also had the privilege of being invited to speak by Matt O'Connor, founder of Fathers for Justice, and George Galloway, multiple-former MP, at a meeting entitled 'Fatherless London,' in April 2016. Galloway has for years been campaigning for better outcomes for children within the UK family court system and views mass state sanctioned fatherlessness as a major problem for society. Galloway is not everyone's cup of tea, but his consistency towards shared parenting puts the vast majority of Members of Parliament to shame.

Matt O'Connor needs no introduction as he has made F4J an international brand and regularly appears on talk shows and writes excellent newspaper articles on the subject. The panel also consisted of John Waters, renowned writer on fatherlessness, Kevin O Brien, Antiknife UK campaigner, and Mo George, Eastenders actor who successfully sued the Sun newspaper for record damages after falsely portraying him as guilty of domestic violence.

My modest contribution on the night consisted of the following:

'Thank you. It is always a pleasure meeting Matt, he frequents the best places. The first place I met him was under a bush opposite the Prime Ministers house, the next place was Buckingham Palace, Marylebone Magistrates Court twice, Houses of Parliament and now the King Soloman Academy.

What's more important is the question on the top of the poster announcing this meeting Fatherless in London, *'are anti father government policies creating a social crisis in London?' Well, I'm not an expert on social crisis but I am an expert on the anti-father government policies in the UK. I say this because I have 5 Ombudsman Investigations to my credit, (3 Parliamentary Ombudsman) and I have twice presented to the Petitions Commission of the European Parliament on its motion of 'Systemic Failings in UK Family Courts.'*

Some of you here will be unfortunate enough to know me as Chair of Central and North London Branches of Families Need Fathers where we have approximately 900 – 1,000 attendees per year.

On the specific question of ant- father government policies in London here is how it works. Let us assume a father has concerns about his children. He may even be the primary carer. In London, all of these policies are operated under what is known as the M.A.R.A.C (Multi Agency Risk Assessment Conference) process which operates under B.O.C.U (Borough Operational Command Unit) which is the operating mechanism of all London Boroughs. It may not be fully utilised, it may exercise only parts of it, but that process is how so many fathers are removed from the family home.

*I see people from Families Need Fathers here in the audience with years of dedicated experience of helping fathers dealing with this brutal discrimination turning up at our meetings week in week out under this system. We're all sick of hearing how fathers are processed: served non – molestation orders, injunctions prohibiting access to the family home under Family Law Act, which are **criminal proceedings** and nearly always a 'Without Notice' hearing. This means that if the father even waves to his children he is guilty of a criminal offence, and can be automatically arrested and imprisoned.*

The father is ousted from the family home by the mother exercising her gender advantage of accessing these agencies who in constitution and practice will only help fathers. I have this information under the Freedom of Information Act and also the Domestic Violence Corporate Strategy of so many of these Boroughs. This means that the father is discriminated against because the mother can exercise her gender advantage by accessing these agencies. This opportunity is denied to the dad. These agencies, in constitution and practice, will promote and facilitate ANY false allegation against the dad, doesn't matter how ridiculous. We are in Alice in Wonderland here. This means that under Article 6 of the European Convention on Civil Rights he is denied access to a fair trial. This nearly always applies to fathers and very occasionally in Private Family Law to mothers. Mothers lose out terribly in Public Family Law (Forced Adoptions).

This promotion of false allegations from one gender only also means that ever since LASPO in 2012 (Legal Aid, Sentencing and Punishment of Offenders) the mother is entitled to Legal Aid by claiming domestic abuse which is denied to the father. This makes a complete mockery of Article 6 of the ECHR and right to a fair trial as these agencies will promote ANY false allegation by the mother against the father. We are sick of fathers attending our meetings believing this has only happened to them, that they will have a fair trial and get a proper opportunity in Court, that they are equal in the eyes of the law, so on and so forth. The problem is explaining to them the actual process.

If the father is very resilient and capable, can access Fathers 4 Justice and Families Need Fathers, has good support from family and friends and is well off, which is always a big help, he can try and deal with the Court process, where he will meet Cafcass.

The greatest sick joke ever perpetrated against children and fathers in the UK was on April Fool's day 2001 when Cafcass was set up. They are formally known as Children and Family Court Advisory Support Service. It would be far more accurate to describe them as Children and Fathers Court Abusing Separation System. I know what I'm talking about because I've had 2 Parliamentary Ombudsman investigations into Cafcass. Some of my best friends in this business are ex-Cafcass Guardians who left in disgust. They have a conscience. Cafcass work closely with these single gender agencies and they are masters of negative linguistics. The most innocent comment by the father is misrepresented. For example, instead of "he responded" we will have "he angrily retorted." The promotion and facilitation of any threat to the mother will be eagerly pursued, doesn't matter how false. Most Cafcass reports follow this trend.

If the father gets to court and obtains an order, probably for supervised contact with his children because of the facilitation of false allegations, and then after still more hearings he may be lucky to have a good Judge, a good Barrister or a good McKenzie Friend (see Chapter 25) and get what we call the 'default position' which is every second weekend and some holidays, he is doing very well. Sometimes it takes 10, 20 and even 30 or 40 hearings to get this order. Some never even get this order.

So, the father has this order and let's assume the mother decides she will not comply with it. He has the option of making an enforcement application C79 under the Children Act. C79s are one of the greatest jokes played upon fathers and the general public because the enforcement is close to ZERO.

If you don't believe what I say check what Tim Loughton, MP and former Minister for Children and Families, had to say in *the House of Commons in February 2013, 'In 2011 there were only 53 successful commitments for breaking court orders in the UK'. (Ref: Hansard, 25th February 2013, Column 113 at 8.46pm) There are approximately 44,000 or so cases every year.*

When Matt and Fathers 4 Justice say that there are 200 children every day who lose contact with their fathers in the family courts, this is not because the Courts make orders denying the father contact with his children, rather they will refuse to enforce their own orders. The Sunday Times in 2004 reported that over half of all family court orders for contact are broken.

Now, let's get into pantomime here. Lots of fathers will say they have equal rights, have parental responsibility, etc. Let me educate you, they haven't read Section 2 (4) Children Act 1989. This states,'For the avoidance of doubt the father is no longer the legal guardian of his children.' This whole process makes a complete mockery of the European Court of Human Rights, Article 6 - Right to a fair trial, Article 8, Right to a family life, Article 9.3 of the UN Convention on the Rights of the Child to have a proper relationship with both parents. This is done because the Children Act 1989 triumphs over all other laws.

Now, I am not a father's rights campaigner, I'm a children's rights campaigner. Can anyone tell me that the process I have just outlined is not anti- father. Much more importantly, can anyone look me sincerely in the eye and tell me the Welfare of the Children is Paramount here?

I thank George and Matt for inviting me onto this panel, it is a pleasure meeting the other speakers, but I want to say one last thing. George Galloway and Matt O Connor did brilliant work in getting George's Early Day Motion (EDM 210) signed by 104 MPs. This is nearly as many as the female MPs, mostly Labour, who voted for an illegal war in Iraq. It is the portrayal of all men as being violent that underpins so much of this anti father and child discrimination. This rotten system needs to be taken down, smash the malpractice. We need to make it fit for purpose as originally intended because until we do we are failing as parents. Thank you.'

John Waters, fellow panellist in the Fatherless London debate, said in his piece, *'the public and fathers believe this is a fair fight between the mother and the father. It is not. It is a fight between the father against the mother backed by the state to see if she will allow him any relationship with his children.'*

I wrote to Theresa May, PM, before the International Men's Debate in the House of Commons on 17th November 2016. Very few male MPs attended that debate though great credit to Philip Davies MP and others for doing so much to bring this debate about. This was a complex letter which included the following topics:

- male suicide (4,630 per annum in the UK, 900 male suicides per year because of the Family Courts. Sunday Express 2001.

- UK children having the worst outcomes for relationships with both parents post separation and divorce in the Developed World

- institutional malpractice in the provision of domestic abuse services, social workers attitudes and malpractice against fathers exercised by Cafcass

- abysmal enforcement of court orders by the family courts

Some people may say the letter was too intense with too much information in a small space. It was also sent to MPs who have expressed at various times an interest in this subject. If I am deemed too intelligent for those MPs their special researchers and personal assistants, then prayer is necessary for everyone.

Several weeks later I received a reply from the office of The Prime Minister. I was thanked for corresponding with them and my letter was being forwarded to the Department for Education who have responsibility in such matters. I'm still waiting for a reply as of October 2020. I guess that one either got lost or is filed in the wrong tray, or perhaps fell down the back of a cabinet. My letters need a homing pigeon.

I have also managed to be invited to attend the All Party Parliamentary Group (Children) House of Lords which meets every so often in one of the committee rooms in the big house by the Thames. No, I have not been invited to the full chamber of the House of Lords just yet, though having said that I have some unopened post. Unfortunately, most of the business conducted within that Parliamentary Group is of the 'hail good fellow, or lass' old pals act. Too often it appears to be an exercise in self-congratulation, but then what do I know about affairs of high government. What I do know is that those who criticise are politely listened to and then ignored. One of the Chairs of the Parliamentary Group definitely does not like me - what a surprise: she is an ex-Chair of Cafcass. Never have I seen a more determined individual who is willing to protect institutional malpractice within Cafcass than her.

I managed to meet Baroness Howarth, ex-Chair of Cafcass, after one of the parliamentary sessions. I politely thanked her for sparing me a moment and asked her if she is the person I should bring my concerns to about Cafcass as I've had two PHSO investigations into them.

I received that frozen smile which never gets to the eyes and she assured me most forcefully that Cafcass do excellent work in the most difficult of circumstances. I replied that as I had two PHSO in my favour finding fault with current Cafcass practice perhaps she needed to reconsider. In a moment of inspiration, she informed me that she is no longer Chair of Cafcass. I had already known that and also who the new Chair of Cafcass was, Baroness Tyler, who earlier had been at the same large table as Baroness Howarth but who had disappeared after I explained to the panel that I had two PHSO into Cafcass out of five Ombudsman Investigations into malpractice by children's services.

After Baroness Howarth informed me that she was no longer Chair of Cafcass I apologised for my error and asked who her replacement was? She thought for a moment, still with that frozen smile, and apologised to me for having a 'senior moment' as she couldn't remember who her replacement was, before promptly leaving my company.

I didn't know whether to feel sad or happy. Here's me, an ordinary Joe who has been lied to by every agency throughout the UK children's services: plus, the solicitors and Brent Primary Care Trust. Then, when I finally get to meet someone of real responsibility in the House of Lords I am apparently lied to there as well. If I played poker I'm assuming that would be the full house.

I have no doubt whatsoever that in any other walk of life, based on what I have seen, that some Cafcass officers' behaviour within the family court process on occasions would be sued, found guilty of perjury, sacked for gross negligence and dismissed without a pension. But we are dealing with the UK family courts system and this is far too often totally unrecognisable from any concept of professionalism.

After the next session, I tried to have a brief word with Baroness Tyler, Cafcass current chair. Most regrettably she said she was terribly busy after I had introduced myself and couldn't meet me as she had to rush to another meeting. For anyone who believes it is possible to reform this system by lobbying, you are having a laugh. Removal of budget and considerable changes of personnel and training are urgently required if children are ever going to benefit from a proper child centred court advisory service within the UK.

In 2018 my campaigning for better outcomes for children within the UK family court process began to gain some momentum. However, my computer luddicy remains a problem. As there are certain dull sparks of intelligence within my make up I decided to ask those who know for help with the preparation of slides for my presentations. My first presentation was to the University of Surrey Law Faculty. The people I asked were Dr John Barry of Male Psychology Network at University College London and Martin Daubney journalist and all-round commentator with a high public profile on men and boys issues. Dr Barry as is his profession focused on the emotional impact and trauma plus the high suicide rate especially among fathers who are litigants in person within the family court and up against state funded lawyers.

Daubney was quite remarkable when I brought this to his attention in his study. Once he grasped it and started to improve the presentation, I could quickly see why he had been an award winning editor. At one stage he was working from about 8 minimised screens on his computer and was astonishingly focused. When we had finished the 20 slides, he read them again and loudly exclaimed 'a father has as much chance in the family court as a one-legged man in an arse kicking contest.' Astonishingly apt comment in my opinion. After all, one could hardly expect delicate phraseology from the son of a coal miner when faced with the horrible reality of circumstance for so many parents.

Later in 2018 I had the privilege of presenting these slides at Families Need Fathers 2018 conference and also a brief presentation at University College London Male Psychology Network 2 day conference in June 2018, and a longer presentation in 2019 co-presented with Dr John Barry. In November 2018 I had the pleasure of presenting a 'comedy sketch' at 'Messages For Men' mini conference in London. Nigel Pankhurst, descended of Emmeline Pankhurst, Natty Raymond, Elizabeth Hobson and myself were the organisers of the march and conference. My presentation/comedy was videoed by Ewan Jones and put onto Mike Buchanan's Justice for Men and Boys (J4MB) website. So far only J4MB and the Welsh section of Fnf has uploaded and promoted my videos. In 2020 I was invited by Mike Buchanan and Elizabeth Hobson (recent party leader of J4MB) to present a 43 minute video titled, 'the War on Dads and Children, for the International Conference on men's Issues. (Google ICMI20 ear to ear Vincent McGovern, youtube) Ewan Jones, a quiet and very efficient camera man and video artist was also good enough to interview me on camera in November 2020 and this video can be seen on Youtube under, Ewan Jones Interviews Vincent McGovern.

Neil Lyndon a renowned journalist and author asked me to contribute a chapter to his book 'Epiphanies.' The contributors apart from myself were high order, Dr Warren Farrell, Professor Janice Fiamengo, Neil Lyndon and similar luminaries. I'm looking forward to more presentations and opportunities, but my diary is not overloaded. What a surprise!

In 2018 I started coming across court orders that made my blood run cold. Increasingly fathers who are unrepresented and up against lawyers (usually legal aid funded) for the mother are being subject to Finding of Fact hearings. The worst abuses happen with Magistrates courts. The fathers are too often found guilty of arguing with the mother because she is alienating them from their children, and then the father is deemed guilty of breaching the new Coercive and Controlling law because the mother feels abused. This is the equivalent of a thief being bankrolled by the state to sue the victim because the thief didn't get all that they wanted. Justice for children, what a laugh in this situation.

By accident or otherwise, I appear to be ruffling some feathers in the system. In 2019 I found out that a barrister and former legal adviser to an All Party Parliamentary Group on Family law, Natasha Phillips, who also blogs under Researching Reform, and who wrote a public letter to Cafcass and the NSPCC on the eve of our (Central London Branch) conference on Parental Alienation in 2017, had created a website, CSI The Centre for Social Injustice (a ripoff of The Centre for Social Justice) or 2 in my honour. Such flattery could make me blush!

In general, it was a hatchet job on Families Need Fathers and especially me. The excellent Nick Langford (Author of An Exercise in Absolute Futility) and the blogger supreme William Collins (Illustrated Empathy Gap) both of whom I steal some brains from, were also denigrated.

Natasha has apparently spent a lot of time and energy researching my comments on various other blogs and Facebook. They were of course selectively picked to demonstrate her viewpoint, only. I have to say I was most flattered by the photograph of me, if I were on a dating site it would feature prominently. That said reading the comments I had made over the years surprised me, I didn't know I could write that well!

Above all, the intention is to label me an extremist men's rights (MRA) activist and attempt to link me with some

MRA's in the States. It would appear that the love a dad has for his children is now the love that dare not speak it's name, in the UK anyway!

Parental Alienation is a term detested by those agencies and vested interests who so vigorously wish to exercise it and give full support to those who do, usually mothers 95% of the time. Domestic Violence gendered promotion and control of the narrative and funding is their vehicle of choice, and they exploit it brilliantly but quite often to the detriment of children. I hope to give them much more reason to hate me.

For the record I am not and never have been a men's rights activist. I am most certainly a children's right's activist and will continue to be.

Chapter 21

Notable people within UK who seek to improve the Situation for Children and Fathers

'*The only thing necessary for the triumph of evil is for good men to do nothing. Nobody made a greater mistake than he who did nothing because he could do only a little. Those who don't know history are destined to repeat it.*'
Edmund Burke.

There are many heroes trying to improve the situation for children and their fathers within the UK. But top of that list is a heroine, Erin Pizzey.

Decades ago I read about her remarkable campaign to open and keep open refuges for women and their children who had been abused by men. But her keen sense of public duty and common sense quickly made her realise that domestic violence is a two-way street. This is of course totally unacceptable to what Erin so accurately describes as 'Marxist Feminists' and those ruthless gender vigilantes have stolen a complete and total march on society.

We now have the crazed situation where the former extremists on the fringes of society are now the very well entrenched establishment and boy will they keep it that way. If you want to find out how this came about then please read a book called, 'This Way to The Revolution', by one Erin Pizzey. I have had the pleasure of receiving it as a gift from her upon our first meeting. Within five minutes of meeting her, with me already well established as a shared parenting campaigner I quickly realised that if I could learn a quarter of what she knows I would be incredible. So, not wanting to be too hard on myself I decided to settle for 20%. After all, one has to deal with reality.

Another stalwart of meaningful shared parenting is the six times elected Member of Parliament George Galloway. Currently not sitting as an MP but with George anything is possible.

Galloway and Matt O'Connor teamed up and brought the Early Day Motion (210) in 2013 to the House Of Commons. Beautiful in simplicity and perfectly succinct, despite Galloway being a firebrand Independent MP, it still gained 104 MP signatures. My respect to each and every one of them. However, there are 650 Members of Parliament so 546 are not apparently too interested in shared parenting, or fearful of the feminist anti-shared parenting lobby. As for the House Of Lords, that is where the real anti-dad and anti-shared parenting opposition lies. If you require evidence look at how watered down the alleged revisions of 2014 to The Children Act 1989 became once the House Of Lords got near it.

Early day motion 210 Primary Sponsor, George Galloway

'That this House notes that many fathers convicted of no criminal offence have very limited access to their children as a result of decisions made by the family courts following separation or divorce; further notes that the family courts operate in conditions of secrecy in which there is a lack of public accountability for the decisions they make; believes

that mothers, children and fathers all have rights in relation to family contact and access where there has been family breakdown; further believes there should not be a presumption that family breakdown is the primary responsibility of either parent; further believes that where there is palpably no threat to children from their father in the context of family breakdown, the courts should try to maximise reasonable access in the interests of the children; and calls on the Government to review the operation of the family courts in general and their decision-making in relation to fathers' access to children in the context of family breakdown in particular, taking into account the testimony of the many thousands of fathers who feel their rights are being ignored or abused in relation to their children and in particular the organisation Fathers4Justice and the 36,000 families it represents.'

Total number of signatures:**104**

There are many individuals who in their own way fight against this anti-father monstrosity. The best known is Matt O'Connor head of Fathers for Justice (F4J) for many years, very ably aided and abetted by his second wife Nadine O'Connor. Among the more colourful, and certainly the bravest, individuals fighting would be Jonathan 'Jolly' Stanesby. He is one of the UK's leading father's rights activists and has been involved in some pretty daring stunts.

Yet another outstanding father fighting for equality is former barrister Michael Cox, now a mechanic on oil rigs. Here's the story from The Telegraph, by Bonnie Malkin (26 June 2007):

'A lawyer was jailed yesterday for refusing to pay child support to his former wife, despite her pleas not to give him a custodial sentence.

Michael Cox, 43, has failed to pay child support for the past 12 years because he says his three children spend half their lives with him.

Mr Cox said that despite looking after his sons he is still expected to pay child support for the time they spend with their mother.

A court heard that while he is asked to pay £365 a month, his ex-wife Lesley Peach, 39, is not expected to pay anything. In March this year Mr Cox, a father of five, was handed a suspended sentence of 42 days in prison for failing to pay the charge.

The sentence was suspended on a condition that he begin paying monthly instalments, but he continued to refuse to make the payments.

Yesterday he heavily criticised the Child Support Agency (CSA) as he was jailed for 42 days. Mr Cox, who represented himself, told Southampton Magistrates Court: "I have been referred to as an absent father, but that's not what I am.

"I'm a father who well knows the obligation to his children and I discharge that obligation. I feed all of my children, I clothe them, I house them - that's what I spend my money on. The Child Support Agency gives me no assistance for that and requires me to spend the money twice."

The agency was "oppressive, unjust and discriminatory in its action", he said. "In this case you have two established families living in equilibrium. My ex-wife lives a mile away from me and the children pass easily between the two households. They spend half of the time with me and half of the time with their mother.

"My ex-wife is not a little old lady living in a shoe, reaching in the back of a cupboard for the last tin of beans. This is not about the law, according to the law I'm dead in the water, I'm bang to rights."

Mr Cox asked magistrates to show discretion and spare him jail so that he could continue to earn money to pay for the care of his three sons who are aged between 13 and 16. Tom Concannon, prosecuting, said that since the couple split in 1994 Mr Cox had racked up a debt to the CSA of around £45,000. The court heard that Mr Cox was required to pay because the children are officially resident with their mother. But in a letter to magistrates Mrs Peach begged them not to jail Mr Cox because in his absence she would have to give up her job to look after her children full time.

Reacting to the sentence, Mr Cox, of Hythe, Southampton, said: "It is outrageous that people are released early from prison for serious crimes and yet I'm being locked up, as a caring father." Mr Cox was supported in court by his current wife Beth Cox, 32, who sobbed as he was jailed.

Outside court, members of the campaign group Fathers 4 Justice, to which Mr Cox is legal advisor, reacted angrily to the sentence. The group's founder Matt O'Connor said: "It is utterly disgusting to jail a very courageous and brave individual and a loving father who cares for his children."

I have no words which can be printed to describe this absurd gender discrimination by the state.

Bobby Smith, a lead campaigner for fathers and children, of New Fathers 4 Justice, along with his sidekick Martin Matthews, have been atop Buckingham Palace and Jeremy Corbyn's house and engaged in other incidents involving ladders. Bobby Smith, an ordinary truck driver of average education and, he would say himself, average ability has with his one-man campaign derailed Harriet Harman's (MP for Camberwell and noted anti-men campaigner) Pink Bus Tour during the 2015 general election. He also stood in the then Prime Minister's seat, David Cameron MP, Theresa May MP and Boris Johnson MP, dressed as the cartoon character Elmo which is his registered political party made up from letters of his daughter's names.

The best speech I have ever heard against the myriad failings of the family court system was from Rosy Stanesby in the Gladstone room of the House Of Commons, an event organised and hosted by George Galloway and Matt O Connor (F4J) in 2012. Rosy is the daughter of the legendary Jolly Stanesby. Her along with Aimee Nicholls and other children featured in a brilliant video where children denounced the harsh and cruel treatment they were subjected to by Cafcass and family courts because they wanted to see their dads. Aimee Nicholls is now an adult living with her elderly father Pete in Australia who campaigns very effectively down under for Shared Parenting. He and I met under the same bush near David Cameron's house in 2010 during Matt O'Connor's hunger strike. I dieted as well...for a day. Nobody noticed any difference in my appearance afterwards. So disappointing.

Glen Poole, author of 'Inside Man' and 'Equality for Men', is a quality commentator in various newspapers and is at the highbrow intellectual end of the equality debate. A comment of his that I love is 'Women have problems, men are the problem'. Glen initially started International Men's Day in his local park in Brighton and kept pushing until it is now happening in the main chamber of the House Of Commons. Glen did a brilliant presentation in UCL on the 5th January 2018 re the social determinants concerning suicide between Australia and the UK.

Nick Langford, author of the truly excellent book which I often refer to, 'An Exercise In Absolute Futility', also co-wrote another book called 'The Family Law A to Z' with his wife Ruth MacKay-Langford to help litigants negotiate the family courts (and she is not a daughter of Mr MacKay the Scottish prison warden in the hit TV series Porridge). Ruth is a former 'Paralegal of the Year' winner and knows this business very well.

A former Patron of Families Need Fathers, before his desire to get things done collided with some FNF trustee's general inability, is best-selling author Louis De Berneires (Captain Corelli's Mandolin). A robust character, who looks more like a shire farmer than a writer, he has campaigned for this misery so often unnecessarily inflicted upon children and fathers to be changed.

Richard Nixon of the Crawley branch of Families Need Fathers (no, not the very naughty American) has done extraordinary work on non-molestation applications via the family courts. He revealed the 'surprising' increase in 'without notice' non-molestation applications after legal aid was stopped, apart from cases where domestic violence featured. What a surprise. So, to obtain Legal Aid nowadays women are being forced to claim domestic violence. At the same time, the definition of domestic violence was heavily altered, and effectively unlimited. From my experience, virtually no father qualifies for legal aid this way: a great many mothers do.

Paul Apreda, boss of Welsh FNF, does an incredible amount of work towards shared parenting, repeatedly lobbying ministers and appears to work without ever sleeping. Dr Sue Whitcombe helps him with some excellent research on the negative effects parental alienation has on children. Her lectures on the subject are truly excellent.

In 2017 a Welsh grandmother Anne O'Regan, who is also a volunteer and Trustee of FNF Both Parents matter in Wales, forced the Equalities and Human Rights Commission in Wales to cease discriminating against male callers to a domestic violence helpline. Male callers were 'screened,' female callers were not. Anne is a former nurse. Looks as if she is still nursing, men! Apart from the staggering gender discrimination at the highest level in society, what does it say when a grannie accomplishes far more than most able-bodied men on an issue that affects them so badly?

A relatively recent convert, and a very effective one, is the son of a Nottingham coal miner who years ago was editor of 'Loaded', a lad's magazine that I can truthfully say I have never read. The onset of maturity and fatherhood has set Martin Daubney on a mission to help working class boys who are so discriminated against. Within a few years he has risen from relative obscurity in this business to being a very effective champion of working class boys and their increasing underachievement because of gender politics in education and opportunities in life. He will be busy!

Another hilarious character who looks like an elderly refugee from a pirate film is Swayne O'Pie. Despite appearances, to the best of my knowledge, he is the only man in the UK with a Masters in Gender Studies. He also wrote a large book titled, 'Why Britain Hates Men' which undoubtedly has the best cover photograph ever seen. He claims it is more of a manual than a book intended to be read cover to cover, as he told me after I had read it cover to cover. Ohhh, I so love hard work.

One of the most effective campaigners for reform and improvement in the UK family court system is the former solicitor Oliver Cyriax. Very effective campaigning by him forced the former department known as Court Welfare Office to be renamed Cafcass. He has always championed his version of a programme called 'Early Interventions' which if ever the UK decides to improve outcomes for children in UK family courts will have to be implemented. The repeat and biggest opposition he has always faced is the impregnable wall of vested interests which Early Interventions mainly bypasses in its working method.

A gentleman whom I know quite well and who has a degree in Psychology is Stuart Hontree. Stuart has written two books, the first one titled: Parental Alienation, Attachment and Corrupt Law, the second is titled, 101 Dirty Tricks of Secret Courts Private Family Law. Such information in the public domain is vital for knowledge gathering.

The internationally renowned men and boy's campaigner Dr Warren Farrell wrote a very comprehensive book titled the Boy Crisis. Heavy going but incredibly well referenced,

There have of course been many other men and women who have taken huge personal risks and sacrifice during demonstrations, campaigns, etc, attempting to get public attention focused on the failings within the family court process.

Quite often when attending talks and seminars led by some of the most active thinkers and intellectuals within this business I often feel like shaking them. So much navel-gazing and pained analysis linked to hugely complicated lengthy statements complaining about how bad the system is. I am not their natural bedfellow intellectually. I believe in getting things done. Talking and analysing is so often just that. After all this is a target rich environment. Sadly, modern education seems to remove the ability to think clearly from so many men. Guess I'm lucky, semi-ignorant and in my very early 60's. I obviously benefit from a simple country upbringing uncluttered by higher education or too often what appears as cultural indoctrination. I was even more convinced of that after attending 'Being A Man' (BAM Festival) at the Southbank arts centre London in November 2017. I was astonished by the supine acquiescence to the 'men are bad' I witnessed speak at the event. In my opinion these men are pursuing an evolutionary, emotionally and culturally cul de sac. Slaves on the wheel of endless appeasement and endless denigration of their fathers for not being 'emotionally' aware! Of what, I ask?

One thing that has always really annoyed me is the lack of fight by so many men in society who are so obviously being taken apart piece by piece as individuals and fathers. If a person with my background and education can obtain five Ombudsman investigations into the myriad failings of this sick sideshow of society, what are the others who are so effected doing? Apart from Shadow the phantom dog I allegedly kicked and killed, nothing else is unusual about my case. The processes I have exposed apply to all. Cafcass Section 7 reports, and I have seen hundreds, are far too often just an exercise in dad demonization. Usually in my experience, when the Cafcass Officer has nothing better to say they hide behind spoof research or utilise one of their highly gendered toolkits. As Nick Langford points out in his book, 'An exercise in absolute futility', research so often depended upon by Cafcass, 'Sturge and Glazer', has neither been debated nor adopted by the authors' ruling body, the Royal College of Psychiatry. It is, in effect, a personal belief. Yet, so many judges in the UK family court accept recommendations from Cafcass Officers using this research. What good is this for children?

My five Ombudsman Investigations, and especially the two PHSO into Cafcass, could be obtained by most fathers in their cases if they only stood their ground and fought. The pantomime Local Children Safeguarding Board in Brent and elsewhere are what passes for child protection agencies throughout the country. It is an absurd joke and a poor reflection on society that a semi-ignoramus such as myself has managed to get so far. Which I suppose means I can include myself in this chapter as a notable person fighting to improve outcomes for children and fathers.

Unfortunately, like cancer, society in the main wants to hide away from the reality which of course leaves the door wide open for the professional and ideological beneficiaries of the system. For example, Covid has been ruthlessly exploited by the anti-shared parenting lobby. And children lose.

'Nobody made a greater mistake than he who did nothing because he could do only a little.'
Edmund Burke.

Chapter 22

Academics and Notables who question and dissect false statements/publications and seek to establish accuracy

Unlike my attempts to correct and expose false and child endangering misandric work throughout the system, for real intelligence one needs to read the work of William Collins. This man has the capacity to take apart false evidence and propaganda better than anyone I know. The sad thing is this should be done by the myriad legal eagles and politicians who have such generous funding for research purposes.

Polly Neate, former CEO of Women's Aid, effectively wrote UK Government Policy and many of the recent changes within private family law are at the behest of, among others, Women's Aid, who totally oppose shared parenting by using the statement 'where safe to do so' against fathers. If they don't oppose shared parenting why don't they use the same phrase 'where safe to do so' against mothers? The anti-shared parenting apostles mercilessly abuse that desire within humans, especially men, to protect women and children and have huge influence because so many journalists and commentators perpetuate the *'male monster, female victim'* narrative. For them, demonising fathers and their desire to damage and destroy the nuclear family, and especially the child-father relationship, is central to their existence.

Gender Equity Network

John Barry, Belinda Brown and Geoff Dench set up the *Gender Equity Network* which has now become the Male Psychology Network with excellent lectures, seminars and conferences given at University College London.

For a simpleton such as myself it is a privilege to be invited to attend these lectures. I have listened to and learned from: Karen Woodall of the Family Separation Clinic; Martin Seager, Consultant Clinical Psychologist and Adult Psychotherapist; Dr Warren Farrell; Dr Richard Bradford; Professor Gigsbert Stoet; Dr John Barry, Chartered Psychologist and Honourary Research Associate UCL; Dr Ben Hine of West London University, Dr Sue Whitcombe, parental alienation expert; Belinda Brown, Honourary Research Fellow UCL; Paul Apreda, Welsh FNF supremo; Glen Poole and Mark Brooks of Mankind Initiative. I have also met many men and women with an interest in genuine equality of the sexes rather than the current dominant toxic narrative.

Dr Warren Farrell is an American educator, activist and author of seven books on men's and women's issues. He is often considered "the father of the men's movement" but he started out as a vocal feminist. During a lecture at UCL he gave us an example of the damage decades of anti-father discrimination has done in one part of the western world. Over the past forty years the very wealthy state of California has built thirteen maximum security prisons for men. During that time, it has built one new university. Says it all really.

I also had the pleasure and privilege of attending an excellent film at UCL Gender Equity Network called 'The Men's Group'. It was put together on a tiny budget by film director, actor, and film maker, etc, Joseph Culp. This brilliantly acted film, and done to great comic effect, explores issues around modern men's dilemmas and coping mechanisms. Joseph Culp was present himself and as usual a very enjoyable talk plus question and answer session followed.

Another film, and one I cannot praise enough, shown by UCL Gender Equity Network is 'The Red Pill', to a packed auditorium. It is a truly remarkable ground-breaking film which has been much criticised by gender vigilantes masquerading as feminists who, for example, tried to block Cassie Jaye, the maker of the film, from entering Australia. Cassie Jaye is a former feminist who has made films on women's issues.

I had also been present when the very first viewing of The Red Pill in the UK was shown at a private event in Bath courtesy of the remarkable Richard Elliott. Some people seriously walk the walk and Richard is one.

Another father who is determined to forensically dissect the systemic failings within the UK family court system is Stuart Hontree. On 22/2/18 I had the privilege along with others of being present at a UCL event where he quite brilliantly demonstrated the damage parental alienation and loss of emotional attachment at an early stage in a child's life. Hopefully the video will be made available for all to view and learn. Stuart is also the author of the book, Parental Alienation, Attachment and Corrupt Law, also 101 Dirty Tricks of the Family Courts.

For a short while Bob Geldof really rattled the cage containing UK family law court personnel and their plethora of faux professionals as he called them, who do so much harm to children. One particularly telling comment he made was that upon entering the family court building a friendly male working in the building advised him to; *not tell the court he loved his children.* This is the new love that dare not speak its name in modern Britain, a father's love for his children.

For foot soldiers, and sergeant majors such as myself, it is so refreshing to listen to and afterwards to chat to those of real intellect and ability who are taking an interest in this business. In my FNF capacity when dealing with an endless procession of disbelieving terrified newcomers, and knowing only too well how rigged the system is against fathers and children, it is gratifying to know that others of serious ability are working on this most contentious of issues. Attending these lectures and events opens the eyes. This is where the real battle for improvement will be fought. You need big guns to deal with big guns. I'm looking for a cannon.

People often say to me, why do I bother? There is huge vested interest, the system will never change, ordinary people have no chance against all these lawyers, vested interests, etc. My response, if I bother, is very short. "Should either of my two sons have this disaster befall them in years to come, they can never say to me, "Dad, this happened to you. Why didn't you do something about it?" Another reply I sometimes give is, "you can be happy with you and your sons being second class citizens. I'm not".

As examples of inspiration for me, probably the best ones are: Dan Carder, who exposed Volkswagen's cheating of emissions test results in the United States; Anne Williams, now passed away, who was so inspirational and effective regarding the Hillsborough tragedy and official cover up; Andrew Jennings, the awkward old reporter who exposed International Olympic Committee and FIFA corruption; and too many others to mention here.

Dan Carder, for example, hunts wild bear with a crossbow barefoot in his spare time. His official job is running a small vehicle testing laboratory in West Virginia with two other part timers on a miniscule budget. He appears to work on 'hunches'. He ignored the official test results re Volkswagen and used his own. He discovered that Volkswagen had installed software in their vehicles which enabled them to cheat the tests. Long before Volkswagen he had caught large US truck manufacturers cheating their emissions tests.

In late 2019 I attended a presentation by Jan James, CEO of Good Egg Safety at an FNF conference. Good Egg Safety is heavily involved with children's safety in car seats, etc. Jan has taken on the job of campaigning against Parental Alienation as she sees the damage it does to children. I can assure you, this woman and her team will be effective in this arena.

So, what are you doing?

Chapter 23

Litigants in Person within Family Court

Reading the preceding chapter and various others may have had a discouraging impact upon Litigants in Person or fathers who wish to remain in their children's lives. It is from my perspective quite simple. You can approach this business with a delusion of equality of opportunity or form an understanding of the system you are up against and why it behaves this way. Your choice on how you fight for your children.

I have seen so many worthwhile quality fathers fight ineffectively against NMO's esp ex parte. Have you read the rest of this book! You are not even as advantaged as a one-legged man in an arse kicking contest. The odds against you are worse, so chose your battles. The Judiciary work hand in glove with the DV agencies to boot the fathers from their home on the pretext of protecting the mother. Then they decide how much if any contact the father should have after the dad removal. Even a 3 year old child knows you have to pick your battles. Don't be falling into the traps the mother and the system lays out for you. Pick the battle, which is ongoing relationship with your children. Of course, you are perfectly free to ignore my advice. Too many who have later suffered mental breakdowns, bankruptcy, suicides, homelessness, sacked, business going bust, double mortgaging, parents pension payments, self-destruction driven by what???? Ego, revenge, or delusions of equality!

Assuming you are still with me, you have decided not to be the toddler, here is what you need to do.

If you have been arrested by the police at the mother's request on a trumped up accusation or received a non-molestation application howsoever obtained, you are completely wasting your time by fighting the NMO itself. Of course, solicitors and barristers will advise you should fight it. Damn right they will, money for old rope. They have devised this minefield and you are now in it. The non-molestation order should have a return date to court. I have seen some that didn't, fortunately LJ Mostyn put a stop to that illegal nonsense. Prepare yourself mentally and logistically for the most horrible experience of your life. Get accommodation sorted for yourself, friends and/or family the usual refuge here. Then prepare yourself as good as you can for the hearing. If unrepresented by barrister or solicitor and even if you are, you will have to learn how to conduct and give instruction for your case. When attending the return hearing for the NMO request that the matter be brought into children proceedings. The longer you fight the NMO without being in children proceedings the more you handicap yourself. And make a C100 application for a Child Arrangements Order if the mother has not already done so.

Phone the Fnf helpline 0300 0300 363 (7am to midnight 7 days a week) attend every Fnf meeting you can and avoid the angry men's rights websites. Many of them helped in their own misfortune. Unless you have £25,000 plus to spare forget about legal representation if mummy has played dirty. And forget about you getting legal aid, the system is designed to boot you not help you. Prepare a Position Statement for your first hearing, I have written bloody hundreds. The format is simple: (when you know how).

A sample:

In the Somewhere Unpleasant Court; Case No: 1234567

Date of Hearing:

Matter of: Child's/children's name/s and D.O.B.

Applicant Father:

Homer Simpson

And

Respondent Mother:

Saint Marge Simpson

Position Statement of Applicant Father Homer Simpson

The first/second paragraph should give the court an effective but brief outline of when/where you two met, nationality race etc, how/where you lived/together/separate/ married work/ careers/children's schooling if applicable- the court knows nothing about you remember-you will not have time or the ability in court to get this across verbally in court without handicapping yourself because of the emotion involved.

The third paragraph should deal with the problems, usually the mother has made (being advised) various allegations about you-usually a few outright lies and many exaggerations with a few honest truths. Above all appear calm and sensible, do NOT NOT NOT attack or denigrate the mother as that is a huge help to her, focus on being calm and child centred despite the huge pressure. Refute the biggest allegations WITHOUT getting bogged down in the detail.

The fourth paragraph may add to matters within the third one. Who looked after the children, collections to and from school. Bring proposal as to how YOU may be involved in this. Bring solutions if at all possible!

By the fifth paragraph you should be requesting the orders you want the court to make regarding you and the children. If there are too many allegations against you (quite common) seek interim contact with your children at all times. Emphasise you only wish to love and co-parent the children and are ABSOLUTELY not a threat either to the mother or the children. Finish the statement with:

I make this statement believing the contents to be true to the best of my ability.

Signed: Date:

It is crucial to NOT have a position statement longer than two pages and not closely typed either. For reasons unknown the judges and magistrates don't seem to like those that are. And make certain you attend court well in advance, sign in with the clerk, hand a copy of your signed and dated position statement to the clerk and also one to the other side WITHOUT GETTING INTO AN ARGUMENT. When you are called into court ask if your position statement is in the courts possession when the judge or magistrate address you. So many LIP position statements seem to get lost??

A comparison I often give to newcomers in this business is the example of the American TV Comedy show The Simpsons. The mother and the system will portray the mother as being like Marge Simpson, fragrant beautiful and a saint who has for too long tolerated an idiot and violent husband. Social services and Cafcass are like Marge's twin sisters. The family court agencies and the mother will probably try to convince the court that you are Homer Simpson, a heavy drinking, violent child strangling lunatic. You will either harm the children or their mother, or possibly worse and kill them (according to Women's Aid), should the court allow you unsupervised access to your own children or, worse still, overnight stays at your home or holidays?

They will probably insist that the children will turn out like Bart Simpson if you have any access or exercise any decision making regarding the children. The mother plus the twin sisters/services will insist that Lisa the beautiful angelic little girl, Bart's sister, is what the children already are and will continue to be if the mother keeps you away from them. The judge is a simple one, Montgomery Burns, and his hapless clerk, Smithers. Actually, most court clerks are fine in my experience.

Who do you as the dad who is seeking to continue the relationship with your children have to be? Quite simply, Ned Flanders. A goody-goody two shoes, who would seek counselling if he harmed a fly. Sad to say the average man in family court is expected to be too much like our good Christian friend Ned, a cartoon do-gooder.

My first experience of this was on 6th July 2007. Despite many years of motorbike racing, including road racing in Ireland, this was a whole new experience in fear. Six weeks earlier I had been booted from the family home via Brent's M.A.R.A.C process and kangaroo case conference, co-ordinated by Brent's Social Services. At a hearing, ex-parte (without notice to me), my wife and her legal team using the notes from the above process obtained several orders against me. Now we had a hearing listed for 30 minutes!

It was a good first experience of the Central London Family Court in Holborn. The District Judge was very angry at the back-door justice I had been subjected to, giving me some much-needed confidence in the judiciary. The next half dozen hearings were all progressive despite Cafcass (Guardian Ad Litem) determination to force me onto their wonderful domestic violence programme costing then £2,850 for an eight-month assessment. Of course, at the end of the assessment I would be portrayed as a serious perpetrator of domestic violence. North Korean style mind adjust.

The reason I write the above is to give hope to Litigants in Person who find themselves in the family court, usually to their total surprise after being kicked out of the family home and served with numerous orders and injunctions usually obtained ex-parte (without notice to the other side). Much as I detest the bias within the system I have some respect for the judges. Yes, they are part and parcel of the anti-father, kick him out of the family home and keep him out crew, but you are infinitely better off normally in front of a judge than the local gender vigilante services co-ordinated by the Local Authority and Social Services. But bear in mind that the shock and trauma especially at the early stages will reduce your intellectual capacity by at least 50%. Emotion overrides logic and learning to control this is vital.

Every parent in this business has four choices:

1. Hire a Solicitor and Barrister.

Better known as being represented. Most London solicitors charge around a starting fee of £250ph plus VAT. Same for the barristers. You will need a minimum of £10,000 for a few directions hearings. Plus, if you are married and there are Ancillary (financial) proceedings these easily double the costs. The family assets will easily be depleted by £30,000 as a starting figure. The highest I know of is £6.5 million in costs in the notorious Whyte case, later reduced to £5.0 million on appeal.

2. Hire a good McKenzie Friend (Lay Advisor in Family Court).

A McKenzie Friend can assist you in the preparation for the court and case bundle where applicable; advise when dealing with solicitor's letters, Social Services, Cafcass, domestic violence agencies, etc, from the other side; and provide vital assistance at the hearing and especially with the horse trading that sometimes goes on outside the court chamber.

The price of commercial McKenzies that I know of vary from £20ph to £80ph. Some are qualified paralegals and a few are qualified barristers. Families Need Fathers has a list of commercial McKenzies advertised on its website. Obviously, the charity cannot take responsibility for them but it does remove those who have been found useless. I know many of them personally, have used five of them in my own case over eight years, all of whom I would happily work with again if necessary. Most of the remaining McKenzies on the list also have my appreciation. A few I don't know, so I cannot comment. I was on Fnf McK list for years until 2019, my wish to remain half sane prevailed and I stopped McKenzieing. But do attend the meetings I chair if your love for me cannot be otherwise satisfied.

Some ex-solicitors and barristers also work as commercial McKenzies. Also, some former social workers and even some former Cafcass guardians (higher level social worker) are McKenzies. I have worked with several former social workers and a few ex Cafcass officers, now McKenzies, and I have always found them excellent. The latter specialise in children's cases, as I do, not financial proceedings.

3. Learn how to conduct your own case.

This is extremely difficult and quite often a shortcut to failure. Plus, once you have lost, it is almost impossible to recover. That said, Families Need Fathers, Fathers for Justice and Dadshouse give invaluable assistance. The central London Branch of Families Need Fathers meets every Monday apart from Bank Holidays. There is a list of all branch meetings nationwide on the very good FNF website (fnf.org.uk). There are many children who would have lost all contact with their fathers but for that charity.

Whether you are exercising 1, 2 or 3 above I urge you to utilise the information I now give.

I come to the greatest single source of support there is for Litigants in Person and McKenzie Friends, and much used by magistrates, barristers, solicitors, and social workers who find it both quicker and easier to access than the government's own information websites. The excellent Custody Minefield website (thecustodyminefield.com) is a free tool of priceless quality. Its author is Michael Robinson. His Family Law guides for separating and divorcing parents cover all major topics, including child arrangements and contact.

Sometimes in life circumstances create or force unique situations, which is normally where unique people come in. Michael Robinson, author of The Custody Minefield, is one such man. He is larger than life: a perfect portrayal of a pub landlord or a successful pirate, especially when wearing a bandana and regaling all around the campfire as the excellent rapscallion he is. A bald, heavily bearded round bellied man, who undoubtedly if he had chosen could have had a successful career as a stand-up comedian. From personal experience, he determined that people who find themselves in the horror of the family court process, as it so often is horrible though not always, would have quality up to date information available for free at their fingertips. All this despite the man suffering with a severe debilitating illness. He lives in remotest Cumbria, where the local air ambulance for sick sheep is a farmer's wheelbarrow. Who says there's no technology in the countryside?

And the best book I have found on the subject is Lucy Reed's, 'Family Courts Without a Lawyer: A Handbook for Litigants in Person'. Lucy Reed is a very experienced Family Law barrister who several years ago became aware how disadvantaged Litigants in Person (LIP) were in the family courts because of not just their complete lack of knowledge but even worse the dearth of information available to them. Some years ago, her and I were meant to produce training videos for FNF members and the wider public who would be going through the family court process. FNF was providing all the funding, a video production company was organised, Lucy Reed and myself had provisionally sorted out the modular formatting of the videos, and personally I saw this as extremely beneficial to FNF members. I was doing the work for free and I believe so was Lucy Reed, to her great credit.

But, as usual, the enemy within sabotaged excellent work. One in particular notorious idiot caused Lucy Reed such problems that she briefly gave up altogether. Congratulations clown, you know who you are.

I have read her handbook (Family Courts without a Lawyer) and unhesitatingly recommend it to anyone going through the family courts, especially if starting. For experienced McKenzies it may be considered lacking in depth but by then you should know the system very well.

4. Give up.

This is hardly a surprise and a very common reaction. How on earth can the average working-class father who finds himself homeless and quite often penniless possibly have a chance against the might of the state and a malevolent mother determined to destroy his relationship with his children. This also happens occasionally to mothers in private family law but the state far too often treats mothers appallingly in what is called public family law i.e. care proceedings, adoption or foster care. For example, read Dame Justice Pauffley's exposure of the 'cut-and-paste' adoption process.

The problem with giving up is that quite often the father, haunted by failure, will phone me and other organisations in bits or appear months or years later at FNF meetings, hoping against hope that they can get back into their children's lives. Pain, and brutal pain, is a given in this business. This applies to the children even more so.

I always say people should fight as good as they can to remain in their children's lives for three reasons. One, it is easier to live with failure knowing you have legitimately tried your best. Two, living with failure knowing you gave up too easily takes a drastic toll on a parent. Three, children hate feeling abandoned by a parent, they may reject that parent but still love him. They just have to suppress it because of huge pressure. I believe this is a major cause of male homelessness and suicide.

The four options I've outlined are the choices I and other FNF officers have been using for years at FNF meetings to newcomers. For those who have already been blooded in family proceedings the advice is tailored to their individual circumstances. I know of many within FNF who have far better knowledge of what goes on within family proceedings than many highly educated and seriously well-paid lawyers, mostly at public expense.

If you opt to go down the route of being Litigant in Person and wish to do so with the help of a McKenzie Friend, you are still described as a Litigant In Person. Very occasionally the McKenzie Friend will get Rights of Audience, meaning they can talk in court, but usually this only applies to those Litigants with very poor English or those who are obviously unable to represent themselves in proceedings in any form of a meaningful manner. There is much inconsistency within the courts here.

Focus and discipline are unquestionably the most important qualities you need. You are almost undoubtedly having the worst time of your life, the woman (or man) you may still possibly love has become an unbelievable monster, your children who you love far more than life itself are showing signs of hostility towards meeting you, and family and friends are in disbelief and sometimes unwilling to share your pain.

In such circumstances, you have to empty your mind. Think of the ancient Spartan warrior code, if you die then at least die fighting. But fighting for parental involvement with your children involves much more that shouting about the horrible injustice you and they are subject to.

Please don't do what one emotional father did when he met the Cafcass officer who moonlighted as a violent fiction writer in his report. This father decided to literally shake the truth out of the (male) Cafcass officer when he met him outside a contact centre. A criminal conviction is guaranteed in this situation.

Marshall your defences. Get independent witness statements if there are false allegations against you where these can help. DON'T get friends or family members to give you character references, that will only annoy the judge. And above all DO NOT procure witness statements which are purely a character assassination of the mother. That is the shortcut to failure.

Get professional assistance whether from FNF, which I heavily recommend, or any other charity or organisation which is dedicated to shared parenting. AVOID the angry men's groups in all forms. They have huge exposure on the internet and some, though not all, are architects of their own failing. Empty buckets make a lot of noise.

It is very important that you learn to compartmentalise your feelings. DON'T fall out with family or friends. DON'T lose your job, which is easier said than done. A friendless dad who is unemployed is not much use to his children or himself. If in doubt stop and have a chat with Big Issue sellers or homeless men: there is a huge choice to pick from these days. Many I have chatted to have, after a while, admitted they suffered from the above system. Try to avoid joining them full time.

Above all, learn how to control your emotions and then learn how to fight. I mean really fight, not self-indulgent tantrums or shouting at social workers, Cafcass or court staff. Ironically, though I certainly don't advise it, probably the safest place to be over emotional is in court. Judges are broadly humane people and at times I have been impressed by how they have tolerated genuine emotional outbursts. But do not be so stupid as to use it as a tactic, judges have years of experience and can spot the difference between tactics being used and genuine emotions a mile off. The same person is not just determining your future, he or she is also determining the future of your children.

I most strongly urge you to bring solutions to the court: mummy and her team will, I assure you, usually bring the problems. If you are a mother who is an unrepresented Litigant in Person and the non-primary parent the same advice applies. Focus purely on a solution for the child.

Your duty is to seek a child centred solution which is the best in the circumstances, not just what you want or feel you should have. In this business by far your best bet is to bring solutions and in that way let the court see you are the sensible parent and the children would benefit from a continuing relationship with you.

Remember and, most importantly, remember twice, contrary to popular misconception you have no right to a relationship with your children. That right is with the children, your duty is to enable their right to be fulfilled. In the event that you are a father and you still have delusions as to your parental rights let me educate you.

'The rule of law that a father is the natural guardian of his legitimate child is abolished.' (Section 2, subsection 4, Children Act 1989)

Some fathers phone me or attend FNF meetings wanting to seek primary residence of the children. Some of these dads are well educated and have a deep belief in the English judicial system. Officially of course you have equality before the law, which in itself is one of the greatest jokes going. So, to remove confusion, let me make it crystal clear where a father stands regarding residence or seeking primary care of his children.

Bar a very, very, few exceptions, unless the system i.e. social services and or police have taken the child off the mother or are looking at care proceedings, you have no chance of getting residence. In the UK family courts *'mothers care and men provide'* is the overwhelming motto. The professionals within the system will usually exercise many negative tactics to do all they can to facilitate and promote false allegations against you if you seek residence initially. You are infinitely better off seeking what we call the default position i.e. every second weekend and half of the holidays plus, if circumstances allow, an evening or in some cases a night preceding the weekend when the children are with the resident mother.

However, I have known of cases, and been a McKenzie in some, where the mother was so implacably opposed to contact and her extremism was very noticeably having a negative influence upon the child that a transfer of residence took place. The scene here is a mum with uncontrollable lunacy and a father of unimpeachable behaviour and quality professionals. A very rare combination.

Ironically, despite common belief, mothers do not have natural guardianship. They have automatic Parental Responsibility upon giving birth, which I agree with. Parental Responsibility is different to guardianship. In reality, the state has guardianship powers and delegates which parent should be the child's carer when disputes occur. In this arena, back door social engineering dominates. For most fathers who are LIPs all this talk about guardianship and parental responsibility is incomprehensible, they just love their children and want to stay involved in their children's lives.

Most fathers, and a few mothers, find out the very hard way how Family Courts operate in private law. For many it is the sudden arrival of a brown envelope at home or at work containing a plethora of court orders obtained ex-parte (without notice).

Usually the mother has been in contact with the local gender vigilante agencies and domestic violence charities, and their twin, Social Services. Quite often after such guidance she sets a scene, calls the police and the father is arrested. Duluth model and derivatives are doing their job here. Quite often the father has called the police but then he is amazed when he is the one who gets arrested because of the policy called 'powers of positive arrest', the favourite excuse when the police exercise gender bias. He is usually forced from the family home and will be arrested under the Family Law Act if he attempts to have any contact with the mother or the children, or asks anyone else to do so, if she obtains a non-molestation injunction, occupation order, etc, usually ex-parte. The father having been arrested is very handy for this purpose as this greatly assists the mother obtaining Legal Aid. Many solicitors, whilst harvesting the Legal Aid crop, will assist pro-bono at the ex-parte hearing and then reap the financial rewards in lengthy proceedings.

Many a father has attempted to get a family member to negotiate or has texted/phoned the mother trying to seek a solution and found himself being arrested and prosecuted for breaking an injunction. Suspended prison time and community service is quite often the outcome here.

After recovering from the initial savage shock, the best that a father can do is seek help from FNF, especially if he cannot afford a solicitor. Forget everything you understand about justice, innocent until proven guilty, human rights under the law and all that nonsense. As for guilt, that is determined by gender, and you, if a dad, are the guilty focus. You are now in the clutches of the UK family court system and that is akin to Alice in Wonderland on a bad day. Hopefully you will have a return date in court, though this is not always the case. Some ex-parte non-molestation orders had limitless time unless the father could make an application himself and challenge it.

Faced with such judicial force, with only one side having been heard, many fathers give up immediately and some have committed suicide. You may have to make an application to the family court yourself upon receipt of an injunction without a return date hearing listed. This normally takes 2 months for a first hearing which will be listed as a FHDRA (First Hearing Dispute Resolution Appointment). My personal nickname for FHDRA is HYDRA, the mythical many headed serpent from Greek mythology. And much more apt in too many circumstances.

At this first hearing if you are an LIP, but hopefully have a McKenzie Friend with you, I cannot stress enough the importance of keeping a cool head and not be ambushed by the counsel for the other side. They earn a living from destroying people outside and inside court and have all the advantages. The system most sadly and wrongly is based on the adversarial. An utter joke in the circumstances when you have an adversarial system and one side, because of gender, usually has such advantage. As a Cafcass lawyer once said to me, 'A litigant in person against a state funded lawyer is the equivalent of a spectator at a concert being asked to compete against the orchestra'. So compete well!

Above all, DO NOT discuss your case alone with the lawyer for the other side before you enter the courtroom unless you have a good McKenzie Friend. Notice I said courtroom, not court building. The number of fathers who get shafted by stupidly giving their case to the other side before the hearing is something that always sickens me. I observe it regularly when I'm attending court in the hallways and waiting areas. Self-handicap is a gift for the opposition and they already have enough advantage. This system is brutally adversarial.

If there are any allegations against you and quite often these may be only handed to you just before you enter the courtroom, **keep very calm**. This late handing over of surprise 'allegations' is standard malpractice and deliberately designed to make you lose your cool. Deal in a practical manner with these allegations, notwithstanding the huge emotional pressure you are suffering from. Have confidence in your desire and ability to explain to the court that you love your children, want to have a proper parenting involvement in their upbringing and that the allegations which are usually lurid and sickening are either entirely false or grossly exaggerated. Above all, seek to get interim court ordered contact, time lost nearly always leads to consolidation of parental alienation. This may mean a contact centre and too often the other side, if represented, will be tasked with organising this. Too often they will throw up so many obstacles the contact will either not happen or be so expensive and deliberately designed to cause you maximum disruption with your work, etc, it will be exceedingly difficult.

As a rule of thumb, where there are lurid or many false allegations and gross exaggeration these are the cases where Parental Alienation takes place. Far too often fathers acting alone, because they cannot afford legal representation, will, when there are lurid false allegations against them, take part in a contested Finding of Fact hearing where the mother has state funded lawyers and support services. This often ends in disaster for the father and the children, the element of institutionalised gender discrimination in particular makes a mockery of any concept of justice. Lambs to the lions.

But some fathers, myself included, have done the best we could with a contact centre and a good McKenzie Friend, and been quite successful at a Finding of Fact hearing. In fact, despite many misgivings, I found the contact centre very professional and well run, plus they gave me a glowing report. I know of several instances where a professional contact centre with well written notes have been the difference between fathers losing all contact with their children and having meaningful involvement.

Unfortunately, sometimes there are rogue contact centres. There used to be one of these beside me in Brent. But Brent is Brent. Sometimes I hear of cases where fathers, and the occasional mother, have spent years in a contact centre. Four years is the longest I know of. Utter and complete child cruelty when this occurs.

Here is the wording from the Children Act 1989, Section 1: Welfare of the child.

(1) When a court determines any question with respect to—

    (a) The upbringing of a child; or

    (b) The administration of a child's property or the application of any income arising from it, the child's welfare shall be the court's paramount consideration.

(2) In any proceedings in which any question with respect to the upbringing of a child arises, the court shall have regard to the general principle that any delay in determining the question is likely to prejudice the welfare of the child.

Will someone please tell me how years of contact centres without the father being found guilty in any court is obeying or complying with the welfare of the child being the paramount consideration?

Quite often there will be a Section 47 investigation by social services as many mothers seeking to avail themselves of free legal aid will up the ante as advised by local agencies and to reduce your chances in court. Section 47s do not require a court order.

There will definitely be a Safeguarding Report from Cafcass. This is mandatory whenever an application concerning children is made to the family court. When the fathers read this Safeguarding Report that is usually when the fathers go into shock when they discover what the mothers have accused them of.

Often there will also be a Section 7 report ordered by the court where the court feels the situation warrants it at the early hearings. This has to be done by a social worker which may be from the local authority or Cafcass. This report is meant to be the eyes and ears of the court by looking into the circumstances of the family.

Section 7 reports normally take 10-16 weeks. Often in these reports social workers and Cafcass consolidate false allegations against the father. Usually by page 3 or 4 the mother has 'disclosed' whereas on page 2 she 'alleged'. This is a perfect example of consolidation of the mother's allegations. What started off as just her word, an 'allegation', has suddenly become a revealing of what 'really' happened: - a 'disclosure'.

'Allegations' are suddenly evidence and the report's conclusions all too often accept mother's allegations as fact and make recommendations accordingly. This alone destroys many fathers as it consolidates their view that the entire system is heavily rigged against them and their children.

If the case gets messy then there may be a Guardian Ad Litem, a court appointed Guardian for the children. The really messy cases may also have what is known as a Part 25 Application. This requires an outside expert, usually a psychologist or psychiatrist, to investigate one or more of the parties according to a court instruction. This report must be made available by a certain date to all parties and also for the author to be cross examined in open court by the parties. A Part 25 normally costs close to £5,000 and is usually payable by all parties. If a Part 25 is ordered, there will usually be a Guardian already appointed for the children, almost always from Cafcass. This Guardian appointment also means that the children are now party to the proceedings with their own solicitor and barrister, though increasingly represented by what is known as a solicitor advocate. Nowadays with fewer parties represented this can sometimes mean the only represented parties in proceedings are the children.

There are often 'uncontested' hearings (FHDRAs and DRAs) where the judge gives 'directions' as to how the case will proceed. This can develop to a 'contested' hearing which involves hearing evidence from the parties under cross examination. These 'contested' hearings can sometimes be a Finding of Fact (FOF) if the court believes the allegations of domestic abuse are serious enough. Final hearings are sometimes added onto FOF and sometimes final hearings and FOF hearings can last for days. The longest I know of is eight days. A final hearing may be listed for a half, full or several days. If the court feels the party's positions are not that far apart then it may involve a lot of horse trading in various corridors or waiting rooms with an occasional usually brief return to the judge or sometimes magistrates for what is known as Guidance.

This is often when the Family Courts are at their best. The court clerk or usher checks with the parties at the court's request and the court and the lawyers move towards solutions rather than the usual extension of problems. When the court decides it wants a solution it can put great pressure on the obstinate party to become sensible.

The other time I feel the family courts sometimes work well, is when usually the mother makes myriad accusations against the father and denies the child all contact, often for months. I have seen an experienced judge at the first hearing take a mother's counsel apart, and the parties walk out with the default position, every second weekend and half the school holidays, with possibly another evening during the week. It saddens me that despite over 350 hearings as a McKenzie Friend the above, in my experience, has only happened twice. Out of all those hearings I have only met a handful of barristers or solicitors who sought solutions. The vast majority seek to delay and add immeasurably to the problem. This leads to more hearings and therefore income. The more professionals involved in a case the slower it will be, with associated damage to the children. Which is why I always emphasise to fathers - bring solutions to the court!

Both as an LIP and primarily as a McKenzie I have participated in variations on all of the above. Many fathers get blown out at the early stages. The mothers usually hyped up or false allegations and excess facilitation of them by all or many of the agencies involved break a great many fathers. However, if he can stay the course and conduct his case the wheel quite often slowly begins to turn. Sometimes when the mother realises the wheel is turning she will suddenly see sense and solutions can come quite quickly. Sadly, too many are just too nuts to see sense and they are the implacable hostile ones. So much depends on the father being a remarkably steadfast parent.

Sometimes after many years of intense litigation a transfer of residence from one parent to the other is ordered. Then much remedial work is needed to take the child away from the toxic environment it was subject to for so long. The problem is too often not immediately solved by transfer of residence because the child is too damaged. This is where interim foster care can take place.

Most distressingly, however, is the simple sad fact that far too often an implacably hostile mother will succeed in not just breaking the relationship between the child and other parent, the child will begin to make false allegations after months and years of intense emotional abuse. They are the truly messy cases and far too often judicial inertia and a flaccid approach by the professionals involved give the green light to these alienating mothers. For that, the courts and pseudo professionals involved have my utter condemnation.

Quite simply, the facts don't lie. In the UK family courts whether you call it custody, residence or primary care in 95% of cases the mother becomes the resident parent irrespective of the previous parenting arrangement.

The figure is undoubtedly higher outside of the family court. The mother's willingness to abuse the father and terrorise him into vacating the family home, knowing she holds nearly all the cards if police and local agencies are brought in, is central to so many outcomes.

However, what contempt I have for mothers who so aggressively alienate children from their fathers is matched by the deep loathing I have for the very few dads who alienate the children from their mother without serious safeguarding reasons.

Many people who find themselves thrust into this business will not have the money for a solicitor. However, if you do have the money, or can borrow it, try and make sure he or she specialises in children's proceedings and avoid the 'we do everything' high street solicitors as they usually are not good enough if the situation gets messy.

If choosing a McKenzie Friend a few simple guidelines:

DO:

1. Telephone several and trust your instincts.
2. Establish costs, method of working, payment.
3. Try above all, despite the emotion, to answer to the best of your ability any questions asked.
4. Be absolutely honest with your MF as the other side will gleefully make hay in court and your MF will be caught unprepared.
5. Establish and stick to a working pattern. No wild diversions or escapades as they ALWAYS bite back far harder.
6. When in Court have a good position statement or skeleton argument plus a crib sheet of do's and don'ts, PRINTED if possible, not just a scribble on a page.

DON'T

1. Work with them if they are obsessed with their own case.
2. If they just want to use you as a proxy for revenge against the system.
3. Go to those who assure you they won every case. That is utter bullshit.
4. Pay large down payments in advance.
5. Be choosy about the gender of the McKenzie.
6. **DON'T PISS OFF THE JUDGE or Magistrates!**

Chapter 24

McKenzie Friend for LIP
within Family Court

I have had over 350 appearances as a McKenzie Friend within the Family Courts. The advice I give is not aimed at experienced McKenzies who should already know. It is for the benefit of Litigants in Person and inexperienced McKenzies. So, a few simple do's and don'ts for new McKenzie's:

Do.

1. Avoid the few angry men who just want to get back at the mother by using you because you are much cheaper than lawyers.
2. Avoid the very few smartasses who drip feed information to you and who you catch out lying. If they lie to you, what chance in court?
3. Many parents will be emotional and desperate. Try to get them focused as easily and effectively as possible.
4. Purely focus on each case, leave your own completely out of it. That is history.
5. Think of what the court wants in the circumstance. Work towards that.
6. Always be polite to court staff, magistrates and judges. They talk among each other and you need to be perceived as a solution, not another headache.
7. Above all protect the LIP when meeting lawyers, Cafcass, etc, before the hearing. This is central to your duty.

8. Establish a practical working relationship. Keep good notes especially of court orders and dates/times, as this is where a McKenzie truly earns their keep. Sometimes the order agreed in court and the order drafted by counsel for the other side have surprising variations. Check this carefully. Protect the LIP at all times.
9. If asked by the court to help e.g. meditate between the parties, suspend your duty as a McKenzie Friend to the LIP and FOCUS on the best outcome in the circumstance for the children. It is crucial that the mother feels she can trust your impartiality.
10. If granted rights of audience either formally or informally (much more common) exercise it professionally. It's imperative the court views you as being helpful to the court.

Don't;

1. Use the LIP to pursue your own agenda.
2. Let you or him be bullied by the other side playing games outside the courtroom.
3. Lose your cool no matter what the provocation.
4. Get confused between being a McKenzie Friend and his sudden new best friend.
5. Be a headache for the court, but at the same time be steadfast and effective at protecting against sloppy magistrates or lazy judges who let the counsel for the other side rule the roost.
6. Ever work with anyone whom you don't trust, especially if you have reservations regarding children's safety.

As a McKenzie Friend, every case you become involved with has variations and will be a learning curve. A major part of that learning is not just educating and improving the Litigant. You as the McKenzie have to learn how he is developing, his strong points and his weak ones. An experienced Litigant with good ability usually only happens when their case is finished. Some nervous, terrified litigants could not be managed or watched closely enough, the sheer savage pressure crushes many. Others become blooded and develop very well, the good ones are very easy to work with. It is too often the sheer force of personality of a good McKenzie which involves a LOT of hard work that will determine the outcome by keeping the litigant protected and focused in the early stages. Learn quickly regarding who you are working with.

It is also very important that you as the semi-detached but knowledgeable one realise what sort of case this is. Is the mother a bundle of nerves? Does she want rid of the father from her life but not necessarily from the children's lives? Or is she determined to break the relationship between the children and their father? This is most noticeable where the father has been the primary carer or the mother has undiagnosed/diagnosed personality disorders. Some mothers decide that the children must love only her. These are the worse cases.

One of the things I often curse is the inadequate assistance for mothers and children, many of whom are foreign and perhaps lonely, who may be suffering from post-natal depression.

Other things to watch out for are the amount of agencies mummy has involved. The smart and vicious usually make hints about the father inappropriately touching the children when playing or bathing them and then hide behind the agencies verdict which was reached based on her evidence only. Many malevolent mothers regularly set scenes. The father, or social services/domestic violence agencies, may have been told by her she was abused as a child by someone who always seems to have died or has gone far away. These are the worst cases because in my experience many of the mothers who make the most vicious of false allegations have either undiagnosed personality disorders or bipolar tendencies and this is something which Lord Justice Wall commented on many years ago. Quite often the more driven they are the more successful they will be, especially in the early stages of proceedings.

I have often observed that the courts are not nearly as obliging of the legal professionals, or indeed professional women in general, who seek to break the bond between children and their father. It is as if the courts have higher expectations of these parents. As the McKenzie, you will have to identify the type of person, the type of case, whether to fight hard or to seek to ameliorate, all these have to be considered. And you will have to educate the litigant dad here as well. Good luck.

Let the LIP always feel you are supporting him, that you can protect him from bullying and harassment by our learned friends, and above all NEVER be late. A nervous LIP is easy meat for unscrupulous counsel from the other side. After the first hearing, you will know the calibre of person you are working with. Some wonderful speakers just talk rubbish in court, the pressure gets to many. Some totally freeze and then when they speak you might wish they had remained frozen. Have him well briefed as he will have limited opportunity within court but make good use of that time when the court does hear from him.

There are differences between McKenzieing for fathers and mothers. Women are usually more driven but also can be more emotional. Hence, they can more quickly 'veer' off course when cross examining their ex. Also, they are more prone to the 'but I'm the mother' type comment. Above all, don't be distracted by her gender and start behaving like an old-fashioned chauvinist who believes her ex is a monster and you are Sir Galahad to the rescue. Understand she is in a desperate situation, if the secondary parent, and your job is to remain purely child focused. If she tries the tears rather than listening to you especially when she 'detours' from previously agreed path, then take a short walk and on return continue as if nothing had happened if outside court. You are not a tear wiper, and don't be a tear jerker either.

Quite often people ask me what legal studying or qualifications I have. I always reply, 'too much from experience'. There is not much law involved in Children Act matters under Section 8 Orders (the main one for children in private law) that most half intelligent members of the public could apply with a bit of experience. The real problem I often find in this business is not the application of the law, rather it is the quasi legal stitch up done by local services before the action begins proper. So, McKenzie Friend to the rescue it is.

Don't be too worried about counsel for the other side opening the case. Judges and magistrates like to hear from lawyers rather than LIPs, in general. This quite often applies even if your LIP is the applicant in proceedings. Have him and you focusing on substantial errors or deliberately misleading comments made to the court by our learned friend. But also make certain you focus on what I call the 'gold dust' and not the coal dust. Less is more and make it quality. Usually if the court finds that he is sensible then the court will give him more opportunity to speak. Angry men go nowhere in this environment, except backwards.

No position statemen or skeleton argument, which sets out your position, should ever be more than two well-spaced pages. For both LIPs and McKenzie Friends, the position statement should be in the following format:

1. Court heading at the top with the words 'Position Statement'

2. The first two paragraphs should give the court a snapshot of the parties involved and the history regarding the children
3. The next one or two paragraphs should outline the current situation and the problems
4. Then focus on bringing solutions to the court in a practical manner in the circumstances.
5. Request the orders you wish the court to make. Interim contact is always crucial.
6. DON'T JUST DENIGRATE THE MOTHER OR THE SYSTEM.

Always make sure you have met the LIP and gone through the case and worked out how the two of you are going to proceed. Being a McKenzie is not nearly as stressful as being a LIP. However, being a McKenzie with rights of audience is damn hard work. Never take on any case half-heartedly, piss poor planning ALWAYS leads to piss poor performance: The six Ps rule.

Some of my most successful hearings were where we had entered a short position statement and just sat back and watched as a good Judge took the opposition counsel apart. Judges like solutions too. Probably the two best cases I McKenzied in were where neither myself nor the LIP uttered more than a few words.

It all depends on the calibre of the judge or lead magistrate and clerk, and a good one is priceless to watch. I have seen some of the very best in action and what a pleasure to witness. Unfortunately, they are the minority, usually very senior, and the tragedy is such good practice is unusual. The sure sign of a hopeless judge is bluster and bluff, delay followed by prevarication, followed by delegation, followed by vacuous lectures on the need for good parenting. Christ, I have listened to some bullshit at times from judges within courts, and not just district judges.

The worst judges of all are those whose opening comments are, especially regarding enforcement applications, that they have no authority to enforce it, or this should be sorted between the parties. A green light to the alienating parent here! This is what I mean by delegation of authority and prevarication. I'm talking about enforcement applications where the hostile parent blatantly breaches the court order and usually hides behind the child in an exercise of 'disguised compliance'. Such cases are very demoralising but there are ways and means of getting around them, usually. However, the delay and damage to the child-parent relationship in such cases is central to the image that the UK family courts are disastrous and only work for the mother or the resident parent. Unquestionably, the courts biggest failing is here.

On a few occasions, I actually felt I was in the presence of evil when a malevolent or incompetent judge totally let the children down. When it gets bad it can get very bad. In the worst cases, your LIP may be heading for mental breakdown territory or becoming a suicide risk. So, don't casually decide to become a McKenzie Friend. There is far too much at stake for a light-hearted approach. I also have the personal satisfaction of knowing that many children have good relationships with their fathers, and a few mothers, because of my work. As a parent, it is very satisfying to sometimes meet at various events, or when shopping, these children and their former alienated parent just being normal happy individuals. The children don't know who I am and neither should they. There is a bigger picture here.

A few paragraphs below is the excellent McKenzie Friend guidance copied from the Families Need Fathers website regarding McKenzie Friends. I cannot emphasise enough how important the FNF Charter and Guidance for McKenzie Friends is. To my mind any McKenzie Friend who breaches this charter should not be a McKenzie Friend.

I have a certain sense of ownership here because many years ago, around 2009, I was the driving force behind FNF publishing a list of McKenzie Friends and guidance in keeping with the FNF Charter. My thanks to Jon Davies, Chief Executive Officer of FNF at that time, and Jeff Botterill, then FNF regional co-ordinator.

'*At all times the litigant in person must accept responsibility for running their case, and for covering all aspects of it. MFs are not necessarily legally qualified (usually they are not) and the things said by the McKenzie Friend are only to be considered as suggestions. The litigant must assess for themselves its value and applicability to their case. The litigant should before accepting the services of a McKenzie Friend explore with them their knowledge, experience and approach and enquire as to whether they require reimbursement for costs (travel etc). The Litigant must accept responsibility for all decisions.*

'*There are two types of McKenzie Friends: Volunteers and those who charge for their services. Volunteer MFs will McKenzie for free but we strongly encourage you to pay for any expenses they incur whilst helping you, such as travel, meals, printing costs and so forth. They can be contacted via the FNF Branches. We do not list them here.*

Below is a list of MFs who offer their services for a fee, often described as Commercial McKenzies. We cannot recommend individuals. It will be up to you to make a judgement on them and to find out how much their fees are likely to be. Families Need Fathers has no control over their work but we welcome feedback, good or bad.

McKenzie Friends who are listed by FNF, are required to be committed to Shared Parenting as laid out in Families Need Fathers' Charter.

In particular, Paras 1 to 6 of the FNF Charter are expected to be considered by McKenzie Friends listed by FNF at all times and they will <u>not</u> assist a parent or other in a case or actions that oppose the principles laid out in the FNF Charter (and in the FNF Guidance) as follows:

1. *No child shall be denied a full and proper relationship with his or her parents unless it has been proved that such a relationship presents a risk to the child. Any attempt to deny or obstruct this relationship should be regarded as unacceptable.*
2. *There should be a presumption of shared parenting and this should be the starting point when parents separate.*
3. *Children must feel that they have two properly involved parents, with free access to both.*
4. *The importance of grandparents and the wider family must be recognised and addressed.*
5. *Children should spend enough time with both parents to be able to negate any attempts at 'parental alienation'.*
6. *Preventing a child having a relationship with both parents by breaching a court order is unacceptable and the law should treat such breaches promptly and severely.'*

Chapter 25

Families Need Fathers

Families Need Fathers is a shared parenting charity set up in 1974 by a Guardian journalist and a child psychologist. They have many detractors, including myself at times. For all their faults, they are the only charity within the UK holding regular meetings in over 48 areas throughout the UK, including Scotland, Wales and Northern Ireland. Below is some advice from their website outlining what the branches can and cannot do:

'*Important - The FNF Branch Officers organising FNF meetings cannot charge for support or advice given at the meeting and on the meeting premises. However, there may be solicitors and/or McKenzie Friends present who may wish to provide visitors with services outside the meeting. The organiser has the responsibility to ensure that no business is solicited by anyone during meetings. FNF does not recommend the services of such providers who may be present although we maintain a <u>McKenzie Friends Listing</u>. who have undertaken to abide by the FNF McKenzie Friend Charter Please note that any such providers provide their services <u>entirely independently of FNF</u> and it is the responsibility of any prospective service user to ensure that the provider has the qualifications and experience necessary to meet their needs. Providers should always provide users with full service and fee information before entering into any commitments to provide services. FNF generally advises against paying in advance for any services.*'

And here is a small piece courtesy of The Custody Minefield website and Mr Robinson once again explaining what I do and also the committee of Central London Branch Families Need Fathers:

Monday, 15 September 2014

'Face to Face Support - FNF Central London

The primary goal of The Custody Minefield is to provide family law information for those without legal representation, lay advisers and charity sector staff (some in the legal profession and other professionals find it quite handy too).

Other organisations provide 1-to-1 support, and one of these is the charity Families Need Fathers (FNF). FNF, despite its name, helps both mums and dads, and in addition to a helpline and internet based forums, has local branches across the country where you can meet with other parents going through separation and find face-to-face support. A vital lifeline for many litigants-in-person.

Much of this work is done by volunteers, who receive no plaudits, little public recognition, but who work to help others, year in, year out.

One such is Vincent McGovern, Chair of Families Need Fathers' largest and oldest branch, who we've invited to explain what his branch does, his personal role and work, and that of the Central London Committee.

FNF's Central London Branch have their own web page, with details of Branch Meetings.

Visit: Families Need Fathers - Central London Branch

We're happy to publicise details of organisations which support parents ...and after this brief introduction, I'll leave you in Vincent's hands...

FAMILIES NEED FATHERS®
because both parents matter

Branch Meetings

The Central London Branch of Families Need Fathers is the founding branch of FNF established in 1974. It is also the busiest and largest with between 900-1,000+ attendees each year.

We have meetings to offer separating and separated parents support, every Monday at 8 pm apart from Bank Holidays and Christmas. Meetings are held in a private function room at The George, 1 D'Arby Street, W1, London.

Newcomers are not obliged to speak and are welcome to observe – we like to provide a relaxed, pressure free forum for discussion.

Our Attendees

People often ask me what type of person attends our meetings. My reply always is "normal people unfortunate enough to find themselves in unfortunate circumstances."

The majority of our attendees are dads, but we are gender blind and help any mother who is the non-resident parent. Quite often younger dads have their mothers or sisters accompanying them. Our whole raison d'etre is to support the children having a proper involvement with both parents, post divorce or separation, unless there is proven danger.

Legal Support at our Meetings

We have a specialist Solicitor clinic on the first Monday of every month for members only from 6-8 pm. We owe a deep appreciation to the family law firm Anthony Gold and Co, who have provided this important pro bono service for decades. Quite often we have the benefit of a senior partner from that firm which is very helpful for nervous frightened attendees. For the past year at most meetings we have also benefited from the assistance of Austin Chessell, a family law solicitor and mediator, also a Trustee of FNF, which enables whoever is Chairing the meeting that night, giving advice, to have a professional referee for validity of comment.

As well as solicitor support, McKenzie Friends (lay legal advisers) are on hand to provide support and assistance.

We wish to make clear that no adviser (solicitor or otherwise) charges for their time at our meetings, and again sincerely thank all, who over many years have given up their time to help thousands of parents and their children.

Confidentiality

All of our meetings are held under Chatham House rule, no repetition of discussions outside of the meeting, no recording, first names only and NEVER ever reveal the names and addresses of parties to anyone. This basic housekeeping causes some problems for newcomers who are quite often emotional (understandably) but it is an absolute requirement for us as a branch and helps the attendee to focus as sometimes they are in deep shock. Confidentiality is important not just to these parents, but their children as well.

Work of the Central London Branch (CLB) Committee

We hold committee meetings every three months dealing with such matters as housekeeping, rota for chairing meetings, liaising between ourselves and FNF HQ, also other branches, financial management etc. The committee of CLB never charges expenses for attending all these meetings, a considerable burden in itself. However, this means CLB has the funds for limited campaigning, assisting some truly desperate members with court fees, train fare to and from meetings, etc and on occasions helping the national charity at AGM's etc.

We normally have the full contingent of seven committee members at each branch meeting, as meeting every week requires considerable time input from officers.

Committee members are elected, each year, at the Branch AGM. We're a democratic group!

About Me

I first joined FNF/CLB in December 2007. Ironically, I delayed joining as I discovered they met above a pub and I incorrectly assumed they were just a bunch of angry dads drinking and 'sounding off'. That false impression was quickly dispelled at my first meeting. A few months later I was invited onto CLB committee.

My views on post-separation and our legal and welfare system

It remains a perversity that, especially when parents are likely to be in heightened emotional state following a relationship break up, the court too often encourages post-separation dispute by handing control and a means of punishment to one over the other.

As Sir Nicholas Mostyn, a judge in the High Court, said in a past judgment, "if parents were behaving well, they'd probably still be together" but ours is an adversarial legal system. My own view is that the term adversarial should have no place in the family courts. Our family courts should be inquisitorial and facilitative.

I can say, with clarity, that too often our family law system does fail children and still contains elements of gender bias. I've seen house husbands relegated to alternate weekend contact parents after separation, with little thought to maintaining the status quo for the children. Why... because of their gender and some judges remaining out of touch with the contemporary household. In so many homes across the country, both parents take an active role in their children's lives. In the new millennium, research finds mums and dads equally involved (Equalities Commission Research, 2008), yet after court, too often arrangements are imposed which hark back to a 1970s ethos. Countless studies confirm child welfare benefits when both parents are fully involved in their children's lives.

I've seen too many instances where there has been malpractice in welfare services, and four Ombudsman Investigations (with findings against) in a single case I've had involvement with. Findings confirmed institutional malpractice within children's and legal services. Two of these were Parliamentary and Health Services Ombudsman investigations with findings against Brent Primary Care Trust and Cafcass. Sadly, findings such as these, while a moral victory, result in zero change on the ground. We need an ethos within UK Children's Services where the primary motivation is raising standards rather than defending reputations.

Too often, our courts fail to safeguard a child's relationships, or protect them from the emotional harm caused by an alienating parent. There is too little enforcement of Court Orders (Ref Hansard 25 February 2013, column 113).

So much opportunity for a more family friendly legal system was lost with the final revisions to the Children Act in 2014. UK MPs were too influenced by powerful lobby groups, and misinformed. An example being their holding that a presumption of shared parenting was unsuccessful in Australia, when no such finding existed. Such was the opinion of Professor Parkinson of the Sydney Law School, whose criticism included that the UK Family Justice Review misrepresented the findings of Australian research. At our branch, we deal with the fall out of political failure. The expression 'Welfare of the Child' has become an expression of convenience quite often unrelated to children's welfare or needs but most beneficial, ideologically and financially, to the myriad virtually unregulated and effectively unaccountable services involved. Big business meets a nigh on unaccountable public sector lacking in checks and balances. As an MEP said to me in Brussels, "when income generation is more important than welfare of children then we have systemic failing."

The difference with Westminster could not have been more stark. The MEP's have extensive knowledge of the shortcomings within UK Family Courts and associated services. Fortunately, Ombudsman Investigations mean something in Brussels, and the fact I could submit details of four (mentioned above) leant weight to my submissions. On March19th this year I had the privilege of briefly addressing the petitions Commission of the European Parliament on its motion 'Systemic Failings within UK Family Courts and Children's Services.' The title was apt. I am deeply grateful to FNF's Central London Branch for always supporting my work attempting to bring about the much-needed improvements in these services.

Our branch and other FNF branches help parents navigate the courts as they stand today. My hope remains for a better system in the future.

By now you have a good idea of what FNF does at branch level and what I and many other FNF officers who run the branches and groups do. There are several FNf Branch Officers with more technical knowledge than I have of how the system and law should work. That gives you an indication of the calibre of people involved. Despite being few in number, some of our best officers are female - FNF is totally gender blind.'

I first went to an FNF meeting in Central London Branch (CLB) in late November 2007. Previously a very good friend had sent me a list of men's groups in the UK. When I rang them most just seemed to comprise of an angry man in a bedsit with a computer giving out about the system. Mankind were sensible and they suggested FNF. When I phoned FNF HQ I was astonished at the professionalism and ability from the office staff and their IT support and above all patience. Andrew Casey and Peter Hill were their names, sadly due to budget cuts both have left.

I attended my first meeting in November/December 2007 above a pub in a very dingy part of Leather Lane, London. About twenty or so men were at the meeting and the chairperson was a smallish stocky man with apparent unlimited knowledge and practicality. I assumed he was a builder's foreman; I had known many of them. It was a game changer for me. I drove home buzzing that night. The man who so effectively chaired that night's meeting was Steve Stephenson and he is still despite serious illness provides assistance for parents. He was a teacher formerly.

A few months later I was asked to join the branch committee. CLB has always prided itself as being the flagship branch of FNF: well, it is the founding branch, the busiest, the largest and benefits from location and has the largest committee. There are always new faces at the meetings. I feel sorry for the officers in the small FNF branches and groups in remote locations who too often see the same sad desperate cases every month. Far too often we meet desperate and destitute fathers depending on friends and families to keep themselves functioning. Some who attend use food banks to supplement themselves. Too many are effectively homeless once they have been booted from the family home.

There is however a huge difference in ability between FNF officers at branch level and some trustees who run the charity. The tragedy, and it is a tragedy, is that a few dud trustees have ensconced themselves in senior roles and by unique interpretation of the electoral rules manage to always stay there. This means there is a virtual logjam. Several times I have seen men and women of huge and proven ability become a trustee and give up after a year or so utterly frustrated with what I call the deadwood trustees. There are a few quality trustees currently who run branches on the board but they are a frustrated minority. They have my deepest sympathy. Of course, far too often when capable people become frustrated they then leave the charity altogether.

I long ago realised how useless some FNF trustees are, especially after they refused to give me a short letter of support despite my repeated requests when I managed to get invited back to the European Parliament in November 2014. The European Parliament motion on that day was 'systemic failings in the UK Family Court system'. This is sadly only one example of their, I have to use the word, incompetence.

That said, in December 2020 at the FNF AGM, three new Trustees were voted in. They are John Baker, Paul O Callaghan and Emlyn Jones. I nominated two and am delighted that such a trio of proven experience and ability are now Trustees. My very few appearances on Radio and TV since 2014 were co-ordinated by others. I always appreciate the invaluable support of the two branches which I chair, Central and North London branches of Families Need Fathers.

Those committee members truly understand the bigger picture and some have spent decades working totally for free, not even charging expenses to attend meetings and help parents stay involved with their children. Among the longest serving is John Baker, currently Secretary and Treasurer of Central London Branch and formerly CEO of FNF years ago when it was much more effective. All of these ten committee members from both branches have been thrown in at the deep end of the family court process themselves and have managed to retain a relationship with most of their children. So, we certainly are not sad desperate losers. We believe in results and for us a result means a child retaining a productive relationship with both parents pos- divorce or separation. What a tragedy the many too often pseudo-professionals involved throughout this vast dad desert landscape do not exercise the same views.

Despite the enormous difficulties FNF face I have absolutely no doubt that the charity has saved many lives and has kept many children in contact with both parent's post-divorce or separation. Despite zero government funding for several years many times the administration work at FNF HQ in East London has often been done by volunteers. Some have given their labour free for months and some helpline volunteers have spent years assisting desperate parents and are deserving of the highest credit for doing so. Contrast that with the vast funding given to Women's Aid Federation of Charities, in the hundreds of millions. So much for gender equality within the UK.

FNF's excellent helpline is staffed by unpaid but trained volunteers who deal with several thousand calls per year. In 2019 Fnf organised a conference and AGM in Central London. I was particularly impressed by the presentation from Jan James, CEO Good Egg Safety marketing campaign. She has serious ability in marketing re child safety and has fully grasped the issue of parental alienation. Her presentation was incredible. Erin Pizzey also became a Patron of FNF in 2019. Despite my criticism of a few at the top of FNF I have one very simple comment to make to the angry men's rights activists who denigrate all of FNF by dismissing us as puppets or Government stooges: how many parents have you helped? If none, then shut up criticising Families Need Fathers.

Chapter 26

Complaints and How To

First of all, here is a copy of my Complaints Template. Reading it you will yet again come across my comment about five Ombudsman Investigations, three PHSOs and twice addressing the European Parliament Petitions Commission.

Nobody is as sick as I am of repeatedly writing about this to various regulatory bodies and individuals within the UK and being rebuffed. And as to the best of my knowledge I'm the only individual within the UK who has five Ombudsman Investigations to his credit plus two presentations to the European Parliament Petitions Commission. I will keep banging on about it until I bring about improvement by removing as much as I can of the institutional malpractice within the system. Of course, if any reader has a better idea based on their accomplishments then please contact me.

Complaints template:

'The following template has resulted in over twenty complaint inquiries and 5 Ombudsman Investigations, which are a Local Government Ombudsman, a Legal Services Ombudsman, and Parliamentary and Health Services Ombudsman (PHSO) three times. There was also an investigation under Special Amendments 2006 of the Children Act 1989 as advised by the Local Government Ombudsman. This led to a sincere apology in writing from the Director of Social Services and the Regional

Director of Children and Adolescent Mental Health Services (CAMHS).

The malpractice by the Local Primary Care Trust resulted in 3 investigations culminating in a Parliamentary and Health Services Ombudsman. These complaints were focused on the *Child Endangering Gender Discrimination* policies and practices of personnel in the above agencies.

The Parliamentary & Health Services Ombudsman ordered the local Primary Care Trust to acknowledge wrongdoing, give a full written apology, pay compensation of £250, instigate a 90-day action plan to demonstrate change in procedure and future verification to the satisfaction of NHS London, The Health Service Ombudsman, The Care Quality Commission, and myself. The Ombudsman investigator found the Primary Car Trust (PCT) standard so poor that it amounted to maladministration and injustice, causing frustration and distress.

In another complaint, there were 3 investigations into malpractice by my ex-wife's solicitors as a result of their actions. Two of these investigations were a pretence as the Legal Complaints Service and the Solicitors Regulatory Authority refused to investigate my concerns properly. The Legal Services Ombudsman formally criticized the Solicitors Regulatory Authority for refusing to investigate. That weak telling-off hardly stopped all further solicitor malpractice.

There was also a PHSO assisted investigation into Cafcass Guardian malpractice and the protection of such by Cafcass management. This led to 5 'apologies', 3 'sorries' in a letter from Anthony Douglas Cafcass CEO, and a separate complaints department being set up within Cafcass to properly address complaints in 2011. In 2015 due to Cafcass repeat failings there was a 2nd PHSO investigation leading to financial compensation to me and recommendations forced upon Cafcass by the PHSO.

On the 19th March 2014 and 11th December 2014, I was allowed to briefly address the Petitions Commission of the European Parliament in Brussels because of my then four successful Ombudsman Investigations. This and other petitions led to an investigation by the EU into 'Systemic Failings in UK Family Courts', but only on Public Law.

I am trying hard to have the domestic violence agencies which act on behalf of the Local Authority forced to comply with The Gender Equality Act of April 2007 and 1st October 2010, and *most importantly*, The Children Act 1989. Their current constitution and practice is to accept evidence from *females* only and, if serious enough, to process this through their Multi Agency Risk Assessment Process (MARAC). This is done in secret without the father having any notice. The verdict (*only*) on this evidence, which is not seen by the father as he is deemed a 'perpetrator', is then brought before the case conference via social services and, surprise surprise, the father is then deemed a risk to his children and with this choreographed discrimination he is then booted ex-parte from the family home.

Please bear in mind that where Cafcass are concerned their complaints process will only deal with the **Conduct** of the officer and not the Content. Also, according to the Ministry for Justice (What Do They Know) there are no records of a judge recommending that a deceitful or disingenuous Cafcass/ social services official be retrained or sacked. *Where is the welfare of the child paramount here?*

Social services are, since 2014, regulated by the Health and Care Professional Council (HCPC). Their predecessor, the General Social Care Council (GSCC) routinely refused to accept complaints about social workers. The HCPC are as skilful at protecting malpractice as the GSCC were but perseverance *and* a legitimate complaint will get results.

The Complaints template is as follows:

1. Conduct 2. Requirement 3) Consequences 4. Remedy

(*In short C.R.C.R*)

The procedure for complaint re social services employers: the '3 stages'. The local authority are the employers of social services so all complaints have to be processed locally first. The words of utmost importance are "*I wish to formally lodge a Stage 1 Complaint*' . Without these words your complaint will just gather dust.

The local authority has 10 working days to deal with your stage 1 complaint under statutory guidelines. Make your complaint absolutely precise and brief, less than 2 typed pages if at all possible. Any loose language will be seized upon and used against you.

If unsatisfied with Stage 1 then do a stage 2 with the formal wording as in Stage 1 except now use the words 'Stage 2 complaint'. They have 15 working days to respond. If unsatisfied then do a Stage 3 using the formal wording 'Stage 3 complaint'. They have 20 working days to respond here. If still unsatisfied you may only then approach the Local Government Ombudsman.

Very Important Points

The skill and willingness of local authorities and agencies to deceive, manipulate, procrastinate, inveigle and lie is astonishing. For reference, read Lord Laming's (Victoria Climbie) investigation into Brent and Haringey in 2001. He was lied to so often by so many e.g. social services, police, NSPCC, and local authorities, that in the end they were reduced to accusing each other of lying. He had to threaten several with imprisonment before they would even attend. I believe they **brought lying into disrepute.**

At all times have evidence of document delivery and keep hard copies. Never engage in telephone conversations unless recorded and/or notes taken. Bring a note-taking friend or McKenzie to any meeting. Above all protect yourself and never ever raise your voice, no matter what the provocation. Remain purely child focused.

Conduct:

Your complaint has to show that the **conduct** of the social worker was not of the required standard.

Requirement:

Look up the HCPC Codes of Practice for social service workers and employers. Also check the Equality Act April 2010. Bear in mind that apart from Article 8 of European Court of Human Rights (Right to Family Life) human rights acts are subservient to the Children Act 1989. The rights are with the children: you and, technically, the mother have almost none. You both however have duties as parents which the local authorities have to consider. Article 6 of the ECHR also applies.

Consequences:

Your complaint will go nowhere unless you can show that the children suffered as a consequence, or were put at increased risk of harm due to social services/local authority action/malpractice. This is absolutely pivotal.

Remedy:

Among the solutions are the following: retraining, referral to the HCPC, Local Government Ombudsman investigation (possibly using Special Amendments 2006 of the Children Act 1989), a written apology, acknowledgement of wrongdoing, verifiable change in procedure and work practice, financial compensation and sacking are among the options.

Your complaint has to be based on Conduct – Requirement – Consequences - Remedy. At all stages copy in the leader of the council, the chief executive of the council, the councillor responsible for social services and the director of social services. Letters only.

Proof of postage, which is free, will do. Otherwise deliver by hand, if necessary at night time, with photographic evidence e.g that day's newspaper, to their office. At Stage 3 you should include your MP. Only bring specific questions to him/her to deal with, not the kitchen sink and all emotional baggage.

Date and keep copies of everything. Your future relationship with your children might depend on this.

Cafcass: (Children and Families Court Advisory and Support Service)

If it makes you feel any better the Government's own regulatory body OFSTED has been very critical of Cafcass. I quote OFSTED's beautiful description of Cafcass – "their conclusions are not reasoned." A House of Commons committee in January 2011 was equally scathing about Cafcass: *'Cafcass, as an organisation, is not fit for purpose'*.

Cafcass's own complaints procedure is clear - only complain about **Conduct,** not **Content.** First of all, during court proceedings discredit the report if inaccurate or unprofessional, not the official. If necessary to do a formal complaint, link dishonest/unprofessional content to conduct. Once again expect to be rebuffed, dismissed and fobbed off. Persevere using the **Conduct Requirement Consequences Remedy** template. Once again, keep all copies of letters or if telephoned request that it be followed with a letter when the complaint is in process. Take notes during the call surreptitiously.

Of great importance is the fact that malpractice by Cafcass/ Guardian Ad Litem can now be referred by your MP to The Parliamentary & Health Services Ombudsman. Cafcass's own revised Complaints and Compliments Policy since 2014 is to respond once to a complaint and then suggest if still dissatisfied you complain to the PHSO via your MP. Be very precise in language when bringing matters to your MP, above all you have to prove **wrongdoing** to him/her for a referral to be made on your behalf.

Domestic Violence Agencies

Let us be crystal clear here, there is no place in a modern society for gender vigilantes, who are usually unregulated and unaccountable, getting control of local authority guidelines and practice. Many of these agencies in constitution and practice demonise men and heavily discriminate against fathers. Many refuse to help fathers at all, fobbing them off with "signposting to a solicitor", etc. Using the Freedom of Information Act (FOI), and your MP and councillor, establish whether they offer equal services to both sexes. If not, establish their funding base using FOI and what statutory authority the local authority may have conferred upon them. Then attack them using the Equality Act 2010 and also the Children Act 1989. Pull the rug from beneath their child endangering gender discrimination. Also remember that the councillor with statutory authority for social services has extra legal responsibilities here. Reduction/removal of funding focuses their minds very well and is the only method of enforcing gender-neutral impartial professionalism. Where local services e.g social services, health, educational, etc, allow the domestic violence agency to take the lead bring this matter to their own regulatory/funding bodies. This particularly applies where false allegations or absurd exaggerations are being facilitated and promoted purely on ideological, gender, or funding grounds. Once again Conduct – Requirement – Consequences – Remedy.

General Practitioners

The General Medical Council guidelines for GPs is very clear. Paragraph 55 GMC guidelines 0-18 years states: "divorce or separation does not affect parental responsibility and you should allow both parents reasonable access to their children's health records". Sometimes the GP and/or their staff may have a female only viewpoint. If necessary a copy of the above and proof of Parental Responsibility plus appropriate ID should suffice. If not, contact the local Primary Care Trust complaints department or the General Medical Council as a last resort. Failing that then bring the matter to your MP and ask for a referral to the PHSO. Once again in writing only if rebuffed. Remember: Conduct – Requirement – Consequences - Remedy.

Schools

Please bear in mind that schools, doctor's surgeries, etc, are usually quite busy places and staff will sometimes take the easy option. Occasionally there will be downright hostility shown towards a father usually where a malevolent mum has falsely portrayed him as abusive, etc. The Department of Education guidelines updated 4/1/2011 and January 6th 2016, are very clear here. Look under their definition of Parent, Parental Responsibility and General Principles for Schools. Effectively, if you are a non-resident parent you are entitled to all correspondence of importance. If sharing residence or overnight contact, particularly at weekends, you should be equally entitled and involved with all relevant school matters.

If you absolutely feel that you have to make a complaint because of malpractice by a professional involved in your case always consider the following first:

- All actions will have a consequence, usually unintended.
- The professionals are not responsible for your painful divorce or separation.
- They are however absolutely obliged to act in the children's interests where they are involved.
- Do not let satellite litigation (complaints) interfere with your own family proceedings unless absolutely necessary.
- Do not make a half-hearted complaint just for the sake of it. Only complain if there is malpractice. If your complaint is more than 2 pages it will almost definitely be counter-productive. Only start what you mean to see through to conclusion. Above all, be thorough, honest, calm, sensible, and exercise the highest standards of focus and discipline. At all times Conduct – Requirement – Consequences - Remedy.

I wish you well and hope this improves you as a parent. Above all never give up on your children, they deserve the best of both parents.

It is perhaps worth noting that one of the Legal Services Ombudsman investigators told me that my complaint was the best they had ever seen. This was the complaint where my learned highly intellectual friend managed in two short brilliant paragraphs puncture the armoured wall of resistance.

These two paragraphs to the Legal Services Ombudsman were distributed to other investigators because of their quality.

Several have complained that my template is too long, too deep and intense. Some have tried to turn it into a flowchart to make it easier to understand. I have news for you, there is only two pages of the template that apply to most. The first page describes its relative success as people were saying why should they accept it without proof of achievement. And the last half page is very general advice. So effectively only half a page is what you want to learn. If you cannot or are unwilling to grasp the C-R-C-R concept, then give up.

This criticism is NOT aimed at the many desperate fathers who find themselves thrown into the horrible deep end of the family court process. It is however directly aimed at those who have survived and wish to make this system fit for purpose. Unless you are prepared to go through what I did then don't bother. When engaging in battle you don't decide to half-fight. Either fight totally or give up. After all, when giving birth, the mother couldn't give up!

The few examples below are some of the letters of complaint which I have sent over the years to various organisations who basically put gender politics and revenue collection above children's safety. You will have already seen my letter of complaint to Brent about its laughable Local Children Safeguarding Board in Chapter 10.

This next one is a copy of the letter of complaint I made to the NSPCC about their Christmas poster campaign on trains and stations in 2012.

'Dear Sir/Madam,

I have difficulty composing my thoughts and it has taken me a week to formally complain about this grotesquely discriminatory portrayal of dads alone being abusive towards children. I have had 15 official enquiries and 4 Ombudsman investigations, (2 Parliamentary and Health Services Ombudsman) with findings in my favour against ALL children's services in London Borough of Brent, who regularly quote the NSPCC when defending their institutional child endangering gender discrimination. I add that Lord Laming's 2001 investigation into Brent and the NSPCC was damning.

I will also be sending a copy of this complaint to the Advertising Standards Authority as so many of their guidelines are breached.

My complaint is as follows:

The NSPCC breach the ASA standard for; Legal, Decent, Honest and Truthful. It wilfully breaches NSPCC duties under Social Responsibilities re ASA.

1.2, All ads must comply with the spirit and not just to the letter.

1.3, The NSPCC has abused its sense of responsibility by solely portraying dads as child abusers when all official research and statistics totally contradict this.

3.1, Any ad must not materially mislead. The above totally misleads as it solely depicts dads as abusers.

3.3, Must not mislead the consumer by omitting material information. The above ad which is crudely and illegally (Section 5 Public Order Act) gender biased in the extreme deliberately omits and wilfully ignores the NSPCC own research into child abuse, as well as all official research.

4.1, The above ad causes harm and offence on grounds of gender.

4.2, This ad makes a shocking claim designed to attract attention and maximise revenue income by pandering to the crudest form of gender stereotyping.

5.2, The NSPCC ad exploits children by taking advantage of their credulity, loyalty, vulnerability and lack of experience.

5.3, This ad breaches the ASA guidelines for marketing communication addressed to or targeted directly at children.

I am appalled at such crude child endangering gender discrimination by the NSPCC. This most sadly, follows on from their deep hostility towards shared parenting as in their submissions to the House of Commons when it was looking into shared parenting. The NSPCC had absolutely no research to present to justify its objection to shared parenting.

The above ad is grossly misleading, is consistent with the NSPCC having allowed itself to become involved in gender politics at children's expense and that of wider society.

The law insists on Gender Neutral Impartial Professionalism in all matters (my words).

I request this deeply misleading ad be removed from all NSPCC literature and sites, an appropriate apology in its place, and all future working practice be in children's interest. I abhor child abuse and domestic violence. I have even greater abhorrence for those who seek financial, ideological, or political gain from such.

Children's safety and welfare is far far too important to be used as an income generating political football.

Yours Sincerely

Vincent McGovern
(Chair, Central London Branch Families Need fathers)

It normally takes several letters and usually I have to go further up the chain before any improvement or semi apology happens. And from too much experience of the alleged regulators further up the chain will readers please remember my opening chapters in this book. However, perseverance and a bit of ability can go a long way. Several intellectuals have told me my complaints are too emotional, too personal, etc. I always ask them how their complaints went. Silence.

This next complaint was against the Independent On Sunday which as it had become prone to doing, did a hatchet job on men and fathers by two female journalists in a lead story. To my surprise a few months later one of the female journalists involved did a very good and accurate story in the same newspaper. Results in this business come in different forms. This is an example where I got a result but, of course, they wouldn't credit me with it. Guess what, I couldn't give a damn who gets the credit, I just simply want an accurate story written and corrected if obviously inaccurate. Other officers within FNF quite often take up complaints against the BBC and other organisations and wherever there is obvious discrimination against fathers which disadvantages children. They do a lot of behind the scenes work with no acknowledgement.

Here is my letter to The Independent on Sunday (IOS):

Dear Sirs/ Madam

It has taken me several days to recover from the shock of reading such a gender discriminatory and brutally misleading article as this headline portrayal on domestic violence in the UK by Emily Dugan and Jane Merrick. I felt like a Jewish person during 1930's Germany or a black man during the segregationist era in the Southern states of America. I was an avid daily reader from 1986 until 2007 of the Independent newspaper. Now I am ashamed and appalled at what a child endangering gender discriminatory vehicle the IOS has become.

I now draw the attention of the IOS Editor and PCC complaints officer to the following;

British Crime Surveys, Home Office Statistical Bulletins, England and Wales 1995-2010/11 published February 2012.

1, Male victims are 35-50% of victims from female perpetrated assaults.

2, Female victims are twice (2) as likely to tell someone and three (3) times more likely to report to the police.

3, Male fatalities from female assault are 40% whereas female fatalities of male assaults are 60%.

The offending IOS article of 25/11/12 completely ignores the UK governments own statistics on Domestic Violence by female perpetrators. The IOS article is deliberately fostering gender hatred by deliberately misrepresentation, miss-selection, and omission of commonly available factual information from UK Government.

I have one request of the IOS Editor;

1, When will a corrective article be published in the same format and apology issued to misrepresented males in UK?

2, If such is not done then I formally request that the PCC intervene under Article 1 (i);

'The Press must take care not to publish inaccurate, misleading or distorted information, including pictures'.

This article is very misleading and distorted since it most strongly implies that the only domestic violence in the UK is by men against women.

Article 1 (ii) It must be corrected

Discrimination: 12 (i) The press must avoid prejudical or perjorative reference to an individual's race, colour, religion, gender, sexual orientation or to any physical or mental illness or disability.

The IOS article is totally perjorative as they imply throughout that men are always responsible for violence against women and are never the victims. This article reinforces prejudice, severely hinders male victims reporting abuse, handicaps charities helping male victims of DV, and fosters false allegations of DV by violent females who benefit from such discrimination as perpetrated by the IOS article.

I abhor domestic violence and condemn it in all forms. I have stronger abhorrence of those with influence e.g newspapers, financially benefitting from misrepresentation and discrimination.

I request an acknowledgment of this email complaint and corrective action in keeping with the PCC guidelines.

Yours Sincerely

Vincent McGovern.
(Chair, Central London Branch Families Need Fathers)

Marilyn Stowe is one of the UK's leading family lawyers who has built up a large practice and she also writes a very good blog. I have always noticed that when she writes her blog it is of a very high standard. The same cannot be said for some of her staff and colleagues whenever they write her blog. Ms Amy Foweather is a solicitor with Marlilyn Stowe Solicitors and the first article that I was aware she wrote is this one. Basically, a quite false portrayal of domestic violence within the UK. But hey, solicitors know there is much money to harvest from the gendered promotion of domestic violence.

To her credit, and I thank her for this, Marilyn always allowed my comments on her blog to be published. However, the offending article and my response I was told had 'disappeared' off Marilyn Stowe's blog. Just as well I kept a copy then. And when Marilyn retired in 2017, I discovered my comments were blocked from their blog!

As family law solicitors, we deal with a vast amount of cases. Most common, perhaps, are divorce, finance and disputes regarding children. However, **beneath the surface of many of these cases, there is quite often an underlying issue** which relates to some form of <u>domestic abuse</u>. In many cases, that abuse is actually the central issue. Having had a great deal of experience in working with victims of domestic violence, I have always been concerned about the lack of recognition and support when that abuse does not ticked the box of physical or sexual assaults.

The criminalisation of 'coercive control' in section 76 of the Serious Crime act 2015 is therefore greatly welcomed. It is a step in the right direction, towards the **acknowledgment and prevention of other forms of abuse.** We <u>recently saw this new law in action</u> with the conviction of a man who had 'controlled every aspect of victim's life.'.

Karen Renshall, a reviewing lawyer at the Crown Prosecution Service, said:

"Controlling or **coercive behavior can have an extreme psychological and emotional impact** *on victims. Today's conviction shows that this behavior will simply not be tolerated. No-one has the right to restrict someone else's freedom. [The convicted man] controlled every aspect of his victim's life. He prevented her from seeing her friends and questioned where she had been if she came in late. He stopped the victim from using her mobile phone and controlled her social media, such as making her delete friends on Facebook."*

Domestic violence has become an increasingly worrying problem in the UK, with more and more awareness of the issues being raised. It is a <u>concern for both men and women</u> and can have devastating effects on the entire family.

Let's take a look at some of the statistics:

- **Two women are killed every week in England and Wales by a current or former partner** *(Office for National Statistics, 2015)*. One woman is killed every three days
- One in four women in England and Wales will experience domestic violence in their lifetimes and **eight per cent will suffer domestic violence in any given year***(Crime Survey of England and Wales, 2013/14)*.
- Globally, one in three women will**experience violence at the hands of a male partner** *(State of the World's Fathers Report, MenCare, 2015)*.
- Domestic violence has a **higher rate of repeat victimisation than any other crime** *(Home Office, July 2002)*.
- Every minute police in the UK receive a domestic assistance call – yet only 35 per cent of domestic violence incidents are reported to the police *(Stanko, 2000 & Home Office, 2002)*.
- The 2001/02 British Crime Survey (BCS) found that there were an estimated 635,000 incidents of domestic violence in England and Wales. **81 per cent of the victims were women and 19 per cent were men.** Domestic violence incidents also made up nearly 22 per cent of all violent incidents reported by participants in the BCS *(Home Office, July 2002)*.
- On average, a woman is **assaulted 35 times before her first call to the police** *(Jaffe, 1982)*.

It is step in the right direction that domestic abuse is now being recognised in its many forms. However, **not all cases will receive the assistance of the criminal justice system.** In my experience, there are many cases where victims are advised by the police to seek help from a family solicitor.

Some protections are available under family law. **Victims can seek advice regarding a <u>non-molestation order</u>.** This is an injunction against the perpetrator and can prevent any form of contact, intimidation, harassment, threats or violence. In urgent cases, a <u>family law solicitor</u> can file your application and seek the order from the court within a matter of hours. If breached, this can carry sanctions through either the criminal or family courts.

Any case of separation or divorce can be a very difficult time. However, in cases where there has been abuse, it is inevitably even harder. Any one **experiencing such difficulties should seek advice from a family law solicitor.** Not only can you seek urgent protection by way of court orders, but you can also seek advice and assistance in relation to all other issues arising from the separation.

If you or anyone you know is experiencing difficulties, then please do not hesitate to contact a specialist family law solicitors for a confidential chat.

Vincent McGovern - May 8, 2016 at 10:43pm

<u>Report/Reply</u>

I had assumed this article was a wind up when I read the statistics of the British Crime survey dated........2001/2. I notice the current one from Feb 2012 dealing with DV is significant by omission. Perhaps this is because it severely contradicts the 2001 edition. And let me take a wild guess, most if not all of the research statistics Ms Foweather quotes were done by feminist academics justifying standpoint research? And then I discover Ms Foweather is a Family Law Solicitor. And as usual the harvesting facilitation and promotion of (usually) false allegations against men and fathers is a source of much needed income to lawyers. And then it made sense.

I'm reminded of my much better- known countryman Oscar Wilde and his comment "there are lies, damned lies and statistics." And there are misandric family law solicitors who exercise child endangering gender discrimination. But who cares when there is income to be derived.

When Marilyn Stowe writes her blog, they are normally excellent. John Bolch much less so. As for this portrayal 'male beast-female angel' model it demonstrates the crudest anti man bigotry I have ever read since Spare Rib magazine in the 1970's.

The above response was accepted by Marilyn Stowe blog and posted after some correspondence between Ms Stowe and myself. A part of me thinks that as Marilyn is smarter than the average solicitor, she sensed a complaint to the Solicitors' Regulatory Authority about her Ms Foweather demonstrating a very strong bias against fathers when as a solicitor she is meant to exercise impartial professionalism.

And yes, I would have initiated a complaint to the SRA if denied right of reply. Ms Stowe's instincts are good.

Chapter 27

My 10 solutions

1. Abolition of all agencies via withdrawal of funding which operate in the shadow of the family court while constitutionally and in practice discriminating on grounds of gender in service provision. No more bigotry, Gender Neutral Impartial Professionalism only.
2. Cafcass to be either remodelled and appropriately regulated or abolished.
3. From first application for a Child Arrangement Order to final order be completed in less than 26 weeks.
4. Family courts to adopt Early Interventions as proposed by Dr Hamish Cameron, Consultant Child Psychiatrist, also by Oliver Cyriax Solicitor and others to enable the above 26- week target.
5. An automatic presumption of shared parenting from between 50:50 to no less than 35% unless circumstances e.g. geography, work, etc, determine otherwise. Obviously criminal convictions would alter this outcome.
6. Allegations of domestic violence to be processed within criminal courts. If found malicious then the force of law should apply.
7. The Duluth Wheel Model on domestic violence, and derivatives, be brought to the middle of the Atlantic and wheeled overboard. All police stations, GP surgeries, hospital reception areas, public broadcasting services and all media outlets to either exercise gender neutral impartial professionalism or face hate crime charges.

8. Family Courts to move from near zero regarding enforcement to a reversal of that figure - *1.24% of 4,654 applications were enforced in 2015. Ref: Hansard 28/3/17, Column 148.* These orders were made in the 'best interests of the child'.

9. Appropriate funding as therapy for children so damaged by the court process. Currently there is not ONE PENNY available within the UK family court for children's therapy. So much for *'the welfare of the child is paramount'*. In the interim a simple transfer of funding from the myriad legal eagles and pseudo professionals to purely children's needs. This transfer of funds is long overdue as these 'professionals' have caused so much of the problem.

10. A resolute determination by the UK to move from being at the bottom of international tables showing one child in three living with their natural father in comparison to the EU average (Ref: Office for National Statistics 2010 *Labour Force Survey).* The picture for children remaining involved with both parent's post-divorce or separation is uniquely disastrous. One in four children didn't consider their father to be even part of their family (Childwise, BBC Newsround Programme 2007). The UK should move to at least mid-table of the OECD countries (Organisation for Economic Co-operation and Development) within five years for children staying involved with both their parents and matching the best within ten years. In Finland, the figure is 95% and the OECD average is 85%. The UK is the second wealthiest nation in Europe but has the worst outcomes for children in so many international tables.

For those who will say, how can this be so complicated and time consuming, I have a very good answer. Just look at the Brexit negotiations in the UK parliament as of March 2019.

When a body of people with the reins of power don't want to do something, they can find many reasons for not doing so.

As an example of enlightened thinking, just look at what the Finnish Government stated it would do regarding shared parental leave when a child is born. Bear in mind this is a Government of 5 political parties all led by women. Unlike the 1970's feminist mindset which is so dominant within the UK and especially family court support systems, these Finnish women think of children and families first.

Finland has just announced an increase in parental leave, equalising entitlements of mothers and fathers. The decision was made by Finland's coalition of five parties, all led by women, taking the view that gender equality had to take a priority. Aino-Kaisa Ilona Pekonen Finland's Minister for Social Affairs and Health said that this is an "investment in the future of children and wellbeing of families". She also added that "sharing parent responsibilities in everyday life will become easier, and the relationship between both parents and the child will be strengthened from the early childhood". Just consider the likelihood of the UK government doing similar!

Of course, you don't have to believe me! Then please check the ratio of teenagers from single parent homes versus the ratio of those raised by both parents who are doing so many of the stabbings in London. There are other factors but the common one is fatherlessness. Do you get the point before more teenagers get the sharper point!!

Chapter 28

Some Actions I initiated or helped to address the problem

On Saturday 14th October 2017 John Baker primarily and myself on behalf of the Central London Branch, Families Need Fathers organised a Parental Alienation Workshop in Central London. We invited Cafcass, N.S.P.C.C, HHJ Stephen Wildblood, Dr Hamish Cameron FRCP FRCPsych, Consultant Child and Adolescent Psychiatrist, Dr Sue Whitcombe Chartered Psychologist, AFBBsS and PA expert. Also invited were Joanna Abrahams Head of Family Law, PA specialists, Setfords Solicitors, and the irrespressible Francesca Wiley QC, Barrister at 1 Garden Court. To our delight they all attended, Chris Cloke Head of Safeguarding in Communities at NSPCC presented on their behalf. Paul Apreda CEO of Welsh Fnf gave an excellent closing address, my minor contribution after his was made unscripted and unaware it would be widely distributed. Well, that's my excuse for being only average.

As an example of the remarkable entrenched hostility against any improvements for children's outcomes being actively considered, a female *barrister Natasha Phillips* wrote an open letter to the NSPCC and Cafcass requesting they not attend our event because she claimed among other things that; *MP Glenda Jackson in 1994 reported in Parliament that Fnf advised fathers who were not allowed access to their children to 'kidnap' them. If that failed and nothing else could succeed, it advocated the murder of the mother."* This is available for your viewing on 'Researching Reform open letter to Cafcass and the NSPCC.'

According to the Family Law publication Natasha is a non-practicing barrister and Editor in Chief of *The Encyclopaedia on Family and The Law*. Natasha also runs the family law project, <u>Researching Reform</u>, which is dedicated to child welfare inside the family justice system. She is the Consultant for the All Party Parliamentary Group on Family Law and The Court of Protection.

On the day two groups Legal Action for Women and Women Against Rape protested outside the venue including handing out leaflets containing Glenda Jacksons scurrilious comment.

As one can see, the slightest hint of possible change and improvement for children within the system sought by a Shared Parent Charity representing mainly fathers will be denounced from the highest office in the land and repeated. Parliamentary privilege means the charity cannot sue Glenda Jackson. The source is of course unverified, what branch he attended ditto, who the presiding Chair of the meeting was ??? Effectively just vile propaganda.

The protestors were complaining that 2 women are killed every week by their partner/boyfriend or husband. They were also complaining about 19 children having been killed by their fathers. Surprisingly they overlooked the following; the much greater amount of children killed by mothers; children killed by mothers while on court ordered contact, the amount of men killed by women and to my mind the biggest killer of all, the amount of fathers who commit suicide because of the trauma after separation from their children (approx. 900 pa) which appears to be 8-9 times greater per year than the amount of women killed by men (100 pa).

Domestic abuse by men against women featured heavily in their protests. The British Crime Survey published February 2012 quickly corrects that gendered misrepresentation. Personally, I consider the DV figures since 2013 to be highly procedurally factored because of the LASPO element since April 2013.

HHJ Stephen Wildblood really gave an excellent talk, he seriously recognises the issue of parental alienation and the huge obstacles facing mostly fathers who are litigants in person. Anthony Douglas Ceo of Cafcass to his credit attended and gave a quality talk. No management jargon spoof, and touched upon his own personal experience as a child of parental alienation. Under questioning Douglas admitted that only 2.5% of Cafcass officers have attended their training webinars on Parental Alienation. In 2019 I found out that 99% of Cafcass personnel have done their online training for expenses! Welfare of the Child is Paramount? Much as I hate Cafcass institutional malpractice, detest it in fact, I have to say well done to Douglas and the NSPCC for attending and ignoring the vile propaganda sent to them about Families Need Fathers.

Fran Wiley QC chaired the afternoon session incl the Q&A. Her telling comments about so many Cafcass personnel refusing to recognise parental alienation and Wildblood's beautifully worded criticisms of Cafcass *Wishes and feelings reports* will live long in the memory of those who attended. HHJ Wildblood's and Douglas's presentation are available on youtube as well as Fnf website.

Dr Hamish Cameron, a colossus against parental alienation for decades and Dr Sue Whitcombe gave as expected truly excellent presentations. Joanna Abrahams presented on how Litigants in Person should attempt to navigate the minefield that is the family court system and especially where parental alienation is concerned. Another leading solicitor attending was Kim Beatson, head of the children section at Anthony Gold solicitors who have spent years helping our branch by holding a solr clinic once a month for two hours before the first Monday of every month.

The quality and behaviour of the attendees around 20% female, at the event was as usual of the highest child focused standard. That is the Fnf I belong to.

On Sunday the 19th November 2017 and also in November 2018 I found myself shepherding marchers through Central London, in my capacity as Chief Steward of the International Men's Day march. I was a junior member of the IMD committee, chaired by Nigel Pankhurst (yes, a descendent of herself Emmeline Pankhurst) executive officers Natoya Raymond and Elizabeth Hobson. There was a brilliant march and afterwards a truly high-level conference attended by around 120, the maximum allowed in the venue. In 2018 this was repeated and I presented a semicomedy/education presentation for 25 minutes. My first attempt and I got the legal aid ratio back to front for male/female in 2013. Doh!! This colourfully expressed piece can be seen if you google 'Vince McGovern messages for men.' Someone cannot spell Vincent it appears. And beware, I used colourful language, so bring your smelling salts!

In October 2018 myself and John Baker organised another conference in London, this time titled 'Workshop on Domestic Abuse Allegations' Basically we wanted to highlight the huge increase in DV allegations and enable fathers to have a better understanding of what they are dealing with and how to survive in this arena and maintain a relationship with their children.

John Baker has many excellent connections within the Judiciary and Academia. Are you surprised to know that not one of them attended though many were invited to address us on the subject. Fortunately, I had made some good contacts over the years and we had a very good workshop. CLB as usual pulled out all the stops, supplied the money and manpower to enable the event to take place. Erin Pizzey opened the day, Martin Daubney brilliantly and humorously presented on how men are portrayed in the media, I presented my 30 minutes on how rigged the system is, Stuart Hontree also presented brilliantly, Dr Melissa Hamilton, lecturer at Surrey University Law Faculty gave an excellent presentation on how badly drafted law can be misinterpreted. Paul Apreda the Welsh dynamo and CEO Welsh Fnf, and Michael Lewkowicz director of Fnf UK presented on what they are doing with lobbying etc. Most of these presentations can be seen on youtube if you google the above event. Ewan Jones, the quiet ultra -professional camera man once again spent the day videoing the event and then editing it for free, same as he did in 2017. If only there were more Ewan Jones in society.

Cynics will say, what did we achieve? My answer is, a hell of a lot more than you did or ever will. I have often noticed that those who do the least are the most vocal at criticising those who have done the most. I believe this is a default mechanism within such individuals to deflect from their own uselessness.

I didn't ask for this or any other battle, it came looking for me. I look upon those within the system who exercise what I call 'Child Endangering Gender Discrimination', when they should be exercising 'Gender Neutral Impartial Professionalism,' as being serial assistants to the further abuse of vulnerable children.

It is imperative that whenever a decision is made to improve children's outcomes post divorce or separation in the UK, those current professionals and agencies who have a stranglehold on implementation and legislation have minimal involvement. You don't ask those who have done so much to cause the problem, and who benefit from it continuing, to be a part of the solution.

I hope this book will help people have a better understanding of the Systemic Failings within UK Family Court System and enable them to move the UK from being at the bottom of international leagues where children's outcomes are concerned to nearer the top. In one fell swoop this would do two things of huge benefit to society:

1. Improve children's lives.
2. Save the country £49 billion per year.

If adults and parents don't consider improving children's outcomes worth fighting for, then what is the point of life? Unless selfishness.

Post-Script December 2020
to February 2021

In December 2020 I did a SAR (Subject Access Request) to Brent Council Data Protection Office. I requested full disclosure of all the information Brent Children's Services had about me. I received the information on January 18th, 2021. It was very heavily redacted, and actually quite sickening for me to read what the children and myself went through. Significant by omission was the information the BDVAP (Brent Domestic Violence Advocacy Project (Women's Aide) had about me. It was repeatedly referred to, but not disclosed.

I protested about this omission of information, and also the huge redaction overall. Brent's Data Protection Office informed me via email on 16 February 2021 that Brent is not in control of the BDVAP (Women's Aide). They stated that the BDVAP is under the control of the police and advised me to do a Subject Access Request (SAR) to the police.

I went in person with various forms of ID to Wembley police station that night. Posters for the BDVAP adorned various notice boards: how wonderful I thought. I submitted my request for a SAR to the police officer on duty, explained the recent situation re Brent and my request concerning the BDVAP information.

The police officer, after some checking, told me that the Police were NOT in control of the BDVAP. They had neither access nor authority to release any information the BDVAP had on me. Also, on the police computer I was 'clean'. An email confirming this was sent to me.

I was in shock with this new information. The BDVAP (Women's Aide) are outside the control, and regulation, of both Brent Council, which commissions them, and the police.

This corrupt and gendered malpractice is central to the failings within the family court process. So much for equality under the law!

An organisation which is totally gendered in service provision, in fact, proudly boasts of such, operates in total secrecy, controls the gateway and quite often the outcome within the family courts! It is pivotal in the procurement of both legal aid and injunctions for its preferred clients. Recently, it claims to also offer assistance to male victims. In my opinion, this is a cosmetic exercise to protect its extraordinary budget and retain total control over domestic violence services within Brent.

Back door social engineering and purest bigotry of the worse type is apparent here. By the worse type, I mean such that pursues a gendered ideology at the proven expense of children's safety. Gender-apartheid, appears institutional in Brent. Is your area any different?

What value now for the meaningless phrase, 'Welfare of the child is paramount'.

In February 2021 some friends and I set up two new websites: www.londonfathers.com for the voluntary/charitable work I do, and www.vincentmcgovern.com, which will be my campaign site.

Thank you for reading

Lightning Source UK Ltd.
Milton Keynes UK
UKHW010945130421
381909UK00001B/91

9 781839 754500